SECOND EDITION

Parents and Teachers of Children with Exceptionalities: A Handbook for Collaboration

Thomas M. Shea
Southern Illinois University at Edwardsville

Anne M. Bauer
University of Cincinnati

Allyn and Bacon
Boston   London   Toronto   Sydney   Tokyo   Singapore

Series Editorial Assistant: *Carol Craig*
Production Administrator: *Annette Joseph*
Production Coordinator: *Holly Crawford*
Cover Administrator: *Linda K. Dickinson*
Cover Designer: *Suzanne Harbison*
Manufacturing Buyer: *Megan Cochran*

Copyright © 1991, 1985 by Allyn and Bacon
A Division of Simon & Schuster, Inc.
160 Gould Street
Needham Heights, Massachusetts 02194

All rights reserved. No part of the material protected by this copyright notice may be reproduced or utilized in any form or by any means, electronic or mechanical, including photocopying, recording, or by any information storage and retrieval system, without the written permission of the copyright owner.

The first edition of this book was published under the title *Parents and Teachers of Exceptional Students: A Handbook for Involvement*.

Library of Congress Cataloging-in-Publication Data
Shea, Thomas M.
    Parents and teachers of children with exceptionalities: a handbook for collaboration / Thomas M. Shea, Anne M. Bauer.—2nd ed.
      p. cm.
    Rev. ed. of: Parents and teachers of exceptional students. ©1985.
    Includes bibliographical references and index.
    ISBN 0-205-12789-4
    1. Special education—United States. 2. Parent-teacher relationship—United States. 3. Exceptional children—United States—Family relationships. 4. Parents of exceptional children—United States. 5. Special education teachers—Training of—United States. I. Bauer, Anne M. II. Shea, Thomas M. Parents and teachers of exceptional students. III. Title.
LC3981.S54 1991
371.0'0973—dc20   90-49367
                                                                                                  CIP

Printed in the United States of America
10 9 8 7 6 5 4   96 95

Photos © Frank Siteman 1990

To our families:

Dolores, Kevin, and Keith

and

Riley, Demian, Tara, and Christopher

CONTENTS

Preface   ix

SECTION ONE: *A Model for Parent-Teacher Collaboration*   1

Chapter One: Parenting   3
    Chapter Topics and Objectives   3
    The Family as a Social System   4
    Social Change and Parent Collaboration   5
    The Art of Parenting   8
    Children's Needs   9
    Summary   17
    Exercises and Discussion Topics   18
    References   19

Chapter Two: Parents, Families, and Children with Exceptionalities   21
    Chapter Topics and Objectives   21
    An Integrative Social Perspective   22
    Bronfenbrenner's Social Contexts   24
    The Ontogenic System: Personal Factors for Coping with Stress   25
    The Microsystem: Intrafamilial Relationships   30
    The Exosystem: External Social Supports   34
    The Mesosystem: Interrelationships among Contexts   36
    The Macrosystem: Societal Beliefs and Values   38
    The Impact of a Systems Approach   40
    Summary   41
    Exercises and Discussion Topics   41
    References   42

Chapter Three: Perspectives on Parent-Teacher Collaboration   47
    Chapter Topics and Objectives   47
    The Need for Parent-Teacher Collaboration   48

vi   *Contents*

      Attitudes toward Parent-Teacher Collaboration   49
      Benefits of Parent-Teacher Collaboration   50
      Effective Collaboration   51
      Parents' Rights and Responsibilities   56
      Parents Who Do Not Formally Collaborate with Teachers   61
      Summary   63
      Exercises and Discussion Topics   63
      References   64

Chapter Four: A Model for Parent-Teacher Collaboration   68
      Chapter Topics and Objectives   68
      The Model   70
      Communication Skills and Information-Gathering Techniques   79
      Assessing the Needs of Families   92
      Additional Resources   101
      Summary   103
      Exercises and Discussion Topics   104
      References   105

SECTION TWO: *Parent-Teacher Collaborative Activities*   107

Chapter Five: Written and Telephone Communication   110
      Chapter Topics and Objectives   110
      Written Reports   111
      Notes, Letters, and Notices   119
      Telephone Contacts   127
      Newsletters   130
      Summary   131
      Exercises and Discussion Topics   139
      References   140

Chapter Six: Parent-Teacher Conferences   141
      Chapter Topics and Objectives   141
      Progress Report Conferences   142
      Problem-Solving Conferences   145
      Training Conferences   148
      Individualized Education Program Meetings   154
      Home Visits   159
      Special Issues   161
      Summary   165
      Exercises and Discussion Topics   166

Contents **vii**

        References   167
        Chapter Supplement—
          Psychosituational Interviews   169

Chapter Seven: Group Activities   178
        Chapter Topics and Objectives   178
        Group Size   179
        Large-Group Activities   181
        Small-Group Activities   185
        Summary   191
        Exercises and Discussion Topics   192
        References   192

Chapter Eight: Group Meeting Models   194
        Chapter Topics and Objectives   194
        Informational Meetings   195
        Communication Groups   198
        Problem-Solving Groups   201
        Discussion Groups   202
        Training Groups   205
        Summary   210
        Exercises and Discussion Topics   211
        References   211

Chapter Nine: School, Home, and Community
   Programs   213
        Chapter Topics and Objectives   213
        Parent Training Techniques   215
        Parent Roles   222
        Parents as Instructors   226
        Parents as Volunteers   227
        Parents on Committees   233
        Parents as Home-Based Teachers   234
        Parent Resources   238
        Summary   240
        Exercises and Discussion Topics   240
        References   241

SECTION THREE: *Special Issues in Collaboration*   245

Chapter Ten: Special Issues in Family Collaboration   247
        Chapter Topics and Objectives   247
        Families from Diverse Cultures   248

viii   Contents

       Collaboration with Siblings and Extended Family
          Members   252
       Child Maltreatment and Substitute Care   253
       Counseling Families   259
       Summary   260
       Exercises and Discussion Topics   260
       References   261

Chapter Eleven: Family Transitions   264
       Chapter Topics and Objectives   264
       Transitions in Families with Members with
          Exeptionalities   265
       Perspectives on Collaboration to Facilitate
          Transitions   266
       Strategies to Assist Families in Transition   268
       Summary   271
       Exercises and Discussion Topics   272
       References   272

Chapter Twelve: Programming for Parent Collaboration: An Illustration   274
       Chapter Topics and Objectives   274
       The Class   275
       Program Introduction   275
       Parent Orientation Meeting   276
       Intake and Assessment   280
       Selection of Goals and Objectives   281
       Activity Selection and Implementation   282
       Evaluation   285
       Summary   287
       Exercises and Discussion Topics   289
       Chapter Supplement   291

Appendix A: Cases for Study and Role Playing   301

Appendix B: Support and Informational Organizations   310

Appendix C: Worksheets and Forms   317

Appendix D: Spanish Worksheets and Forms   332

Index   347

PREFACE

In the years since we completed the writing of *Parents and Teachers of Exceptional Students: A Handbook for Involvement* many changes have occurred in the role of parents in special education. Parents have moved from expressing gratitude for being allowed to participate in their children's education to questioning the practices of special education and the provision of services to their children. Parents have moved from involvement, which assumes an invitation, to collaboration, which assumes a true partnership. Special educators have moved from simply informing parents to empowering parents and thus enabling them to fully participate in their children's education.

On a personal level, we, the authors, have changed our life roles. One of us completed a transition to parenting adult children who reside many miles from home; the other began the task of parenting children with special needs. Such changes have forced us to a new perspective on parenting children with special needs and parent-teacher involvement. Our new perspective is reflected in the title of this second edition, *Parents and Teachers of Children with Exceptionalities: A Handbook for Collaboration*.

The use of the phrase "children with exceptionalities" represents our belief that we are writing about individuals who are first and foremost children but who vary from their peers in some manner. By choosing the term *collaboration*, we are suggesting that parents are competent (or have the capacity to become competent) coeducators of their children.

The purpose of the text remains essentially as it was in the first edition. Its purpose is to increase the probability that parents and teachers will work effectively together to benefit the children with special needs for whom they share responsibility. The book is a textbook for college students in special education—preschool, elementary, and secondary education; and in courses on parent-teacher relations and the psychology of exceptionality. It is also a desk reference for special education classroom, resource, itinerant, and crisis teachers; school psychologists, counselors, nurses, social workers; administrators; and other professionals servicing children with exceptionalities and their families. Due to the recent surge of interest in the Regular Education Initiative, we have added information applicable to regular educators working with children with special needs in the least restrictive environment.

The text presents a model and broad range of parent-teacher activities that provide a framework for developing parent-teacher programs. A goal of the model is to provide enough flexibility for parents and teachers to design programs responsive to their needs, the needs of the child with an exceptionality, and the educational environment in which they function.

The first section sets the stage for collaboration by discussing parents' and children's experiences of exceptionality and outlining a parent collaboration model. Chapter 1 describes the family as a social system and the impact of this perception on the workings of the family. The chapter emphasizes that parenting children is an art and that families with exceptional members are, first and foremost, families with needs and desires common to all families. The chapter highlights the current role of the family in society. Chapter 2 applies the family systems perspective in a discussion of the variations in families with members who are exceptional. It discusses the role of the exceptional child's parents, the parents' reactions to the birth and diagnosis of a child with an exceptionality, the coping behaviors parents may use to adjust to their new role, and the impact of the child with an exceptionality on the family.

Chapter 3 discusses the need and desirability of parent-teacher collaboration and its advantages for children with exceptionalities, parents, teachers, schools, and communities. It emphasizes the rights and responsibilities of children with exceptionalities and their parents as key factors governing parent-teacher collaboration. The chapter recognizes that due to a wide range of circumstances, some parents and teachers do not participate in collaborative activities.

Chapter 4 describes a detailed model to help teachers think about and plan a program of collaboration. It defines the model's purpose, limitations, and processes and provides several forms that can guide the writing of individualized parent education programs. The chapter discusses assessment techniques and guidelines for interpersonal communication that are critical to effective application of the model.

The second section of the text supports the model by presenting a broad range of collaborative activities. These activities extend from those placing the least demands on the parents for participation to those that are more complex and thus more demanding of time, energy, and commitment. Chapter 5 discusses approaches to written and telephone communication, including daily and periodic report cards, newsletters, notes, notices, and telephone contacts. It introduces the task analysis report card and the passport for positive parent-teacher communication. Innovative applications of technology to parent-teacher communication are presented.

Chapter 6 discusses parent-teacher conferences, which are essential to effective communication. The discussion highlights progress report, problem-solving, and behavior management training conferences, with special attention to the individualized education program conference and home visits. It also explores two special conferencing issues—the three-way conference that includes the child and working with the negative reactions of conferees.

Chapters 7 and 8 focus on parent-teacher group activities. Chapter 7 establishes a framework and offers guidelines for small- and large-group activities. Chapter 8 looks at specific types of groups, including informational, communication, problem-solving, discussion, and training groups. Again, in this second edition, further research and innovative programs are presented.

Chapter 9 discusses parents as an important resource in the classroom and school, at home, and in the community. It discusses parents' potential contributions as paraprofessionals, instructors, committee members, volunteers, home-based teachers, and home study supervisors. It also looks at resource centers, teaching packages, and training techniques that can help parents perform their roles effectively.

Chapter 10 discusses families who may require special assistance. We discuss working with families representing diverse cultures, families involved in the maltreatment of their children, and families serving as adoptive or substitute families for children. Chapter 11 follows with a discussion of the impact of various life transitions on the family and child. Chapter 12 is an extensive illustration of how to apply the parent-teacher collaboration model in the special education setting.

As supports to our readers, each chapter opens with a statement by a parent recorded during a project with inner-city children in special education and with chapter objectives. Each chapter ends with exercises and topics for discussion that reinforce concepts and provide practice in the techniques described in the chapter. Extensive reference lists lead the reader to additional sources to broaden understanding of the chapter content.

The book includes four appendices. Appendix A presents cases for study and role playing. Appendix B is a resource list of support and informational organizations for parents and teachers. Appendix C provides copies of worksheets and forms used in the text. Appendix D presents the same forms in Spanish in recognition of the unique issues confronting bilingual parents and children in a predominantly English-speaking society.

We hope this handbook enhances parent and teacher collaboration on behalf of all children with special needs. We appreciate the assistance of the parents, teachers, and students who have taught us so very much.

A special thanks to those parents who candidly expressed their feelings and concerns, and to Sue Murphy, through whose credibility we gained access to families. Their feelings and concerns are presented in the statements that open each chapter. We wish to express our thanks to our editor, Ray Short, for his confidence in us and his assistance with this new edition.

Finally, we thank Dolores Shea and Riley Humler for their support in this project and their collaboration in parenting, and our children, Kevin, Keith, Demian, Tara, and Christopher, for their special contributions as we learn together the lifelong activities of parenting.

SECTION ONE

A Model for Parent-Teacher Collaboration

Chapters 1 through 4 offer an introduction to parent-teacher collaboration in behalf of children with exceptionalities. Chapter 1 serves as an overview of families and parenting for all children. The effects of social change on families and parenting are discussed. Throughout this chapter, children with special needs are described as children first and foremost, with needs and desires similar to those of nonexceptional children.

Chapter 2 describes what is special about parents and families of children with exceptionalities. The effects of this specialness on parents, families, and teachers are assessed. Parents' needs for professional support are discussed.

Chapter 3 provides perspectives on parent-teacher collaboration. Guidelines for fostering home and school cooperation are provided. The rights and responsibilities of parents of children with exceptionalities are reviewed.

Chapter 4 concludes this section with the presentation of the model for parent-teacher collaboration and its purposes, limitations, processes, and procedures. Specific information is provided on communication, interviewing techniques, and competencies for parent-teacher collaboration. The section concludes with a description of the use of professionals and paraprofessionals in the parent-teacher collaborative process.

CHAPTER ONE

Parenting

Ms. W., parent of a ten-year-old son with mental retardation:

"Well, we just take it day by day. He's a little stubborn, but you know, it's not too bad. It's not as bad as everyone puts it out to be, really. It's no worse than dealing with my other kids. Really."

Chapter Topics and Objectives

Parenting is a complex, dynamic process through which parents develop and use the knowledge and skills required to plan for, give birth to, and care for children (Morrison 1978). In this chapter, we will explore the nature of parenting and families, using a social systems perspective. We begin our discussion with a consideration of families and parenting in general for two reasons. First, children with special needs and their parents are first and foremost children and parents, and the factors that influence them are the same as those that influence all parents and children. Second, children with special needs and their parents participate in the same parenting processes experienced by all parents and children. Parenting a child with an exceptionality is unique in degree and intensity rather than in kind. Like all children, those with special needs require love, care, guidance, support, protection, and direction. Efforts to address children's special needs cannot ignore their basic human needs.

In this chapter, we will:

- Describe the family as a social system.
- Discuss the impact of social change on parenting and parents' relationships with the schools.
- Describe the art of parenting.
- Discuss the needs of all children.

The Family as a Social System

A family is not simply a collection of individuals who share some biological relationship. Rather, a family is a social system in which each member is affecting and being affected by the other members. It is ever changing and dynamic.

As a social system, the family follows several principles common to all social systems (Minuchin 1974). The family itself is a structured whole, a complete unit. The elements within that unit are interdependent. The interactions within the family social system are reciprocal, representing constant give and take, accommodation and adaptation, rather than linear cause-and-effect relationships. Like all social systems, the family attempts to maintain stability, to remain unchanged. The behavior of family members is seen as purposeful, and resistance to change is natural. Though a family may resist change, Minuchin contends that change within the family is constant.

The family system is composed of subsystems. Within these subsystems, there are specific boundaries. For example, the roles and relationships between father and daughter may be quite different from the roles and relationships between mother and daughter. (This topic is explored in greater depth in Chapter 2.)

When studying the family as a social system, we become aware that a linear cause-and-effect perception of family members' behavior is inadequate (Johnston and Zemitzsch 1988). Rather, each person's functioning within the family system helps to maintain and change the behavior of other family members. Effecting change in one member provides the opportunity for effecting change in another member. As members assume new roles, the family system reorganizes (Bronfenbrenner 1986). Reorganization changes the expectations and attitudes of family members. In addition, reorganization within the family affects other settings in which the child and other members of the family spend time, such as the school.

When professionals collaborate with parents with regard to the education of their children, the workings of the entire family system, rather than individuals or dyads (such as mother-child, father-child) within the family, must be taken into consideration. The family, then, is perceived as a developing social system that is going through transitions and changes overtime. Winton (1986) suggests that some of these changes are predictable, others less predictable. Times of transition cause additional stress within the family system. If professionals are to address the ever-changing family social system, collaboration with parents must reflect family characteristics and needs. Thus, collaboration with the family is a dynamic, developing, adapting process.

Social Change and Parent Collaboration

Social Change and the Family

Families exist within a social context. As Fromm (1956) suggests in his discussion of loving, the capacity to parent an individual living in any culture depends on the influence that culture has on the character of the individual. In the past two generations, changes in society have affected the capacity to parent and have influenced the nature of the family. Table 1.1 highlights several social changes occurring between the 1950s and the 1990s that have influenced parenting and families.

Families are no longer typically comprised of a married mother and father, with two or more children. Rather, most children live in one-parent homes, reconstituted or blended families, foster homes, extended families, relatives' homes, or a variety of other family structures (Epstein 1988). Epstein contends that all families struggle with limited time and need understandable and useful information about how to help their children.

Benson (1988) suggests that the changes that have occurred in family structures are not digressions from the ideal but are attempts of the family to adapt to a rapidly changing society. Many families face limited financial resources, and the struggle to maintain the family day by day may take precedence over concerns related to children's schooling. Families, due to social changes, spend far less time together and are seldom together during the work day. Television has changed the way family members interact. The amount of time young children are spending alone or with substitute caregivers has increased significantly.

Coleman (1987) suggests that social change has reduced the incentives parents have for assuming responsibility for their children and their children's education. The age at which an individual receives autonomy from parental authority has drifted downward, with younger and younger children functioning independently. In addition, an increasingly wide range of socialization activities, such as sexuality and consumer and family-living education, have been granted to schools. With an increased demand for after-school or latchkey programs and summer activities, schools are acting increasingly in loco parentis.

TABLE 1.1 • *Social Changes*

Factors	1950s	1990s
Family	Extended, traditional nuclear	Neolocal nuclear
Neighborhood	Personal, cohesive	Impersonal, multicultural
Neighbors	Concerned, responsible, active	Concerned, defensive, passive or indirectly active
Companions/friends	Close, cohesive, socially and emotionally supportive	Often distant or unavailable, nonexistent for many needing social and emotional support
School	Small, in the neighborhood, personal	Large, outside the neighborhood, impersonal
Teachers	Accepted as friends, neighbors, community leaders	Perceived as strangers, professional, specialists
Knowledge	Limited, manageable within existing standards of behavior and application	Exploding, unmanageable within existing standards of behavior and application
Church	Influential	Relatively less influential
Standards/values	Rigid, widely accepted, emphasizing the normal	Relative, fragmented, emphasizing the bizarre and unacceptable
Work	Simple, personal, available, sufficient to produce needed goods, supportive of artisans	Mechanized, impersonal, automated, specialized, unavailable to many, less supportive of artisans
Material goods	Limited, emphasizing necessities for living	Available to majority, emphasizing luxuries
Mobility	Limited for most people	Nearly unlimited
Communication/transportation	Limited, slow, inefficient	Nearly unlimited, rapid, more efficient
National and world events	Not widely followed or understood	Extensively followed and understood

Glenn and Nelson (1987) classified the social changes that have occurred during the past fifty years into four major groups. First, there has been an "absence of networks," which suggests that due to increased mobility, the present generation is the first to attempt to raise children without the active involvement of networks of extended family members and friends. Without such networks, children and youth have only their peers as a major source of reference. Second, with less stability of family rituals, traditions, and activities, there has emerged an "absence of roles." Rather than playing an essential and active role in their education, children act as compliant and passive recipients of knowledge. Third, Glenn and Nelson suggest that children now receive most of their exposure to life experiences through the media rather than in hands-on or real-life activities. There is an "absence of on-the-job training" for adulthood. Finally, there is a "loss of parenting resources," with few of today's parents having their parents available to provide active support and role models. Many parents raise their children alone.

Social Change and Schooling

Hoffman (1975) contends that the period of time from 1875 to 1914 established the public schools as an integral part of the new, mass, industrialized society. The public school acted as the main socialization agent for U.S. society. Those students who did not adapt to the school's socialization program were segregated or dismissed. Students who challenged teachers as a consequence of their behavior or learning capacity were placed in special classes as early as 1899.

Today, schools continue to separate students who differ from their peers to such an extent that they are considered exceptional. Algozzine, Christenson, and Ysseldyke (1982) reported that 92 percent of all children referred as potentially requiring special education were tested, and that 73 percent of those tested were placed in special education services. The Tenth Annual Report of Congress on the Implementation of the Education of the Handicapped Act (U.S. Department of Education 1989) notes that in excess of 4 million children with handicaps between the ages of birth and twenty-one years were served in special education.

In recent decades, education has become increasingly impersonal (McAfee and Vergason 1979). Schools are no longer in children's neighborhoods, and teachers are infrequently members of the local school community. Given this physical separation between families and schools, parents' associations with teachers and other school personnel tend to be infrequent and impersonal.

The knowledge explosion of the past several decades has led educators to place greater emphasis on developing children's cognitive abilities. Teachers design instructional programs for the accumulation of specific knowledge and skills more frequently than for the development of critical thinking and problem-solving skills. With the emphasis on teacher accountability and competency testing, instruction tends to be test-directed rather than being responsive to students' need and abilities.

The Art of Parenting

Parenting is a dynamic process. Parents constantly adapt their activities to fit their children's emerging needs and interests, to meet their own needs and new learning, and to respond to the demands of the ever-changing influences of society.

Just as artists aim for the ideal in their art, parents try to attain certain standards of effective parenting. They aim for objectivity, trying to see their children, themselves, and society as they are, not as they wish them to be or as they were during their childhood. Just as artists use their canvases to provide a reflection of life, children use the eyes of their parents as mirrors in which they discover themselves (Glenn and Nelson 1987).

Like artists, parents strive for self-discipline in their personal lives and support their children's efforts to attain self-discipline. They concentrate on the art of parenting, devoting time and energy to analyzing their functions and responsibilities.

Parents are patient, accepting that mistakes do occur and that a child's attainment of maturity is a slow, difficult process. They consider parenting sufficiently important to make personal sacrifices to attain their goals. At times, parenting takes precedence over personal, social, and occupational goals.

Modern parents are versatile, able to play numerous roles and juggle many responsibilities (Table 1.2). Indeed, the breadth of their responsibilities makes it clear that they cannot personally meet all their children's needs. Parents must depend on others outside the family to assist with the responsibilities of parenting. Important allies in parents' efforts to raise children are teachers.

No parent is perfect, but many parents are successful. Successful parents perceive themselves and their children as capable, contributing individuals.

TABLE 1.2 • *Parents' Roles in Contemporary Society*

Arbitrator	Healer (doctor)
Babysitter	Homemaker (cook, maid)
Caregiver	House person
Chauffeur	Income provider
Community worker	Janitor
Companion	Lawmaker/judge
Consoler	Learner
Counselor	Listener
Dietitian	Lover
Disciplinarian	Mother
Economist (shopper, budget maker)	Nurse
Entertainer	Peacemaker
Father	Playmate
Financier (budget, bank account)	Psychologist
Friend	Seamstress/tailor
Groundskeeper (landscaper, gardener)	Security provider (guard)
Guardian	Teacher
Plumber/electrician	Volunteer

Source: Morrison 1978, 31. Reprinted with permission.

Children's Needs

Scott-Jones (1988) suggest that if children are to be successful in school, parents must respond to the varying needs that emerge as their children grow and develop. During the preschool years, daily interactions with parents foster the growth of skills that children need much later during their formal schooling. During this time, children need to hear variety in spoken language and be encouraged to express themselves. They need to be read to and observe others using books and print materials. Children should be encouraged to use their memory and explore size, quantity, and patterns. Children should experience both gross-motor and fine-motor activities. Most importantly, children should engage in social interaction and develop persistence at tasks.

During school age, Scott-Jones suggests, the role of the parent changes to helping their children to develop social and emotional skills that will assist them in their new involvement with peers. At this time, children need support to practice self-management skills. Parents transmit values and expectations about school to their children. During adolescence, parental influence must become more indirect, as adolescents internalize values and turn more and more to peers.

Glenn and Nelson (1987) suggest that there are seven essential ingredients to parenting successful children. These include strong personal perceptions that one is (1) capable and (2) needed and able to contribute in meaningful ways. Successful and productive human beings perceive themselves as (3) having personal power over their lives, and (4) able to use their understanding of personal emotions to develop self-discipline and learn from their experiences. Successful persons are (5) able to work with others and develop friends, (6) respond to the limits and consequences of everyday life with responsibility, and (7) have a strong sense of personal judgment. In a supportive parental relationship, children can develop these ingredients for success.

According to Homan (1977), effective parenting is the process of "responding responsibly" to a child's expressed and unexpressed needs for love and emotional security and providing behavior management leading to self-discipline, intellectual stimulation, freedom to explore, feedback on efforts, a joy of living, and physical care, nourishment, and safety. Parents emphasize different needs with different children and at different times during the formative years, in keeping with changing circumstances.

Love

All humans need to love and to be loved. In fact, research has demonstrated that infants deprived of love do not thrive (Spitz 1946); a child's survival depends on the giving and receiving of love.

The love between parent and child is unique. Parental love goes beyond sentiment, however; it is responsible responding to need. This responding is a prerequisite for all of the child's other successes (Beck 1977). Glenn and Nelson (1987) suggest that parental love helps children perceive and experience personal significance, meaning, purpose, and status in life. Love, they suggest, requires three shared perceptions between parent and child: (1) that one is being listened to, (2) that one is safe to risk personal perceptions and feelings, and (3) that others consider that what one has to offer or what one thinks is significant. Love requires unconditional acceptance and approval, rather than limits and restrictions.

Perhaps the greatest deterrents to love between parents and children are overindulgence, domination, disinterest, and an unwillingness to be a model. Loving parents respond to their children as individuals capable of making decisions and judgments in accordance with their maturational level and life experiences. Parents who truly love their children do not treat them as prized possessions who cannot make decisions.

Loving parents avoid dominating their children. They encourage them to make decisions, take actions, and succeed or fail as a result of personal efforts. Of course, parents do not allow children to make decisions inappropriate for their level of maturity; nor should they allow children to fail repeatedly in their efforts. Children who are prohibited from expressing themselves and taking responsibility for their actions often have difficulty learning to love.

Mature, loving parents perceive themselves as loving and lovable. They seek growth in knowledge and understanding of themselves, their children, and their environment. Loving parents respond appropriately to their children's expressed and unexpressed needs and desires. Loving parents see their children as they are and respect their humanness, actively participating in their lives.

Glenn and Nelson suggest that in order to experience emotional stability and a sense of meaning, purpose, and significance in life, one must be listened to. One must be taken seriously, accepted and given unconditional love, care, and respect. They suggest that a child must feel genuinely needed and affirmed in his or her personal worth, contributions, and significance.

Behavior Management Leading to Self-Discipline

Behavior management is acting to help children develop self-fulfilling, productive, and socially acceptable behaviors (Shea and Bauer 1987). Self-discipline is the goal of all behavior management: to allow children to gain control over their behavior in varied circumstances involving many individuals and groups. Self-control develops over many years and includes many developmental phases. During this process, children naturally progress and regress. A child may appear to be in excellent control of his or her behavior one day and out of control the next day. Parents can measure progress in self-discipline—maturing, learning, and growing—by the slowly increasing lengths of time between the occurrences of inappropriate behaviors.

The word *discipline* derives from the word *disciple*, a follower of a master's teaching. Thus, it conveys the idea of learning from the person a child wants to emulate. The most effective discipline grows out of mutual respect and understanding between parent and child. It is voluntary and cooperative, not simply an authority figure imposing limits and restrictions on another person.

Self-discipline involves being able to consider an outcome and select the behavior that will achieve it (Glenn and Nelson 1987). Self-discipline involves both self-assessment, evaluating what one wants to achieve from the experience, and self-control, understanding which behavior is the most appropriate. Glenn and Nelson caution that the most basic level of teaching self-discipline begins with mature parents who love enough to avoid pampering. They suggest that parents who project their feelings onto others, rather than take responsibility for their feelings, provide a barrier to self-discipline. In addition, rescuing children rather than having them assume responsibility for their behavior discourages the development of self-discipline. Parents should allow their children to experience safe consequences so that they will realize that they have control over their personal behavior.

Intellectual Development

Parents have responsibility for their children's intellectual development from infancy to adulthood. Parents first provide their infants with a stimulating environment—a bright and cheerful nursery with attractive furnishings, toys, and pictures that the baby can see, hear, feel, and manipulate. In the early years, the parent is a "loving play partner," sensitive to the child's cues (Gross 1981). As children mature, their parents encourage them to join in exploring the home, neighborhood, and other places of interest. Parents are teachers, helping children identify what they see, hear, taste, smell, and touch.

Young children need play materials that encourage creativity. They enjoy playing with household items such as pots, pans, brushes, brooms, cans, boxes, spoons, and beaters, for example. During the preschool years, parents can offer their children opportunities to develop proficiency with school-related tools, such as crayons, pencils, pens, paper, paints, blocks, puzzles, scissors, and simple construction and kitchen tools.

As children grow older, they benefit from picture books and easy-reading books. These are personal possessions for the children to keep in their toy chests or bookcases. Puzzles and educational games also stimulate children's early learning.

Language skills are critical to success in school and the community. Children learn speech by hearing language used appropriately, and they need opportunities to practice proper usage. Frequent parent-child conversations, discussions, and word games stimulate children's language skills.

Another important parent responsibility is to help develop prereading skills. Reading to children, encouraging them to listen to and discuss stories, gives them an excellent start. Time devoted to studying and discussing the pictures, words, colors, shapes, sizes, and visual configurations in printed material fosters reading skills.

When children reach school age, parents begin to share with teachers the responsibility for their children's intellectual development. Parents who show their interest in their children's school activities, and who assist with home assignments when appropriate, help foster their children's love of learning. The parents have an obligation to provide an intellectually stimulating home environment as well, making available reading materials and educational games, encouraging individual and family projects in animal care, rock collecting, stamp collecting, baking, carpentry, and so on. Family vacations and weekend outings provide excellent opportunities to stimulate interest in learning. Family discussions can become a routine part of a new or unusual acitivity.

Parents should encourage junior and senior high school children to participate in intellectually stimulating school, church, and community activities, such as dramatics, language clubs, sports, science fairs, essay contests, or debate clubs.

The more parents show interest in their children's environment, are stimulated by new ideas, events, and problems, and participate in serious discussions, the more likely their children will model their behavior.

Freedom to Explore

From the day of birth, children need freedom to explore themselves and their environment. Parents can encourage and assist their children in this area of development by providing limits within which they are free to explore and develop their abilities (Brooks 1981).

When their children are infants, parents physically help them explore. Mother and father carry the young child about the nursery, home, or yard, drawing attention to objects and happenings. They encourage their children to use their senses of vision, hearing, taste, touch, and smell.

Even when infants are confined to their crib, playpen, or nursery, they can explore toys, mobiles, pictures, and furnishings in their immediate surroundings. In fact, infants and toddlers need little encouragement to explore their environment. On occasion, toddlers explore too much, too quickly, too carelessly, and in the wrong places at the wrong time. When necessary, parents must restrict or supervise children's explorations.

Although severe restriction of children's freedom to explore is unwise, it is equally unwise to remove all objects or secure all areas of the home that pose potential dangers. As children explore, they learn which objects and areas are dangerous and therefore not available for exploration (electric cords and outlets, stoves, fireplaces, stairways, power tools, and appliances). They learn that they must ask permission or have supervision to explore certain objects and areas governed by other family members (kitchen, workshop, parents' sewing basket or toolboxes, and brother's and sister's rooms and toys). Children also learn that their personal possessions and toys are theirs to explore freely.

As children mature and enter school, parents continue to encourage them to explore their immediate surroundings and to extend their experiences through discussing them with others, reading books and magazines, and viewing plays, movies, and television programs.

In encouraging their children to explore throughout their growing years, parents can follow these guidelines:

- Encourage measured and systematic exploration. Children do not benefit from exploring topics beyond their comprehension nor can they learn effectively if they explore so many areas that they explore nothing in depth.
- Encourage children to explore themselves as unique individuals with special abilities, experiences, and interests. Allow them to devote time to quiet consideration of themselves and their world.
- Protect children from physical and psychological dangers as they explore.

Feedback

Children develop and modify their self-image as a result of feedback from others. Parents provide children encouragement and feedback as they develop their psychomotor abilities to crawl, walk, climb, run, play ball, write, and so on. They offer feedback on cognitive skills, such as language, memory, comprehension, problem solving, reading, spelling, and arithmetic. And they reinforce children's affective learning, such as obedience; thoughtfulness; social and interpersonal skills; home, school, and play behaviors; and values and standards.

Frequent feedback is necessary when a child is learning a new behavior or skill. Once the behavior becomes habitual, parents can reduce the frequency of feedback.

During infancy and early childhood, their parents' pleasure is children's primary reinforcement. Therefore, parents must show their pleasure or displeasure with the child's actions in a manner the child understands. In the early years, a hug, a kiss, a smile, a toss in the air, a drawing displayed on the refrigerator door, a cookie, and so on, are all very rewarding to children. A frown, the removal of an object, a restriction on freedom, or a sharp word is usually sufficient negative feedback. A young child should receive feedback as soon as possible after the behavior occurs so that the connection between his or her behavior and the parent's response is clear.

Joy of Living

Living should be a joy for every child. Children's lives should be exciting, interesting, and satisfying. Parents can raise their children to feel the joy of living rather than to view life as a trial to be endured with caution, fear, and suffering.

For an infant, joy is a smile from a parent, a tussle with a father, a peekaboo game with a grandparent, or a spoonful of favorite food. Joy in childhood is a visit to the zoo, a red balloon on the end of a string, a ride in the family car, a whirl on a merry-go-round, a visit to Santa Claus, or a make-believe tea party. Joy is the new, the unusual, the exciting, and the adventurous.

During the early school years, joy is a family outing, excursions to interesting places, family vacations, family projects around the house, and physical activites. Joy is exploring the neighborhood with a friend, participating in Scouts, 4-H, and Little League. Joy is going to the playground, exploring nearby woods, and participating in after-school games.

In the preteen and early teen years, joy is a pajama party, a phone conversation with a friend, a shopping trip, a ballgame, a hobby, a family gathering, a bike ride, and a chance to do real work.

In the adolescent years, joy is participating in a school club or team, receiving recognition for efforts and accomplishments from people important to you, and exploring the arts, crafts, and music. Joy is a best friend with whom to share life's secrets and a group of friends to "hang out" with. Joy is having important responsibilities, finding a part-time job, driving the family car, selecting and buying clothes, dating, and making important personal decisions. To teenagers, joy is being treated as equals by adults and having parents who try to understand their points of view, who listen, and who express confidence in them.

For all young people, joy is a good joke, an unusual happening, and a good laugh. Children learn that there is a time to laugh and a time to cry and that both are acceptable human behaviors. They learn to laugh with others, not at others. They learn never to take satisfaction in others' failures, faults, personality traits, physical features, and handicaps.

If children are to develop joy in life, parents must refrain from demanding unwanted and undesirable participation, ill-advised competition, and unattainable levels of performance. Moreover, each parent must model the joy of living for his or her child. The parent who sees life as a dark and dreary winter day will raise a child who sees life similarly. The parent who radiates a joy of life and sees beauty in the world will raise a child who shares this view.

Physical Care, Nourishment, and Safety

The child's physical care, nourishment, and safety are basic parental responsibilities. Children's physical well-being not only is important in itself but also has a major impact on all other aspects of their psychosocial development. Chronically ill, undernourished, or abused children have difficulty functioning effectively. Moreover, their pain, discomfort, and insecurity create a distorted perception of reality and a negative self-concept. Children whose basic needs go unmet view themselves as unwanted, unloved, and worthless, and they see their parents and the world as uncaring. Our concern for this less fortunate group of children and parents is discussed extensively in Chapter 11.

Care for children's physical well-being begins before birth. The mother's prenatal care, health, diet, emotional state, and social habits all affect the baby's development, as do her use of alcoholic beverages, tobacco, and drugs. Research has shown that the mother's level of anxiety, stress, and frustration during pregnancy affect the baby's health as well.

After their baby's birth, the parents provide the food, shelter, clothing, and care most appropriate to his or her needs. Most parents in our nation have access to the housing, money, insurance, and transportation they need to care properly for their children. Unfortunately, however, this ability to provide is not universal in our nation and certainly not in the world.

Many children suffer physical and emotional neglect because their parents cannot obtain the basic necessities of life. Some parents are ignorant about what their children need. Still other parents, because of the immobilizing effects of personal and social-emotional handicaps and pathologies, cannot respond to their children's needs.

Parents are responsible for protecting growing children from illnesses and infectious diseases as much as possible. Children need a clean, healthful home in which disease cannot germinate or spread, and they need access to corrective and preventive health care services.

A well-balanced diet is necessary fuel for children's active daily lives. Parents provide healthy food to protect the child from malnutrition (a lack of proper nutrients) and obesity (excessive body fat resulting from nutritional imbalance).

Parents provide a safe environment for their children as well to avoid childhood accidents and injuries that could have a life-long effect. Bumps, cuts, and bruises are a normal part of childhood. However, parents should eliminate as many potential hazards as possible in their homes and teach children to avoid those that cannot be eliminated. If a child is too immature to understand the dangers of certain items and situations, parents must secure them. Safety includes protecting children from their natural curiosity by securing medicines, cleaning materials, and dangerous tools and equipment.

All children need a safe place in which to play, eat, sleep, and care for their body functions. Moreover, parent responsibility extends to teaching children self-care skills, such as toileting, bathing, washing before meals, brushing teeth, keeping their clothing and room reasonably clean, and wearing proper clothing. Parents teach children to care for themselves and to seek care when they are ill or injured.

Summary

This introductory chapter provides a general overview of the art of parenting all children, exceptional and nonexceptional. The discussion establishes premises for the parent-teacher collaboration model and activities presented in the remainder of the book.

A variety of social changes have modified parenting between the 1950s and the 1990s. The chapter highlights changes in families and in schools. The discussion emphasizes that parenting is an art—a complex, dynamic process—and describes an ideal of effective parenting. It discusses the basic human needs of all children to be loved, secure, and guided toward a satisfying life and spells out parents' duties and responsibilities in each category of children's needs.

Chapter 2 considers the role of parents of children with exceptionalities and describes parent reactions to the birth and diagnosis of a child with an exceptionality. It describes the coping and adaptive behavior typical of parents confronted with a diagnosis of exceptionality and assesses the effects of the exceptional child on family functioning.

Exercises and Discussion Topics

1. Discuss the following statement: "Parenting a child with special needs is unique in degree and intensity rather than in kind." Do you agree? Why or why not?

2. Using the social change factors presented in Table 1.1, compare the society of your childhood to the present. Can you add other social change factors or social problems that have occurred in your lifetime?

3. Trace one or more of the social change factors in Table 1.1 through your childhood, your parents' childhood, and your grandparents' childhood. Library research or interviews with your parents, grandparents, or people of similar ages may assist you in this exercise.

4. Research the definition of "art." Discuss or write a report on parenting as an art, describing the ways you think parenting is similar and dissimilar to other arts. In your report, contrast the ideal and the reality of the art of parenting.

5. Research and discuss one of the psychosocial needs of all children discussed in this chapter. Define the need, describe how parents can respond to it, compare its importance in a child's life to that of the other psychosocial needs discussed.

6. This text is for people interested in parent-teacher collaboration to benefit exceptional children. Explain why this chapter, applicable to all exceptional and nonexceptional children and their parents, opens the book.

7. Compare the philosophy and parenting methods presented in two or three articles or books of your choice on contemporary parenting.

References

Algozzine, B., S. Christenson, and J. Ysseldyke. 1982. Probabilities associated with the referral to placement process. *Teacher Education and Special Education* 5: 19–23.

Beck, J. 1977. Looking Ahead To Parenthood. *Parent's Magazine* 10 (1): 13–14, 46, 48, 50.

Benson, H. 1988. The changing American family and students at risk. *Behavior in Our Schools* 3: 7–12.

Bronfenbrenner, U. 1986. Ecology of the family as a context for human development: Research perspectives. *Developmental Psychology* 22: 723–42.

Brooks, J. B. 1981. *The process of parenting.* Palo Alto, Calif.: Mayfield.

Coleman, J. 1987. Families and school. *Educational Researcher* 16: 32–38.

Epstein, J. 1988. How do we improve programs for parent involvement: *Educational Horizons* 66: 58–60.

Fromm, E. (1956). *The art of loving.* New York: Harper and Row.

Glenn, H. S. and J. Nelson. 1987. *Raising children for success.* Fair Oaks, Calif.: Sunrise Press.

Gross, D. W. 1981. *The pleasure of their company.* Radnor, Pa.: Chilton.

Hoffman, E. 1975. The American public school and the deviant child: The origins of their involvement. *The Journal of Special Education* 9: 414–23.

Homan, W. E. 1977. *Child sense: A guide to loving, level-headed parenthood.* New York: Basic Books.

Johnston, J. C. and A. Zemitzsch. 1988. Family power: An intervention beyond the classroom. *Behavioral Disorders* 14: 69–79.

McAfee, J. K. and G. A. Vergason. 1979. Parent involvement in the process of special education: Establishing the new partnership. *Focus on Exceptional Children* 11: 1–15.

Minuchin, S. 1974. *Families and family therapy.* Cambridge, Mass.: Harvard University Press.

Morrison, G. S. 1978. *Parent involvement in the home, school, and community.* Columbus, Ohio: Charles E. Merrill.

Scott-Jones, D. 1988. Families as educators: The transition from informal to formal school learning. *Educational Horizons* 66: 66–70.

Shea, T. M. and A. M. Bauer. 1987. *Teaching children and youth with behavioral disorders.* 2d ed. Englewood Cliffs, N.J.: Prentice-Hall.

Spitz, R. A. 1946. Anaclitic depression. *Psychodynamic Study of the Child* 2: 313–42.

U. S. Department of Education. 1989. Tenth Annual Report to Congress on the Implementation of the Education of the Handicapped Act. *Exceptional Children* 56: 7–9.

Winton, P. 1986. Effective strategies for involving families in intervention efforts. *Focus on Exceptional Children* 19: 1–10, 12.

CHAPTER TWO

Parents, Families, and Children with Exceptionalities

Ms. D., parent of a nine-year-old son with learning disabilities:

"The first thing I thought, was "Why did it have to happen to me?" I've been around a lot of special ed kids, but this was mine, not the others. I was so careful while I was carrying him, why did it have to happen to him? When they said "placement", I just cried. I asked questions, and I couldn't understand why. And then I thought, he forgets a lot of things, he can't remember to do things, he can't sit still. I called my mother, and she said, "Look baby, you got eighteen years of this. You better deal with it. Do what the boy needs."

Chapter Topics and Objectives

The previous chapter communicated our belief that children with exceptionalities are first and foremost children, with needs and desires similar to those of other children. In this chapter, we address the variations in families with members who are exceptional and assess the effects of this specialness on their relationship with parents, other family members, the school, and the community. As Ramey, Krauss, and Simeonson (1989) suggest, studying families must include a recognition of their heterogeneity.

We review the current literature on families with members who are exceptional, using the social systems perspective that was introduced in Chapter 1. This perspective views the family as a social unit embedded within other formal and informal social units. This perspective is reflective of Bronfenbrenner's (1979) conceptualization that parents' functioning and their view of their child are related to external factors such as work, child care, friends and other support systems, the quality of health care and social services, the neighborhood, and society.

In this chapter, we will:

- Describe an integrative social systems perspective of parents and families with exceptional members.
- Describe the social contexts within which families with exceptional members develop.
- Discuss the impact of an integrative social systems perspective on working with families with exceptional members.

An Integrative Social Perspective

Contemporary social attitudes toward marriage and childbirth have a significant impact on the ways families adapt to the birth or diagnosis of a child with an exceptionality. Society views marriage as an eternally blissful union of two adults who then produce physically and mentally perfect children (Greer 1975). With nearly 15 percent of the school-aged population identified as exceptional (U.S. Department of Education 1988), this myth is challenged.

The most common interpretation of the way families adapt to the birth or diagnosis of a child with an exceptionality is based on a progression through a series of psychological stages: shock, denial, bargaining, anger, depression, and acceptance (coping) (Kroth 1975; Creekmore 1988). The theory of chronic sorrow views the grieving process, which is the consequence of the birth or diagnosis of a child with an exceptionality, as continuous throughout the life of the parent and child (Kroth 1975). Grieving is seen as necessary for parents in order to free themselves of the dream of the "perfect" child (Hinderliter 1988).

Though stage theory recognizes the significant emotional impact that the presence of an exceptional member can have on a family, there is little empirical data to support the stages of adaptation and the clinical inferences drawn from them. In an extensive review of the literature, Blacher (1984) concludes that the stages are the result of clinical judgment based on interviews with parents of children with exceptionalities rather than analysis of objectively gathered data. Allen and Affleck (1985) concur, suggesting that theoretical assumptions implicit in the stage construct are not addressed in the research literature. Their review of the literature and data analysis defied any stagelike categorization.

Kratochvil and Devereux (1988) suggest an additional concern when interpreting adaptation to an exceptional family member as a series of stages. Stage theory presupposes a final stage: closure, adjustment, or acceptance of the situation. In interviews with parents, however, they found that despite overall adjustment, all families experienced "down periods." These recurring feelings of grief were triggered by unreached milestones, worries about the future, and introspection.

As an alternative explanation, Bauer and Shea (1987) presented an integrated perspective on family adaptation to the birth or diagnosis of a child with an exceptionality. Viewed from this perspective, adjustment becomes a developmental process that is an attempt to meet both the parents' and child's needs. Family adaptation is seen as occurring within several nested personal, familial, social, and cultural contexts.

As suggested in Chapter 1, an understanding of the family as a social system requires the use of specialized vocabulary. *Ecology*, as we discussed, is the interrelationship of humans with the environment. This interrelationship involves reciprocal association (Thomas and Marshall 1977). From an integrative perspective, *development* is the continual adaptation of an individual and environment to each other. It is a progressive accommodation that occurs throughout the life span between the growing and developing individual and the changing environment. *Behavior* is the expression of the dynamic relationships between the individual and the environment that occurs in a setting that includes specific time, place, and object "props" as well as the individual's previously established patterns of behavior (Scott 1980).

Congruence is the goodness of fit, or match, between the individual and the environment. Congruence occurs when there is harmony between the individual's behavior and environmental norms. The lack of congruence is a result of the individual being out of harmony with the norms of behavior (deviant) or incompetent (lacking the necessary behavior) in the environment (Thurman 1977).

In the discussion of family adaptation, we will apply this systems or ecological perspective. The family's ecology is all of the settings in which the family interacts. The family itself is a reciprocal system—that is, the behavior of one member impacts upon another member. Development, the progressive accommodation of the family members within the system, is also affected by the reciprocal nature of the family; for example, as the child learns new skills, the caregiving role of the mother changes, changing the relationship of mother to child, siblings, and spouse. The concept of congruence helps us to gain insight into why families react differently to children with various disabilities. The match between the child and the family can be either supportive or stressful for the child or family members.

Bronfenbrenner's Social Contexts

Bronfenbrenner (1979) described human development as occurring within a series of nested contexts. His theory has been applied to adaptation to divorce (Kurdek 1981), to day care placement (Belsky 1980a), to child abuse (Belsky 1980b), and to the adaptation of familes with exceptional members (Bauer and Shea 1987).

In a paper applying Bronfenbrenner's theory, Kurdek (1981) analyzed the five contexts that influence adaptation:

1. The ontogenic system, which includes the individual's personal psychological competencies for dealing with stress*
2. The microsystem, which includes the nature of interaction among family members
3. The exosystem, which includes the stability of the environment and the social supports available to facilitate adaptation
4. The mesosystem, which includes the relationships between two or more settings within which an individual functions
5. The macrosystem, which includes the cultural beliefs, values, and attitudes surrounding modern family life.

These nested contexts, as they relate to parents and families of children with exceptionalities, are presented in Figure 2.1

Bronfenbrenner's ecological contexts offer a framework that enables us to simultaneously consider what is taking place within the immediate household (microsystem), the forces at work in the larger social system in which the family is functioning (exosystem), the interaction of these settings with one another (mesosystem), and the overriding cultural beliefs and values that influence the microsystem and exosystems (macrosystem). These contexts operate interdependently, and the nature of this interdependence changes over time (Lerner and Spanier 1978).

---

*This ontogenic system is not a component of Bronfenbrenner's theory but was postulated by Kurdek (1981).

FIGURE 2.1 • *Developmental Contexts as Related to Parent and Family Adaptation*

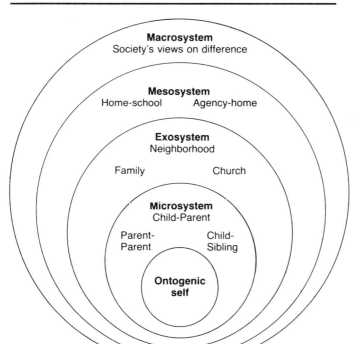

In the remainder of this chapter, we will describe parental adaptation to the birth or diagnosis of a child with an exceptionality as it develops in view of forces within the individual, the family including the exceptional member, and the community and culture in which the family functions. We will provide a detailed discussion of the literature on parental adaptation as it applies to the ontogenic system, microsystem, exosystem, mesosystem, and macrosystem. We will also present a rationale for the application of the social systems perspective to working with parents and families with exceptional members.

The Ontogenic System: Personal Factors for Coping with Stress

The ontogenic system includes personal factors that impact on an individual's ability to cope with stress (Kurdek 1981). Ontogenic development represents what an individual brings to the family setting and the parenting role. Personal characteristics within this system that are explored in the literature include gender, personality factors such as self-worth, religion, and the nature of the child's exceptionality.

Gender

When compared with fathers, mothers of children with disabilities describe themselves as less able to experience personal development or freedom, more limited in how they can use their time, poorer in health or mood, more sensitive with regard to how the child fits into the community, and more aware of disharmony within the family (Holroyd 1974). Cummings (1976) studied four groups of parents of children with mental retardation, chronic illnesses, and neuroses and of nonhandicapped children. He found that the fathers of children who were mentally retarded differed from fathers of normal children with regard to depression, preoccupation with the child, and diminished self-esteem. He hypothesized that fathers, unlike mothers, have fewer opportunities to do something directly helpful to the child, which provides concrete evidence for their loving, caring, and benevolent concern. Fathers have relatively few opportunities to counterbalance their sense of loss, frustration, and anger.

Goldberg, Marcovitch, MacGregor, and Lojkasek (1986) found that among the parents of developmentally delayed preschoolers, fathers reported fewer distress symptoms, higher self-esteem, and more internal locus of control than did mothers. Their results indicated, however, that fathers experience less support. Fathers of developmentally delayed children did not perform more child care tasks than fathers of nondisabled children; in fact, when the child was more seriously disabled, fathers assumed less tasks than did the mothers (Erickson and Upshur 1989). This recent finding concurs with earlier studies that fathers have fewer opportunities to interact with their developmentally disabled child.

Personality Factors

Though professional conjecture has attempted to stereotype parents of children with exceptionalities, empirical data have regularly failed to identify any abnormalities of personality in the parents of children with even severe disabilities such as autism (Cantwell, Baker, and Rutter 1979).

In a survey to assess their perceptions of themselves as teachers, the parents of intellectually handicapped children were found to demonstrate total mean scores within the same range as parents of intellectually normal children (Rees, Strom, and Wurster 1982). The child-rearing expectations of parents of children with mental retardation was also found to closely resemble those of parents of children with normal intelligence (Strom et al. 1980).

Schild (1982) suggests that parents of children with exceptionalities may have difficulty with regard to their personal expectations and feelings of self-worth. They may experience value conflicts, particularly when they are involved in decisions about institutional care for the child with an exceptionality and meeting the needs of other family members. Transitions, caused either by the child's development or by family mobility, contribute additional stress to parents.

Darling (1979) summarized several preexisting parental traits that may affect acceptance of the birth or diagnosis of an exceptional child:

- *Social class.* Parents of lower socioeconomic status appear to be more accepting than parents of higher status.
- *Religion.* Roman Catholics appear to be the most accepting.
- *Parents' personal self-acceptance.* The parents' level of personal self-acceptance appears to be directly related to their capacity to accept the child.
- *Prior experience with children.* Prior experience with normal and with exceptional children appears to facilitate acceptance.
- *Parents' age.* Younger parents are more tolerant.
- *Reason for having children.* The parents' reason for having children, such as to carry on the family name, appears to be related to their acceptance.

The Nature of the Child's Exceptionality

One factor impacting on the parents' ability to cope with stress may be the nature of the child's exceptionality. Considerable research has been conducted in this area, often with contradictory results.

The level of stress was found to be higher in mothers with severely disabled children than in a sample of mothers of nonhandicapped children. Little of the variation in stress could be ascribed to the external social and physical conditions of the family and the child (Bradshaw 1978). In a study of the mothers of children with Down's syndrome, the effect on the mental health of the mother was found to be similar in type and degree to that experienced by other mothers raising small children under difficult circumstances and was not significantly greater than the stress indigenous to raising a healthy baby (Gath 1977).

Frey, Greenberg, and Fewell (1989) found that the child's characteristics predicted the amount of stress parents reported and the amount of psychological stress reported among fathers. Greater stress was reported by parents of boys and of children with limited communication skills.

Holroyd (1974) studied the differences between the mothers of children with autism and of children with Down's syndrome. When compared with the mothers of children with Down's syndrome, the mothers of children with autism were found to have the following characteristics:

- They were more upset and disappointed about the child's condition.
- They were more aware and concerned about the child's dependency.
- They were more concerned about the effect of the child on the family.
- They were more concerned about the lack of recreational and community activities for the child.
- They were more aware of the child's personality and behavior problems.

In contrast, mothers of children with Down's syndrome were more concerned about their tendencies to be overprotective and encourage dependence. They were also more concerned about the limited school or occupational opportunities available for their child.

Irvin, Kennel, and Klaus (1982) indicate that parental reactions to their child's disability are dependent on the characteristics of the disability. The characteristics that they suggest impact on parents' reactions are presented in Table 2.1. In another set of studies, the number of physical handicaps a child presented was found to be related to parental tolerance and pessimism. When a child has fewer physical handicaps, parents tend to be less pessimistic (Holroyd et al. 1975). A child's age also impacts on the family's functioning, in that stress ratings were found to be higher for mothers of older children living at home than mothers of younger children (Holroyd et al. 1975).

Holroyd and Guthrie (1979) compared parents of children with neuromuscular handicaps with parents of children with behavioral

TABLE 2.1 • *Characteristics Impacting on Parents' Reactions to Their Child's Handicapping Condition*

Is the handicap correctable?
Is the handicap visible?
Is the handicap impacting the central nervous system?
Is the handicap life threatening?
Is the handicap impacting on future development?
Is the handicap affecting genitalia or eyes?
Is the handicap evident in a single sign or in multiple signs?
Is the handicap familial?
Is the handicap requiring repeated hospitalization, physicals, or visits to agencies?

Source: Adapted from Irvin, Kennel, and Klaus 1982.

disorders. Parents of children with neuromuscular handicaps were found to be more pessimistic; parents of children with behavioral disorders reported more problems in integrating the child into the family. Parents of children in wheelchairs had significantly higher stress factors related to excessive time demands, overcommitment and martyrdom, limits on family opportunities, physical incapacitation of the child, and lack of activities for the child. In Harris and McHale's (1989) study comparing families of children who were nonhandicapped and those who were developmentally delayed, parents reported stress related to more time for caregiving, concern over present and future needs, and uncertainty over the child's prognosis.

These findings contrast with those of Bradshaw (1978), who found that parents' stress scores did not vary with the child's handicaps, mobility, capacity to communicate, or personal independence. Rather, stress levels appeared to be a function of the parents' personality and physiology and not the burdens imposed by the child or social conditions. The authors believe that if their findings are true, attempts to reduce stress by providing goods and services or other resources would be ineffective. Wikler, Wasow, and Hatfield (1981) maintain that the intensity of the level of stress of parents seems to be a function of the child's developmental stage as well as the parent's individual coping strengths.

Considerations in the Ontogenic System

Our review of the literature suggests that parents' stress is primarily a function of their personality and physiology and not a consequence of the nature of the child's exceptionality. When professionals collaborate with families, then, programs that relieve stress by providing goods, services, or other resources are of questionable effectiveness (Bradshaw 1978). Rather, successful programs may be those that help family members develop effective ways of managing stress.

Although there is evidence that mothers and fathers differ in their needs and perceptions of their child, programs are traditionally designed for either both parents or for mothers only. Fathers are frequently hesitant to participate in available programs, perhaps because such services fail to meet their needs. Thus, designing programs in response to the individual needs of mothers and fathers may be appropriate.

The Microsystem: Intrafamilial Relationships

The microsystem focuses on relationships within the family. It represents the complex interrelationships within the immediate family setting and includes mother-father, parent-child, and sibling-child relationships. Family interactions before and after the birth or diagnosis of a child with an exceptionality have been explored in several research studies.

Mother-Father Relationships

The presence of both parents in the home is a major source of emotional support to the family (Germain and Maisto 1982). Friedrich, Wilturner, and Cohen (1985) found that a measure of marital satisfaction was a significant predictor of the parents' coping with their child's disability. In self-reports, parents emphasized the normal aspects of their families; however, they suggested that maintaining a satisfactory relationship with each other was crucial to their adaptation to the child's exceptionality (Drotar et al. 1975).

Parent-Child Relationships

Harper (1984) analyzed the self-reports of 101 mothers of children with multiple disabilities. The mothers reported on positive relationships, detachment, obedience, independence, and the control problems of their child. Harper found that a positive relationship is contingent upon a combination of compliant child behaviors in association with general child competence. For the mothers, a positive relationship was related to the child's being more compliant and possibly exhibiting a more passive interaction pattern. The mothers' reports were influenced by their child's age, intellectual level, degree of physical impairment, and number of nonhandicapped children in the families.

Cantwell, Baker, and Rutter (1979) found that mothers spent as much as twice the amount of time in concentrated interaction with their child with a handicap than with their normal children. According to Beckman-Bell (1981), the best predictors of the amount of stress reported by mothers were caregiving demands, the child's responsiveness, and the existence of self-stimulatory behaviors. Levy-Shiff (1986) found that having a child with mental retardation was reflected more in mothers' than fathers' behavior, with mothers having fewer positive interchanges with their children. Mothers were found to perform most of the caregiving for their children, even when fathers were at home.

The differences between parents of handicapped children and parents of nonhandicapped children reported by Levy-Shiff paralleled her findings that the interactions of children with mental retardation posed challenges to their parents. These children initiated and sustained pleasurable interactions (such as smiling) less often than their nonhandicapped peers and cried more frequently. Schell (1981) reported similar findings, suggesting that the development of reciprocity and a bond between parent and child is difficult to attain when parents are unable to interpret the infant's signals or when the infant seems unresponsive to the parents' activities.

Sibling-Child Relationships

Siblings may share the stigma of their brother or sister's exceptionality. Featherstone (1980) indicated that brothers and sisters of handicapped children may feel that they live in two cultures: the world of normal classmates and the world of the "exceptional" family. Siblings, however, are accepting and helpful to the handicapped child.

In interviews with children and their parents, Menke (1987) found that school-aged children who had siblings with chronic illnesses worried about them. They reported more changes in their parents than in themselves as a result of their sibling's illness. Children and parents agreed that both worried about the ill child but disagreed on the nature of their worries and concerns. Specific worries and concerns depended on the siblings' age and the ill child's diagnosis.

Sydney and Minner (1984) reported on a form of stigma in the behavior of professionals toward the siblings of children with exceptionalities. In their study, teachers recommended placement in programming for students with behavioral disorders more often for students with siblings identified as behaviorally disordered than for an identically described student with a nonhandicapped sibling. They concluded that in this way, information regarding a student's sibling may influence the placement recommendations of special class teachers. However, Dyson, Edgar, and Crnic (1989) found that the effect of the child with exceptionalities on siblings is mediated by the family's psychological and personal resources. Self-concept was influenced by the perceived family and parental problems, and variations in social competence were accounted for by the emphasis parents placed on personal growth and independence.

Family Functioning

A "new" family unit is formed when an exceptional child is born or diagnosed. In this new unit, there is reduced involvement with other families. More time is given to supervision and entertainment of the child with the exceptionality (Fotheringham and Creal, 1974). Cantwell, Baker, and Rutter (1979) found that families of children with autism were not characterized by abnormality in family life or interaction. Interaction between parent and child was found to be less frequent in families with a child with behavioral disorders than in families without such children (McAllister, Butler, and Lei 1973). A study of eighteen families of children with autism, behavioral disorders, or no handicap failed to demonstrate a relationship between the severity of behavioral differences and abnormality in family functioning (Byasee and Murrell 1975).

Gallagher, Beckman, and Cross (1983) suggested that two factors may influence stress levels in families with a child who is exceptional:

1. The child, as he or she grows older, demonstrates a slower rate of progress, more difficult temperament, stereotyped behaviors, and increased and unusual caregiving demands. Additional and unusual caregiving demands were related to higher stress levels.
2. The parents' view of the cause of the exceptionality may have a significant impact. The strongest predictor of both child prog-

ress and maternal performance was the mother's perception of whether or not they could be effective with their child. The number of parents in the home also affects the level of stress.

Significant Others

Families with exceptional members may experience decreased social interaction outside the family. The impact of this decreased social interaction or loss of social roles is considerably reduced if the parents have a close personal relationships with each other, giving each other social support (Lowenthal and Haven 1968). Social support may be defined as one of the following:

1. Information leading the parent to believe that he or she is cared for and loved
2. Information leading the parent to believe that he or she is esteemed and valued
3. Information leading the parent to believe that he or she belongs to a network of communication and mutual obligation (Cobb 1976).

Cobb contends that social support facilitates coping and adaptation to change. He suggests that there is a biological phenomenon of increased susceptibility to disease when individuals do not receive confirmation that their actions are leading to desirable or anticipated consequence. When an individual does not have this support, protective defenses are exhibited. The lack of a supportive environment in times of stress is a major reason some people respond with increased stress. These comments were confirmed by Minnes (1988) in her study of parents of children with mental retardation. Family social support emerged as a significant predictor of stress in a family, associated with dependency and management, family disharmony, and lack of personal rewards.

Considerations in the Microsystem

Beckman-Bell (1981) viewed the stress experienced by families of children with exceptionalities as the result of an ongoing process of interaction between personal consitutional and environmental influences. It appears, then, that professionals may be more responsive to the issues and concerns of families by analyzing (1) the personal characteristics and environmental influences, (2) the characteristics of the family that may change, and (3) those that are not likely to change. Programs may then be designed to respond to these issues and concerns.

The Exosystem: External Social Supports

The exosystem is the context in which events occur that affect the individual's immediate environment—that is, the individual's microsystems (Bronfenbrenner 1979). Settings within the exosystem may include work, church, neighborhood, school, and community. In this section, consideration is given to the amount of change caused in the exosystem by the birth or diagnosis of the exceptional child as well as the formal and informal support systems available to the family. Significant factors within this context may include professionals, social interaction, and external social supports.

Initial communication to the parents with regard to the child's exceptionality is usually from a professional. Early experiences between parent and professionals are frequently neither positive nor conclusive. Professionals often perceive parents as "shopping," that is, pursuing other professional's evaluations after receiving at least two earlier opinions (Kiern, 1971). However, in an empirical study, only 3 percent of the parents were identified as "shopping parents," and these parents were usually making specific requests for information. Kiern maintained that the term *shopping parent* may be a stereotype that reflects negative bias on the part of professionals and avoids the major issue—responding to a parent's request for help.

Professionals have a significant impact in the parents' exosystem. Donnellan and Mirenda (1984) suggest that due to their negative assumptions, professionals may in fact encourage shopping behavior by initially denying the existence of the child's problem, suppressing information, and disagreeing among themselves. To reduce parents' shopping behavior, they suggest that professionals make the least dangerous assumptions; that is, if an intervention is ineffective, they should assume that the intervention is wrong, not that something is wrong with the parents. Parents are often discouraged or misled by professionals (Marcus 1977).

Professionals have been found to overestimate the negative impact of the exceptional child on family relationships. They appear to overestimate the extent to which parents report community rejection and lack of support, while underestimating the parents' ability to use appropriate teaching and behavior management techniques in the home. The availability of external support systems, including service providers, educational services, medical services, and day care, has been found to be related to the parents' capacity to cope (Schell 1981).

The presence of an exceptional child in a family may modify the family's social interaction patterns. McAllister, Butler, and Lei (1973) indicate that parents of children with behavioral disorders are less likely than parents of other children to visit relatives, neighbors, friends, or co-workers. They are less likely to participate in social clubs or organizations. Although no difference was found among parents who belonged to formal support organizations, families with children with behavioral disorders were found to be less likely to interact frequently with neighbors than families of normally developing children. In addition, parents of children with behavioral disorders were less likely to interact with friends.

Korn, Chess, and Fernandez (1978) reported that in three-fourths of the families they studied, the exceptional child did not impair marital quality or family patterns. Parents felt that the presence of an exceptional child had little effect on the family (Dunlap and Hollingsworth 1977). Yet parents have reported restrictions in family activities (Blackard and Barsch 1982).

Family Resources

The extent of family resources affects its function (Farber 1975). Families with an abundance of personal, social, and financial resources are better able to adjust to the problems of raising a child with an exceptionality because they have the resources to obtain needed services. Families with limited resources were less able to redirect their resources to service needs (Abrams and Kaslow 1977).

Holroyd, Brown, Wikler, and Simmons (1975) found that mothers who demonstrated a high level of stress lacked social support, family cohesion, family opportunities, and financial independence. Chiriboga, Coho, Stein, and Roberts (1979) found that women were likely to seek help from others in many areas of concern. They sought advice and assistance from friends, spouse, counselors, relatives, and partners.

Support systems within the extended family may make a difference in the family's ability to cope with the birth or diagnosis of a child with an exceptionality (Schell 1981). Grandparents, for example, are a potential source of emotional support that enables families to withstand the stresses of maintaining a child with mental retardation in the home.

Considerations in the Exosystem

Members of a family's exosystem, such as friends, relatives, and self-help organizations, may provide support to parents of children with exceptionalities. Most relevant in our discussion, however, is the role teachers may play in assisting the family. If we can determine the environmental changes that result from the birth or diagnosis of a child with an exceptionality, we may be able to design the support systems needed to help the parents and family.

The Mesosystem: Interrelationships among Contexts

The mesosystem is concerned with the interrelationships of major settings in which an individual actually participates. These settings contain the individual at a specific point in his or her life. They may include relationships between school and family and between social agencies and family.

School-Family

Karnes and Zehrbach (1972) suggested that coordinated school-family endeavors serve children with exceptionalities better than school endeavors alone. They maintain that services for exceptional individuals can be improved if parents are meaningfully involved in their child's educational program. Parents and schools need to be mutually involved because they share responsibility for the child (Rockwell and Grafford 1977).

School-family involvement may reduce personal and family problems related to the child's difficulties (Ross 1964). Parents may change their behavior and improve the educational value of the family environment for the child as a consequence of school-family involvement (O'Connell 1975).

Social Agencies-Family

Social agency personnel are frequently the first individuals with whom parents interact about their child. These interactions are generally a result of a follow-up of an initial referral to determine the child's eligibility and acceptance into the service; an ongoing short-term service delivery program; or a response to an emergency or crisis request that demands immediate action (Unger 1974). There is little research on the impact of social agencies on family functioning; however, Levinson (1969) reported that the longer a family received assistance, the more likely it was that the family would have children with serious emotional problems. To parents, agency staff roles are confusing, and staffing is often perceived as inadequate. There seem to be frequent breakdowns in communication between agency personnel and parents.

Parent training may be provided by the social agencies. Parents, however, vary in their ability to profit from training. In a study of 103 families with children with mental retardation, Clark and Baker (1983) found that the families who were less proficient in the skills being taught were of lower socioeconomic status, anticipated greater problems in training, and were less experienced in behavior modification techniques. The parents who had difficulty implementing the techniques they learned during training were those who were less likely to have taught their children before training, to have achieved proficiency during training, and to have intact marriages.

Winton and Turnbull (1981) studied the provision of preschool services for children with exceptionalities. They found that the factors of greatest importance in parents' selection of preschool services for their child were logistics (i.e., location and transportation), respite (65 percent stated that they needed relief), parent-professional relationships, parent involvement activities (all parents liked informal contact with teachers, yet nearly 20 percent expressed that they would prefer having no role in the child's formal education), and the availability of a peer group for discussion and support. Winton and Turnbull concluded that professionals often mistakenly assume that good parents become involved with whatever parent activities are offered, regardless of their needs or desires.

Considerations in the Mesosystem

McAfee and Vergason (1979) make three recommendations to further the coordination of school and home efforts in behalf of the exceptional child:

1. School and family should develop a written or unwritten contract structured to ensure that each contributes toward common goals for the child.
2. Parents should assume some responsibility for their child's education.

3. School and family should seek ways to regain community support for the educational system.

Though the provision of appropriate services for the child is a critical issue, the school (and perhaps social agency personnel) may oversimplify the issue of parent involvement by equating the parents' involvement in formal programs with parents' involvement with their child. According to MacMillan and Turnbull (1983), a decision not to be involved in educational programming with their child does not mean that they are uninvolved with the child in the larger context of home and community. They maintain that parents have the right to choose not to be involved in a formal program when they feel noninvolvement is beneficial to them, the family, or their child. Decisions about the degree of involvement should grow out of parents' individual needs and preferences rather than generalized expectations of professionals.

Bronfenbrenner (1979) indicates that the developmental potential of settings within the mesosystem is enhanced if the person's initial transition into that setting is not made alone but with one or more persons with whom they have participated in prior settings. Development is enhanced if prior to entry into a new setting, individuals are provided with appropriate information, advice, and experience. The developmental potential of the settings within the mesosystem is enhanced to the extent that there are direct and indirect links to power so that participants can influence the allocation of resources and make decisions that are responsive to their needs.

It is essential to respond to the needs of individual parents. In a discussion of parents of children identified as mentally ill, Marcus (1977) suggests that a thorough understanding of the range of pressures and bewildering daily events affecting the lives of these families will enable the professional to deliver services based on parents' real needs rather than their presumed needs. In this way, strategies for intervention can be designed to respond to the family's expressed needs and concerns and their style of adaptation. The impact of the handicapped child on family relationships and the family itself needs to be carefully assessed (Blackard and Barsch 1982).

The Macrosystem: Societal Beliefs and Values

The macrosystem is concerned with the cultural beliefs, values, and attitudes surrounding family life and exceptionality in society. Bronfenbrenner (1977) defines this context as the generalized patterns, overarching ideology, and organization of the social institutions common to a particular culture or subculture. Rather than referring to specific ecological contexts, the macrosystem refers to the general prototypes that exist in any culture or subculture that set the patterns for the structure and activities occurring in that culture or subculture. The macrosystem includes the institutional patterns in which the microsystem, mesosystem, and exosystem are imbedded. Riegel (1975) suggests that though development occurs within particular contexts, an individual's developmental changes must be seen within the context of broad social and cultural change.

Stigma

As suggested earlier, society views marriage as a continuing union that produces healthy, perfect children (Greer 1975). Families not producing perfect children are considered "different" (Darling 1979), and this difference creates a stigma for parents. As a consequence, parents may demonstrate a loss of self-esteem, shame, defensiveness, aloneness, insignificance, or a loss of immortality.

Darling (1979) defines a stigma as a form of social reaction to members who are different and do not conform to an arbitrary set of expectations. Voysey (1975) suggests that parents develop strategies to deal with these societal expectations with regard to their child's exceptionality. Among the possible strategies the parents utilize are the following:

- Accept the inevitable ("It could happen to anyone").
- Don't take anything for granted ("Take it day by day").
- Redefine good and evil ("We didn't deserve this—it just happened").
- Discover true values ("We appreciate the little successes much more").
- Understand the positive value of suffering ("We can understand other people with problems much more").
- Value differentness ("Each person has some special contribution").

Managing a stigma that is a result of the beliefs and values in the macrosystem involves managing impressions projected by parent behavior as well as developing an ideology consistent with cultural beliefs. Parents may manage the impressions they project by conveying to others that the child is manageable and successful, by mentioning the exceptionality informally, by controlling the amount of information relayed, or by seeking information, that is, getting a "real" impression of the child from others (Voysey 1972).

Birenbaum (1970) suggested that parents acquire a "courtesy stigma" by association with their child. The parents' former social identity is not fully retained with the birth or diagnosis of a child with an exceptionality. Gallagher, Beckman, and Cross (1983) suggest that the social factors of mainstreaming may increase parents' stress because they share their child's stigma. Mainstreaming also results in a lack of intimacy with parents of similar children. Parents of older children have been found to be significantly less supportive of mainstreaming (Suelzle and Keenan 1981). Dealing with the public means parents must confront ignorance or callousness, explain behaviors, suppress anger or shame, and develop a thick skin, a sense of humor, or indifference (Marcus 1977). The child's social interactions in the community tend to result more from exclusion of the child than avoidance of the family (Suelzle and Keenan 1981).

Considerations within the Macrosystem

The broad components of the macrosystem involve society's beliefs, values, and attitudes about the family and exceptionality. Positive or realistic changes in society's beliefs, attitudes, and values with regard to family and exceptionality will provide the support needed to assist parents in adapting to the birth and diagnosis of a child with an exceptionality. As professionals working with families with exceptional members, we must recognize our personal assumptions and biases. Open acceptance of family members as individuals rather than as a stereotyped group (i.e., parents of children who are mentally retarded) is essential.

The Impact of a Systems Approach

In this chapter, we suggested that family adaptation to the birth or diagnosis of an exceptional child is influenced by a series of ecological contexts. The assessment strategies we describe in Chapter 4 are designed to respond to the interrelationships among the contexts. Their use will further enhance our understanding of the needs of families. This increased understanding can be used to facilitate individualizing programming in response to parents' needs. The model presented in this chapter delineates the relationships among individual, familial, community, and cultural factors with regard to parental adjustment to the birth or diagnosis of a child with an exceptionality.

The major advantages of a systems model is that it delineates nested relationships and provides a framework for the integration of research and concepts about parental adaptation. The birth or diagnosis of a child with an exceptionality will impact very differently on an individual with effective coping skills (ontogenic system), strong marital relationships (microsystem), supportive extended family (exosystem), and resources for the provision of support services (mesosystem) than it will on an individual under stress (ontogenic system) or a single parent (microsystem) with little outside help available (exosystem and mesosystem).

Summary

A contextual model for parental adaptation to the birth or diagnosis of a child with an exceptionality provides a positive and practical means of interpreting adjustment. The social systems perspective offers a systematic method for organizing and interpreting parents' reactions. The understanding derived from the application of this model will increase our empathic responses to parents of a child with an exceptionality. As Gadlin states (1980):

> In the face of social contingencies over which people have only limited control . . . they struggle to fit and resist the demands made on the form and content of their personal lives. Some lose, many are disfigured in the struggle, but always in their family life people attempt to satisfy their needs as best they understand them, while attempting to maintain some sense of personal and social integrity and keeping in mind the desire for the respect of those who matter most to them. They do this often with the realization that they are not completely in control of the forces they must control to be really satisfied, yet recognizing they cannot await the kind of changes that are necessary before they could live the kinds of lives they would like to. (p. 252)

Exercises and Discussion Topics

1. Discuss the following statement: "Society views marriage as an eternally blissful union of two adults who then produce physically and mentally perfect children" (Greer 1975). Is this statement generally true? False? Are views of marriage and parenthood changing as

time passes? Discuss this statement with your peers, your parents, and your grandparents.

2. Interview the parent of a child with an exceptionality, and discuss his or her first reaction to discovering the child's exceptionality.

3. Divide your study group or class into smaller groups, and have each group interview parents of an exceptional child. Use the contexts described in this chapter to provide a framework for your discussion. Compare and contrast the findings of each group.

4. Discuss this statement: Noninvolvement in a child's educational program does not imply noninvolvement with the child.

References

Abrams, J. C., and F. Kaslow. 1977. Family systems and the learning disabled child: Interventions and treatment. *Journal of Learning Disabilities* 10 (2): 86–90.
Allen, D. A., and G. Affleck. 1985. Are we stereotyping parents? A postscript to Blacher. *Mental Retardation* 23: 200–02.
Bauer, A. M., and T. M. Shea. 1987. An integrative approach to parental adaptation to the birth or diagnosis of an exceptional child. *School Social Work Journal* 9: 240–52.
Beckman-Bell, P. 1981. Child related stress in families of handicapped children. *Topics in Early Childhood Special Education* 1: 45–52.
Belsky, J. 1980a. Child maltreatment: An ecological integration. *American Psychologist* 35: 320–35.
Belsky, J. 1980b. Early human experience: A family perspective. *Developmental Psychology* 17: 3–24.
Birenbaum, A. 1970. On managing a courtesy stigma. *Journal of Health and Social Behavior* 11: 196–206.
Blacher, J. 1984. Sequential stages of parental adjustment to the birth of a child with handicaps: Fact or artifact. *Mental Retardation* 22 (2): 55–68.
Blackard, M. K., and E. T. Barsch. 1982. Parents' and professionals' perspectives of the handicapped child's impact on the family. *The Journal of the Association for the Severely Handicapped* 76 (2): 62–70.
Bradshaw, J. 1978. Tracing the causes of stress in families with handicapped children. *The British Journal of Social Work* 8: 181–192.
Bronfenbrenner, U. 1977. Toward an experimental ecology of human development. *American Psychologist* 32: 513–31.
Bronfenbrenner, U. 1979. *The ecology of human development.* Cambridge, Mass.: Harvard University Press.
Byasee, J. E., and Murrell, S. A. (1975). Interaction patterns in families of

autistic, disturbed, and normal children. *American Journal of Orthopsychiatry* 4: 473–78.
Cantwell, D. P., L. Baker, and M. Rutter. 1979. Families of autistic and dysphasic children: Family life and interaction patterns. *Archives of General Psychiatry* 36: 682–87.
Chiriboga, P. A., A. Coho, J. A. Stein, and J. Roberts. 1979. Divorce, stress, and social supports: A study in help-seeking behavior. *Journal of Divorce* 3: 121–36.
Clark, D. B., and B. L. Baker. 1983. Predicting outcomes in parent training. *Journal of Consulting and Clinical Psychology* 51: 309–11.
Cobb, S. 1976. Social support as a moderator of life stress. *Psychosomatic Medicine* 38: 300–14.
Creekmore, W. N. 1988. Family-classroom: A critical balance. *Academic Therapy* 24 (2): 202–207.
Cummings, S. T. 1976. The impact of the child's deficiency on the father: A study of mentally retarded and chronically ill children. *American Journal of Orthopsychiatry*, 46: 246–55.
Darling, R. B. 1979. *Families against society*. Beverly Hills, Calif.: Sage.
Donnellan, A. M., and P. Mirenda. 1984. Issues related to professional involvement with families of individuals with autism and other severe handicaps. *The Journal of the Association for Persons with Severe Handicaps* 9:16–26.
Drotar, D., A. Baskiewicz, N. Irvin, J. Kennell, and M. Klaus. 1975. The adaptations of parents to the birth of an infant with a congenital malformation. *Pediatrics* 56: 710–17.
Dunlap, W. R., and J. S. Hollingsworth. 1977. How does a handicapped child affect the family? *Family Coordinator* July, 286–93.
Dyson, L., E. Edgar, and K. Crnic. 1989. Psychological predictors of adjustment by siblings of developmentally disabled children. *American Journal of Mental Retardation* 94: 292–302.
Erickson, M., and C. C. Upsher. 1989. Caretaking burden and social support: Comparison of mothers and infants with and without disabilities. *American Journal of Mental Retardation* 94: 250–58.
Farber, B. 1975. Family adoptions to severely mentally retarded children. In *The mentally retarded in society: A social science perspective*, eds. M. Begab and S. Richardson, 247–66. Baltimore: University Park Press.
Featherstone, H. 1980. *A difference in the family*. New York: Basic Books.
Fotheringham, J., and D. Creal. 1974. Handicapped children and handicapped families. *International Review of Education* 20: 355–73.
Frey, K. S., M. T. Greenberg, and R. R. Fewell. 1989. Stress and coping among parents of handicapped children: A multidimensional approach. *American Journal of Mental Retardation* 94: 240–49.
Friedrich, W. H., L. T. Wilturner, and D. S. Cohen. 1985. Coping resources and parenting mentally retarded children. *American Journal of Mental Deficiency* 90: 130–39.

Gadlin, H. 1980. Dialectics and family interaction. *Human Development* 23: 245–53.

Gallagher, J. J., P. Beckman, and A. Cross. 1983. Families of handicapped children: Sources of stress and its amelioration. *Exceptional Children* 50: 10–19.

Gath, A. 1977. The impact of an abnormal child upon parents. *British Journal of Psychiatry* 130: 405–10.

Germain, M. L., and A. A. Maisto. 1982. The relationship of a perceived family support system to the institutional placement of mentally retarded children. *Education and Training of the Mentally Retarded* 17: 17–33.

Goldberg, S., S. Marcovitch, D. MacGregor, and M. Lojkasek. 1986. Family response to developmentally delayed preschoolers: Etiology and father's role. *American Journal of Mental Deficiency* 90: 610–17.

Greer, B. G. 1975. On being the parent of a handicapped child. *Exceptional Children* 41: 519.

Harper, D. C. 1984. Child behavior toward the parent: A factor analysis of mothers' reports of disabled children. *Journal of Autism and Developmental Disorders* 14: 165–82.

Harris, V. S., and S. M. McHale. 1989. Family life problems, daily caregiving activities, and psychological well-being of mothers of mentally retarded children. *American Journal of Mental Retardation* 94: 231–39.

Hinderliter, K. 1988. Death of a dream. *Exceptional Parent* 18 (1): 48–49.

Holroyd, J. 1974. The questionnaire on resources and stress: An instrument to measure family response to a handicapped family member. *Journal of Community Psychology* 2: 92–94.

Holroyd, J., N. Brown, L. Wikler, and J. Q. Simmons. 1975. Stress in families of institutionalized and noninstitutionalized autistic children. *Journal of Community Psychology* 3: 26–31.

Holroyd, J., and D. Guthrie, 1979. Stress in families of children with neuromuscular disease. *Journal of Clinical Psychology* 35: 734–39.

Irvin, N. A., J. H. Kennel, and M. H. Klaus. 1982. Caring for parents of an infant with a congenital malformation. In *Parent Infant Bonding*, eds. M. H. Klaus and J. H. Kennel. St. Louis: Mosby.

Karnes, M. B., and R. R. Zehrbach. 1972. Flexibility in getting parents involved in the school. *Teaching Exceptional Children* 5 (1): 6–19.

Kiern, W. C. 1971. Shopping parents: Patient problem or professional problem? *Mental Retardation* 9 (4): 6–7.

Korn, Chess, S., and P. Fernandez. 1978. The impact of children's physical handicaps on marital quality and family interaction. In *Child influence on marital quality and family interaction*, eds. R. M. Lerner and G. B. Spanier. New York: Academic Press.

Kratochvil, M. S., and S. A. Devereux. 1988. Counseling needs of parents of handicapped children. *Social Casework* 69 (7): 420–26.

Kroth, R. L. 1975. *Communication with parents of exceptional children: Improving parent-teacher relationships.* Denver: Love.

Kurdek, L. A. 1981. An integrative perspective on children's divorce adjustment. *American Psychology* 36 (8): 856–77.

Lerner, R. M., and G. B. Spanier. 1978. *Child influence on marital and family interaction.* New York: Academic Press.

Levinson, P. 1969. The next generation: A study of children in AFDC families. *Welfare in Review* 7: 1–9.

Levy-Shiff, R. 1986. Mother-father-child interactions in families with a mentally retarded young child. *American Journal of Mental Deficiency* 91: 141–42.

Lowenthal, M. F., and C. Haven. 1968. Interaction and adaptation: Intimacy as a critical variable. *American Sociological Review* 33: 20–30.

McAfee, J. K., and G. A. Vergason. 1979. Parent involvement in the process of special education: Establishing the new partnerships. *Focus on Exceptional Children* 11 (2): 1–15.

McAllister, R. L., E. W. Butler, and T. P. Lei. 1973. Patterns of social interaction among families of behaviorally retarded children. *Journal of Marriage and the Family* 35: 359–70.

MacMillan, D. L., and A. P. Turnbull. 1983. Parent involvement in special education: Respecting individual differences. *Education and Training of the Mentally Retarded* 18: 4–9.

Marcus, L. M. 1977. Patterns of coping in families of psychotic children. *American Journal of Orthopsychiatry* 47: 388–98.

Menke, E. M. 1987. The impact of a child's chronic illness on school-aged siblings. *Children's Health Care* 15 (3): 132–40.

Mercer, J. R. 1965. Social system perspective and clinical perspective: Frames of reference for understanding career patterns of persons labeled as mentally retarded. *Social Problems* 13: 18–34.

Minnes, P. M. 1988. Family resources and stress associated with having a mentally retarded child. *American Journal of Mental Retardation* 93: 184–92.

O'Connell, C. Y. 1975. The challenge of parent education. *Exceptional Children* 41: 554–56.

Ramey, S. L., M. W. Krauss, and R. J. Simeonson. 1989. Research on families: Current assessment and future opportunities. *American Journal of Mental Retardation* 94: ii–vi.

Rees, R. J., R. D. Strom, and S. Wurster. 1982. A profile of childrearing characteristics for parents of intellectually handicapped children. *Australia and New Zealand Journal of Developmental Disabilities* 8: 183–96.

Riegel, K. F. 1975. Towards a dialectical theory of development. *Human Development* 18: 50–74.

Rockwell, R. E., and K. Grafford. 1979. *TIPS: Teaching involved parent services.* Edwardsville: Southern Illinois University.

Ross, A. E. 1964. *The exceptional child in the family.* New York: Grune and Stratton.

Schell, G. S. 1981. The young handicapped child: A family perspective. *Topics in Early Childhood Special Education* 1: 21–28.

Schild, S. 1982. Beyond the diagnosis: Issues in recurrent counseling of parents of the mentally retarded. *Social Work in Health Care* 8: 81–93.

Scott, M. 1980. Ecological theory and methods for research in special education. *Journal of Special Education* 4: 279–94.

Strom, R., R. Rees, H. Slaughter, and S. Wurster. 1980. Role expectations of parents of intellectually handicapped children. *Exceptional Children* 47: 144–47.

Suelzle, M., and V. Keenan. 1981. Change in family support networks over the life cycle of mentally retarded persons. *American Journal of Mental Deficiency* 865: 267–74.

Sydney, J., and S. Minner. 1984. The influence of sibling information on the placement recommendations of special class teachers. *Behavioral Disorders* 10: 43–45.

Thomas, E. D., and M. J. Marshall. 1977. Clinical evaluation and coordination of services: An ecological model. *Exceptional Children* 44: 16–22.

Thurman, S. K. 1977. Congruence of behavioral ecologies: A model for special education programming. *Journal of Special Education* 11; 329–33.

Unger, C. 1974. Treatment of deviance by social welfare system: History and structure. In *A study in child variance, Vol. III: Service delivery systems,* eds. W. C. Rhodes and S. Head. Ann Arbor: Institute for the Study of Mental Retardation and Related Disabilities.

U. S. Department of Education. 1988. *Tenth annual report to Congress on the implementation of the Education of the Handicapped Act.* Washington, D.C.

Voysey, M. 1972. Impression management by parents with disabled chidren. *Journal of Health and Social Behavior* 13: 80–89.

Voysey, M. 1975. *A constant burden: The reconstitution of family life.* London: Routledge and Keagan Paul.

Wikler, L., M. Wasow, and E. Hatfield. 1981. Chronic sorrow revisited: Parent vs. professional depiction of the adjustment of parents of mentally retarded children. *American Journal of Orthopsychiatry* 51: 63–70.

Winton, P. J., and A. D. Turnbull. 1981. Parent involvement as viewed by parents of preschool handicapped children. *Topics in Early Childhood Special Education* 1: 11–19.

CHAPTER THREE

Perspectives on Parent-Teacher Collaboration

> Ms. R., parent of an eight-year-old daughter with behavioral disorders:
>
> *"The teachers here, they keep contact with you—they call on you as somebody who knows something. We talk, about what's going on, what Becka needs help in, when she doesn't, what they're working on, what they shouldn't work on. I sit in her classroom, and watch the teacher and how she's doing, and talk to the teacher about what's going on in class."*

Chapter Topics and Objectives

In this chapter, we discuss the value of parent education and parent-teacher collaboration in educating children with exceptionalities. The chapter offers suggestions for parents and teachers wishing to foster home-school cooperation and summarizes the advantages of such cooperation for children, parents, and teachers. The chapter reviews parents' rights and responsibilities—an important issue for parents and teachers who function as advocates for children. The chapter concludes with a discussion of parents who do not *formally* collaborate with teachers on behalf of their children.

In this chapter, we will:

- Describe the need for parent-teacher collaboration.
- Discuss attitudes toward parent-teacher collaboration.
- Suggest several benefits of parent-teacher collaboration.
- Describe the factors that contribute to effective collaboration.
- Discuss parents' rights and responsibilities.
- Discuss parents who do not *formally* collaborate with teachers in the education of their children.

The Need for Parent-Teacher Collaboration

Epstein (1988) describes five types of parent-teacher collaboration in education. The first involves the basic obligation of parents to provide for children's health and safety, prepare them for school, and build positive home conditions that support school learning and behavior. The second type of collaboration involves the basic obligation of schools to communicate with parents about children's programs and progress. The third type of parent-teacher involvement includes volunteering and attending performances, sports events, and other programs. The fourth type of involvement is conducting learning activities in the home with the assistance of teachers who share ideas and instructions for incorporating learning activities into that environment. Finally, parents can collaborate in school governance and educational decision making.

Though parent-teacher collaboration has been mandated since the passage of Public Law 94-142 in 1975, some special educators remain skeptical about its need and desirability. However, experience and research suggest that parent programs are not only needed and desirable but also essential to the development of effective programs for children with exceptionalities.

Parents are effective agents of change in their children's lives. Recognizing the responsibility they share with teachers for their children's social and academic learning, parents have moved, physically and intellectually, into classrooms and schools (Clements and Alexander 1975).

Clark (1983) reported that involving parents in their children's formal education improves student achievement. Parent involvement is most effective when it is comprehensive, long lasting, and well-designed. Involving parents in their own children's education, however, is not sufficient. Clark maintains that parents must be involved at all levels in the school. Schools and homes, he contends, cannot exist in isolation but must collaboratively expose children to the real world.

In her studies of inner-city children, Taylor (1988) found that children's knowledge is not available to the teacher simply for the asking; teachers can only make tentative interpretations based on their observations of children. She maintains that the greatest asset for gaining insights into children is through their families, which can become informants as teachers attempt to interpret the accomplishments of children in particular situations. Taylor suggests that when teachers work with children who vary from their peers, it is essential to know the family. In order to evaluate children, teachers need to build descriptions of the children as they interact in their various social contexts. It is necessary to understand these social contexts to gain some understanding of the social and academic accomplishments of teachers and children in the classroom.

The parents of students with exceptionalities are afforded many more opportunities to collaborate with teachers than are the parents of nonhandicapped children. Salisbury and Evans (1988) compared the mothers of students with severe disabilities with the mothers of nondisabled students and students with mild and moderate disabilities regarding their perceptions of school involvement. In comparison with the parents of students in regular education, parents of students with disabilities were offered more opportunities to be involved, were more satisfied with their involvement, and felt more able to influence their children's education. These differences between regular and special education were true over age groups, with no significant differences in the severity of the disabilities. Parents' satisfaction with involvement was found to be significantly correlated with perceived opportunities for involvement.

Attitudes Toward Parent-Teacher Collaboration

In a survey of special education teachers and teacher preparation personnel, Hughes, Ruhl, and Gorman (1987) found strong support for training special education teachers to work with parents. Little is known, however, about the nature of the actual activities for which teachers should be trained. In a survey of the frequency and types of parent contacts made by teachers, Hughes and Ruhl (1987) found that 42 percent of the teachers averaged fewer than five parent contacts a week; 31 percent averaged five to ten contacts; 11 percent averaged eleven to fifteen contacts; 5 percent averaged sixteen to twenty contacts; and 11 percent made more than twenty parent contacts a week.

Teachers, then, are actively involved with parents. The role they assume in these contacts, however, impacts on the effectiveness of their interactions with parents. Dunst and Trivette (1989) contend that in the most effective interactions, the helping teacher assumes a positive stance toward the parents and families; emphasizes the role and responsibilities of the families for solving their problems and meeting their needs; assumes that the families with whom they are working have the capacity to understand, learn, and manage events in their lives; and builds on strengths rather than attempting to remediate problems. In addition, Dunst and Trivette emphasize that in work with families, it is important to anticipate their needs rather to wait for problems to emerge before intervening. Effective helping teachers use collaborative activities with families to create opportunities for parents to become more capable and competent. As Ayers (1986) suggests, effective teachers perceive their function as one of empowering parents and families, helping them to take control, and supporting them in decisions with regard to their children. Effective teachers make themselves available to parents and interact with them reflectively.

In their role as effective helpers, Firth (1981) contends, teachers are sometimes confronted with being either an advocate for the child and parents or a professional employee who supports the school system. For example, when services are not available, some teachers are instructed not to put a needed service into the child's individualized education program (IEP). Effective teachers need to decide whether their initial loyalty is to the child or to the school system.

Benefits of Parent-Teacher Collaboration

Many authors have documented the advantages of parent-teacher collaboration that accrue to parents, teachers, and children with exceptionalities. This section offers a sampling of their views.

Advantages for the Child

Parent-teacher collaboration has several advantages for the child. It has a positive effect on children's academic achievement (Clark 1983) and enhances the probability they will succeed in school. Parent involvement significantly increases the number of people available to foster the child's development. The availability of additional people increases the time the child can devote to learning and individualized instruction.

Through collaboration, knowledge about the child not usually available to school personnel is communicated by the parents (Scott-Jones 1988; Taylor 1988). Such increased understanding of the child results in more responsive programming.

Parent-teacher collaboration communicates to children that school is seen as important to their families and that family members are an important part of the school community (Scott-Jones 1988).

Through collaboration, parents' and teachers' expectations of children become more consistent, which has a positive effect on learning and behavior (Blackard 1976). This consistency protects the child from anxiety, confusion, and frustration. Collaboration is also related to more positive attitudes and behavior among children (Henderson 1988).

When parents and teachers communicate frequently, children need not experience the anxiety of carrying messages of unknown content to and from home and school (Croft 1979).

Advantages for Parents

Collaboration holds several advantages for parents. Involvement in their child's education helps parents fulfill their social and ethical obligations for the education of their children (Epstein 1988). Also, working with teachers helps parents improve the educational value of the family environment (Murphy 1981). Involvement with understanding teachers and other parents improves parents' feelings of self-worth and self-satisfaction (Murphy 1981).

Parent education increases the parents' competence as their child's primary teacher. Parents learn effective instructional and behavioral management techniques and productive communication skills (Moersch 1978).

Advantages for Teachers

Teachers as well as parents benefit from collaboration. The child's cultural background and family values are infused into the school (Scott-Jones 1988). Parent collaboration provides teachers with information on the child's personal history, current problems, and the family and home environment (Marion 1981).

Collaboration also results in teachers' receiving support from parents for the school's goals. And it allows teachers to devote additional attention to children (Scott-Jones 1988).

Effective Collaboration

Dunst (1987) described effective collaboration as enabling parents and families to become better able to solve problems, meet needs, and achieve aspirations by helping them to acquire the competencies that support and strengthen functioning in ways that permit a sense of personal control. "Cooperation, communication, respect and appreciation are what all adults hope for and want from each other as they work together to meet the needs of children with disabilities" (Klein and Schleifer 1976, 10). Effective parent-teacher collaboration requires trust, commitment, work, appreciation, and communication. The partners are equals working together to set goals, find solutions, and carry out and evaluate these solutions (Rutherford and Edgar 1979).

Parents and teacher must rely on each other's character, ability, and strengths, and they must trust each other. Each must show confidence that the other will do his or her best for the child and the partnership (Stewart 1978). If parents and teachers mistrust each other, tension in the relationship may affect the exceptional child, with the danger that the child will become a pawn in a nonproductive game between parents and professionals.

In effective collaboration, both parties commit themselves to the purpose of the collaboration—that is, to help the exceptional child develop and to support each other's work. Each accepts responsibility for bringing about mutually agreed on plans and actions. Each understands that working together is more effective than working alone. Each is aware of how much there is to learn and appreciates the complexity and significance of the educational process.

As they plan and take action, parents and teachers increasingly become involved in the difficult work of helping the child and maintaining collaboration. They must have the capacity and will to spend the necessary time and energy to make the partnership work. As their relationship develops, they learn to appreciate each other's needs and hopes, and they learn to reinforce each other's efforts and successes.

Communication is the key to developing and maintaining effective collaboration. Parents and professionals must actively listen to each other (Lichter 1976) and understand that trust, respect, appreciation, and collaboration depend on honest communication. Communication dispels mistrust.

Though it is difficult to specify those personal qualities most needed for parents and teachers to work together effectively, several traits and practical skills are common among parents and teachers active in successful parent-teacher programs. The remainder of this section highlights these qualities. (Additional qualities, such as curiosity, willingness to learn, persistence, flexibility, and a sense of humor, are important supplements to qualities discussed here.)

Self-Awareness

Effective teachers have taken the time to examine why they work with exceptional children and their parents and how their work fits into their life-style (Shea and Bauer 1987). They have determined to the best of their ability the extent to which they are motivated by self-interest, a need to help others, or a combination of these motives. Teachers, like parents, are subject to denial and guilt, possibly feeling that they have contributed to the child's or parents' problems (Seligman and Seligman 1980). Thus, effective teachers will explore for negative emotions such as guilt, fear, sympathy or pity, and a need to control others and the extent to which they are balanced by acceptance, empathy, concern, and a desire to help others. They will also be aware of their expectations of children from different cultures and be alert to variations in the instructional activities (Henderson 1980). From this kind of awareness, the teacher learns self-acceptance.

Parents can also benefit from exploring their motives, perhaps working with a professional counselor to sort out their feelings about their children's exceptionality. Often, they will need time to regain their emotional equilibrium, their sense of self, and their commitment to their child.

As they grow in self-insight and self-acceptance, and as they acquire skills and experience, parents and teachers gain self-confidence, which in turn breeds acceptance of each other as partners in helping the child. Teachers accept themselves as they are, while seeking to improve personally and professionally. They are realistically confident in themselves and their abilities but are not so overconfident as to be naive. They do not have an unrealistic "I can do anything" attitude and are honest with themselves, parents, and other teachers about their strengths and weaknesses.

Expertise

Effective teachers are knowledgeable and skilled in the disciplines of child development, exceptionality, behavior management, instructional methodology, counseling, therapy, parenting, and parent education. They know the limits of their knowledge and skills and conscientiously seek to expand them (Lynch 1978).

Parents must also be knowledgeable, making a concerted effort to learn all they can about their child and his or her exceptionality.

They need information on the origin of the exceptionality, it's probable course with and without treatment, and its effects on the child's learning and behavior. They must learn about the impact of the exceptionality on the child's present and future and investigate available medical, social, and education programs (Schleifer et al. 1978).

Control of Emotions

Effective teachers recognize and control their emotions. They cope with the anxiety that frequently accompanies difficult tasks, new settings, or new students and their parents. Moreover, they exercise strict control over negative emotions that may arise during intensive interactions with others.

Although insensitive, incompetent professionals or a dearth of needed services may be extremely taxing, prudent parents also control their emotions. They recognize that anger can accomplish little of lasting value (Odle, Greer, and Anderson 1976).

Compassion

Effective teachers are compassionate and empathetic. They communicate their empathy to the parent who is hurting, sad, confused, or frustrated. They possess an understanding heart and can communicate their understanding and willingness to help. They project a deep concern for the parent, child, and problem. The effective teacher distinguishes between empathy and sympathy; teachers who consistently experience sympathy and pity may not be well-suited to work with children with exceptionalities (Seligman and Seligman 1980).

Parents and teachers must understand that their partners are human beings with strengths, weaknesses, abilities, and emotions. Parents must recognize teachers' limits in knowledge and skills. Parents, too, must be empathetic toward teachers, who can become as frustrated as parents by their inability to provide needed services (Lynch 1978).

Sensitivity to parents is another important quality. Hilliard (1980) suggested that insensitivity, particularly to a parent's cultural differences, will produce professional errors. A sensitive teacher will be open and receptive to the cultural contributions each child and parent can make (Chinn 1980).

Patience and Acceptance

Effective teachers are patient with themselves, parents, and other teachers. They recognize that all parties may make errors and become discouraged. They understand that the seriousness and chronic nature of a child's exceptionality makes instant solutions impossible. Teachers' acceptance of parents as legitimate partners is essential to ensure positive parent-teacher collaboration (Simpson 1982).

Parents in turn need patience. They learn that helping exceptional children is not an exact science and that teachers face many real limits on their ability to bring about change.

Honesty

Harmon and Gregory remarked, "Why is anything as simple and straightforward as honesty so terribly difficult to sustain in our day-to-day human experience?" (1974, 11). Articles by parents and professionals repeatedly emphasize the professional's responsibility to communicate honestly with parents. Professionals owe parents their most honest and complete judgments, including truth about the unanswerable. In fact, Shigley (1980) suggested that dishonesty delays parents' adjustment process. Sensitive teachers will nonetheless present the truth with kindness and consideration and will not indulge in bluntness and brutality in the name of honesty.

Parents benefit from honesty when they communicate with others about themselves and their child. They have the responsibility to let the teacher know when they do not understand something, do not agree with a proposed treatment, or lack the time and energy to participate in an activity. If they are honest with themselves, they can accept that they cannot be all things to their child (Taccarino and Leonard 1976).

Advocacy

Wolfensberger (1978) identified three criteria for effective advocacy. First, advocates possess a special commitment to advance the cause of another person. Second, advocates expend their own time, effort, and other resources. Finally, advocates are free of conflicts of interest and independent of the outcomes they seek.

Effective teachers are advocates for parents and children. They have an idealistic vision of what could be if all individuals and agencies exert maximum effort to help the child. Moreover, they are willing to take risks to serve the child and parent (Goolsby 1976).

Parents serve as advocates not only for their child and for themselves but also for other parents and children. They know their child's legal rights and their rights as their child's principle advocate. They are aware of the federal and state laws and regulations protecting the child and providing needed services. Armed with a thorough knowledge of their rights, parents must then know when to negotiate and compromise in planning and implementing services.

Parents' Rights and Responsibilities

Parents are the first and most essential teachers of their children. As such, they have ethical and legal rights to participate actively in their children's formal education. Nonetheless, many parents feel they have been denied meaningful participation in their children's educational programs. Rowell (1981) stated that all parents have the rights to know, to understand, and to share in all decisions that affect their children's education. Because parents are their children's principle advocates—that is, act on the child's behalf—they in effect must exercise their children's rights for them.

Recent federal and state legislation and several court cases are having and will continue to have a significant impact on parents' role in educating their children. These laws and judicial decisions have already significantly influenced the practices and procedures of special and regular education programs and related service programs.

One of the most important court cases affecting the education of children with exceptionalities was *Pennsylvania Association for Retarded Children v. the Commonwealth of Pennsylvania* in 1971. A consent agreement between the two parties granted all mentally retarded children full access to free public education. This consent agreement and similar suits have influenced educational services for the mentally retarded and other students with exceptionalities throughout the United States.

In 1972, *Mills v. Washington, D.C., Board of Education* affirmed the right of all handicapped children to a publicly supported education, including appropriate alternatives for those unable to attend regular classes or schools. In addition, the decision required school systems to guarantee exceptional students the constitutional protections of due process and equal protection under the law.

These decisions prompted several legislative initiatives by the

U.S. Congress during the 1970s. Public Law 93–112, Title V, Section 504 (The Rehabilitation Act of 1973), established equal rights for all handicapped people. The *Federal Register* expressed the hope that this regulation would "usher in a new era of equality for handicapped individuals in which unfair barriers to self-sufficiency and decent treatment will begin to fall before the force of law" (4 May 1977, 22677).

Several other provisions of Public Law 93–112 are particularly important. Section 501 forbids federal departments and agencies to discriminate in employment based on handicapping conditions. Section 502 calls for eliminating architectural, transportation, and attitudinal barriers confronting people with handicapping conditions. Section 503 prohibits federal contractors and subcontractors from discriminating against people with handicapping conditions in employment and promotion practices.

Public Law 93–380 (Education Amendments Law of 1974) is a major step toward realizing and protecting the educational rights established in the Rehabilitation Act of 1973. Among its major provisions are the following:

- Expenditure of federal monies to provide full service to handicapped children.
- Development of state plans to implement Public Law 93–380, including procedural safeguards for the "identification, evaluation, and educational placement of handicapped children." These safeguards include (a) prior notice to parents or parent surrogates when the educational agency proposes a change in the child's educational placement, (b) the opportunity for parents to have an impartial due process hearing, (c) the right of parents to examine their child's school records, and (d) the right of parents to present an independent evaluation of their child's needs and progress at a due process hearing.
- Placement of the exceptional child in the least restrictive educational setting capable of meeting his or her needs.
- Use of a parent surrogate as an advocate when the child's parents are unknown or unavailable.

The Buckley Amendment to Public Law 93–380 protects the rights and privacy of all students and parents. This legislation states that schools cannot release information or a child's records without parental consent. The amendment establishes parents' right of access to their child's school records and their right to challenge information in the records they deem inaccurate or inappropriate (Fanning 1977; Pasanella and Volkmor 1977).

The legislation reviewed in the preceeding section establishes national policy governing the federal, state, and local rules and regulations for educational service programs for children with exceptionalities and their parents. Public Law 94–142—known as the Education of All Handicapped Children Act of 1975—made these policies operational, mandating a *free, appropriate public education for all handicapped children.* Congress's intent in passing this law was to provide all children with exceptionalities with an education appropriate to their needs, whatever the nature of their exceptionality. Moreover, the public school system is to provide this free, appropriate education.

This act has significantly affected the structure and operation of the U.S. educational system, from preschool to postgraduate levels. It will continue to reshape both regular and special education services and affect all students for many years.

Abeson and Weintraub (1977) highlight the following provisions of Public Law 94–142 as most important to the parents of children with exceptionalities:

- Each child requiring special education and related services is to have an *individualized education program* (IEP) written in response to his or her specific educational needs.
- Parents are to participate in the development, approval, and evaluation of their children's IEP. As partners with professionals in their children's education, parents have other important responsibilities and functions: to participate in assessments of their children's progress, to contribute to placement decisions, and to participate in program evaluations. In addition, parents can participate directly in the child's educational program through instruction.
- Regular and special education teachers are to be full participating members of the IEP decision-making team. As the professionals primarily responsible for delivering services to children with disabilities, teachers have a full and active role in IEP development, implementation, and evaluation.
- Children with exceptionalities are to be served in "the least restrictive environment" necessary to meet their unique educational needs—that is, in an educational setting as close to a normal school placement as feasible that does not sacrifice responsiveness to the child's needs. The special education setting meets the needs raised by the child's exceptionality; the regular class and school setting meets the child's normal childhood and educational needs.

The following section of the law is important to teachers, allied professionals, and parents interested in parent-teacher collaboration:

> *The term "related services" means transportation and such developmental, corrective, and other supportive services as are required to assist a handicapped child to benefit from special education, and includes speech pathology and audiology, psychological services, physical and occupational therapy, recreation, early identification and assessment of disabilities in children, counseling services, and medical services for diagnostic or evaluation purposes. The term also includes school health services, social work services in school, and parent counseling and training. (Federal Register, 23 August 1977, 42479)*

Thus, "parent counseling and training" qualify as related educational services under Public Law 94–142.

Other important provisions of the law call for federal funds to state and local education agencies for early identification and screening programs, reaffirm earlier legislation guaranteeing the accessibility and confidentiality of a child's school record, mandate nondiscriminatory testing, and require "due process" procedures to protect the exceptional child's rights when parents and educational agencies disagree on the child's educational program. Due process protects children with exceptionalities from misclassification, inappropriate labeling, and education unequal to that offered the nonhandicapped (Stewart 1978). Either the educational agency or the parents may request a due process hearing to impartially resolve agreements.

A key provision of P.L. 94–142 is the individualized education program to be written for each child who is declared eligible for special education. The law specifically requires the direct participation of parents, teachers, and when appropriate, the child in the IEP development process. In addition, P.L. 94–142 mandated that a child be integrated into the regular school programs for education activities unless such integration is detrimental to the child's overall educational process.

Analysis of the description of the IEP in P.L. 94–142 suggests the following four minimum requirements under the law:

1. The child's educational performance must be assessed and resultant data included in the written IEP.
2. The results of the assessment must be translated into annual

goals and short-term instructional objectives to form the base on which the child's educational program is designed.
3. The educational program must be written and implemented in response to the child's individual needs as stated in the annual goals and short-term instructional objectives.
4. Objective procedures must be designed and implemented to evaluate the effectiveness of the program implemented in response to the child's individual needs.

The Individualized Education Program provisions of Public Law 94–142 require that parents and educators collaboratively develop and provide educational and related services in response to the needs of each child. The effectiveness of the education and related service program must be objectively evaluated. The IEP meeting is discussed in detail in Chapter 6 of this text.

Public Law 99–457, enacted in 1986, reauthorized Public Law 94–142 and provided a national directive for further services for young children with exceptionalities and their families. All the rights and protections of Public Law 94–142 were extended to children three to five years old in the 1990–91 school year. Parents are to be involved in their child's programs through a written individualized Family Service Plan developed by a multidisciplinary team and the parents.

In addition to the rights afforded to parents by law, parents have rights as human beings responsible for their children's welfare and education. Within broad limits, they have the rights and obligations to decide all questions affecting their family (Schopler, Reichler, and Lansing 1980).

Gordon (1988) described the rights of parents and families with members with disabilities:

- Parents have the right to mourn, to feel sorry for themselves, and to agonize over the question "Why me?"
- Parents have the right to feel they are doing the best they can.
- Parents have the right to organize their own lives to their satisfaction including hobbies, distractions, and leisure.
- Parents have the right to a sense of humor.
- Parents have the right not to be blamed or intimidated by professionals.
- Parents have the right to understand what's going on.
- Parents have the right not to be exploited.
- Parents have the right to accept help without apology.

- Parents have the right to make decisions.
- Parents have the right to a normal family life.
- Parents have the right to live a part of their lives that does not include the child.
- Parents have the right to fake it occasionally.
- Parents have the right to expect miracles.

If they are to function effectively as advocates for exceptional children, parents and teachers alike must be well-versed in the legislation reviewed in this section and in their human rights. Teachers can help parents learn their rights and responsibilities and can function competently and ethically when they know the legal and ethical parameters of their role.

Parents Who Do Not Formally Collaborate with Teachers

Although many parents recognize the need for and welcome professional support, some parents—and some teachers—do not actively collaborate in the education of the exceptional children for whom they are responsible. As a consequence, both may lose their most valuable ally.

Several situational factors may influence the parents' level of involvement (MacMillan and Turnbull 1983). The more severe the child's disability, the greater the demands are on the parents. For some parents, the school day is their only respite, so they seek to remain uninvolved during that time. Family factors—such as the family being a one-parent family, the availability of family support, the fact that both parents work, and the availability of child care—may discourage involvement.

MacMillan and Turnbull (1983) suggest that teachers may oversimplify the issue by equating parent involvement in educational programs with parent involvement with the exceptional child. Parents' decisions not to collaborate in their child's educational program does not mean they are also uninvolved with the child at home. MacMillan and Turnbull maintained that parents have the right to choose not to be involved in educational programming when they feel noninvolvement is beneficial to them, their child, or the family. Indeed, parents forced into involvement against their better judgment may become frustrated, be absent from work or from their families for extended times, have decreased free time, or become an inordinate drain on school staff. Decisions about the degree of involvement should grow out of individual preferences rather than generalized expectations.

Parent involvement in their exceptional child's educational program may be a benefit to some parents and a detriment to others (Turnbull and Turnbull 1982). Because not all parents are suited to be advocates, the Turnbulls pointed out the need to individualize programs for parents as well as for children. Parents' needs, abilities, and preferences and families' expectations are important programming considerations. Professionals must allow parents to remain uninvolved in educational activities if they so choose.

Epstein (1988) agrees that generalized expectations are ineffective for parents. Parent involvement, she maintains, requires site-specific development and leadership. Parent collaboration programs must be tailored to experiences, current practices, and school leadership.

In their study of sixty minority families, Leitch and Tangri (1988) found that work was the major reason given by working parents for nonparticipation. For unemployed parents, poor health was most frequently reported. Many parents felt there was nothing more they could do to help their child in school. For teachers who did not pursue active collaboration, personal family responsibilities were most often reported. Teachers suggested that the barriers to collaboration by parents included the unrealistic expectations of the school and parents' responsibilities to large families. Teachers suggested that parents did not collaborate because they felt that school wasn't important enough to take time from work; they were unable to help with schoolwork; they were jealous of teachers' upward mobility; they felt that long-time teachers were apathetic and unresponsiveness to parents; there was an absence of activities to draw them to school; and they believed that teachers resented or suspected parents who were involved. The most frequent barrier to collaboration as seen by teachers was the parents and their attitudes toward the school. Teachers also implicated the school in terms of apathy, paperwork, cumbersome systems, and intimidation.

Gartner (1988) suggested several tongue-in-cheek guidelines for effective teacher and parent interactions. He suggests that the ways teachers and other professionals actually treat parents may be in conflict with the public position that parents are welcomed, wanted, and needed. A summary of his "ways to exclude parents" is presented in Table 3.1.

TABLE 3.1 • *How to Exclude Parents*

Recognize their rights, when convenient

Teach them, but do not learn from them

Make explicit for them the reasons for their actions (they are denying their child's limitations; they are overprotective)

Invite them in (during school hours, and don't return the visit)

Keep it simple (have the IEP written before the conference, so they need not worry about it)

Source: Adapted from Gartner 1988.

Summary

This chapter considers the need for and advantages of parent-teacher collaboration in the education of exceptional children. The discussion demonstrates that though some professionals resist parent involvement, most parents and educators recognize that services for children improve with parent-teacher cooperation. The chapter points out specific benefits for all groups affected by the parent-teacher relationship—children, parents, and teachers.

Next, the discussion focuses on the necessary components of effective parent-teacher collaborations. Personal characteristics most likely to foster parent-teacher communication and cooperation include self-insight, self-acceptance, and self-confidence; knowledge about exceptionality; emotional control; compassion, empathy, and sensitivity; the ability to communicate support and provide feedback on others' efforts; patience and acceptance of others; honesty; and advocacy.

The chapter includes a brief review of recent judicial decisions and legislative mandates affecting exceptional children, parents, and teachers. Parents and teachers, as advocates for exceptional children, must be knowledgeable about these laws and regulations governing special education. The chapter concludes with a discussion of parents who do not collaborate, formally, in their children's education.

Exercises and Discussion Topics

1. In interviews with the parents of an exceptional child and a special education teacher, explore their positive and negative perceptions of the need for and desirability of parent-teacher collaboration.

2. Select one of the guidelines cited in the section entitled "Effective Collaboration." Conduct a group discussion or write a brief paper relating this guideline to a personal experience with a teacher, colleague, parent, or student.

3. The term *collaboration* appears throughout this chapter and elsewhere in the text. Write a paper or deliver an oral presentation on the meaning of this term in the education of children with exceptionalities.

4. Spend some time contemplating the concept of self-insight. Answer the following questions:
   - What is self-insight?
   - How does an individual develop self-insight?
   - Why did I enter (or why do I plan to enter) a helping profession?
   - Why do I work (or wish to work) with children with exceptionalities?
   - Why do I work (or wish to work) with the parents of children with exceptionalities?

5. Why is it difficult to honestly report negative (or potentially negative) information to parents? Interview an administrator, psychologist, social worker, or special teacher about the difficulties of honest, yet sensitive, communication of negative information.

6. Write a brief paper on the advantages and disadvantages of parent-teacher involvement for the child, parent, and teacher.

7. Write a paper on the legal rights of exceptional children, parents, and teachers in your state, commonwealth, or province.

8. Using Wolfensberger's criteria for an advocate, answer the following question: Can parents and teachers of children with exceptionalities be effective advocates? Defend your position.

References

Abeson, A. and F. Weintraub. 1977. Understanding the individualized education program. In *A primer on individualized education programs for handicapped children*, ed. S. Torres. Reston, Va.: The Foundation for Exceptional Children.

Ayers, W. 1986. Thinking about teachers and the curriculum. *Harvard Educational Review* 56: 49–51.

Blackard, K. 1976. *Introduction to the family training program: Working paper.* Seattle: Experimental Education Unit, University of Washington.

Chinn, P. 1980. The exceptional minority child: Issues and some answers. *Exceptional Children* 46: 598–605.

Clark, R. 1983. *Family life and school achievement: Why poor Black children succeed or fail.* Chicago: University of Chicago Press.

Clements, J. E., and R. N. Alexander. 1975. Parent training: Bringing it all back home. *Focus on Exceptional Children* 7: 62–64.

Croft, D. J. 1979. *Parents and teachers: A resource book for home, school, and community relations.* Belmont, Calif.: Wadsworth.

Dunst, C. J. 1987 (December). What is effective helping? Paper presented at the biennial meeting of the National Clinical Infants Program Conference, Washington, D.C.

Dunst, C. J., and C. M. Trivette. 1989. An enablement and empowerment perspective of case management. *Topics in Early Childhood Special Education* 8 (4): 87–102.

Epstein, J. 1988. How do we improve programs for parent involvement? *Educational Horizons* 66: 58–60.

Fanning, P. 1977. The new relationship between parents and schools. *Focus on Exceptional Children* 9: 1–10.

Federal Register. 1977 (May 4). Part 4. 42 (86).

Federal Register. 1977 (August 23). Part 2. 42 (163).

Frith, G. H. 1981. "Advocate" vs. "professional employee": A question of priorities for special educators. *Exceptional Children* 47: 486–95.

Gartner, A. 1988. Parents, no longer excluded, just ignored: Some ways to do it nicely. *Exceptional Parent* 18: 40–41.

Goolsby, E. L. 1976. Facilitation of family-professional interaction. *Rehabilitation Literature* 37: 332–34.

Gordon, S. 1988. Parents' declaration of independence and bill of rights. *Exceptional Parent* 18 (8): 26–30.

Harmon, M., and T. Gregory. 1974. *Teaching is. . . .* Chicago: Science Research Associates.

Henderson, A. 1988. Good news: An ecologically balanced approach to academic improvement. *Educational Horizons* 66 (2): 60–63.

Henderson, R. W. 1980. Social and emotional needs of culturally diverse children. *Exceptional Children* 25: 8–11.

Hilliard, A. G., III. 1980. Cultural diversity and special education. *Exceptional Children* 46: 584–88.

Hughes, C. A., and K. L. Ruhl. 1987. The nature and extent of special educator contacts with students' parents. *Teacher Education and Special Education* 10: 180–84.

Hughes, C. A., K. L. Ruhl, and J. Gorman. 1987. Preparation of special educators to work with parents: A survey of teachers and teacher educators. *Teacher Education and Special Educaton* 10 (3): 81–87.

Klein, S. D., and M. J. Schleifer. 1976. Editorial: Parents and educators—Bases of effective relationships. *The Exceptional Parent* 6 (4): 10.

Leitch, M. L., and S. S. Tangri. 1988. Barriers to home-school collaboration. *Educational Horizons* 66 (2): 70–75.

Lichter, P. 1976. Communicating with parents: It begins with listening. *Teaching Exceptional Children* 8 (2): 66–71.

Lynch, E. W. 1978. The home-school partnership. In *Parents on the team*, eds. L. Brown and M. Moersch, 21–24. Ann Arbor: University of Michigan Press.

MacMillan, D. L., and A. P. Turnbull. 1983. Parent involvement with special education: Respecting individual differences. *Education and Training of the Mentally Retarded* 18: 4–9.

Marion, R. L. 1981. *Educators, parents, and exceptional children*. Rockville, Md.: Aspen.

Moersch, M. S. 1978. History and rationale for parent involvement. In *Parents on the team*, eds. S. L. Brown and M. S. Moersch. Ann Arbor: University of Michigan Press.

Murphy, A. T. 1981. *Special children, special parents: Personal issues with handicapped children*. Englewood Cliffs, N.J.: Prentice-Hall.

Odle, S. J., J. G. Greer, and R. M. Anderson. 1976. The family of the severely retarded individual. In *Educating the severely and profoundly retarded*, eds. R. M. Anderson and J. G. Greer, 251–61. Baltimore: University Park Press.

Pasanella, A. L., and C. B. Volkmor, 1977. *To parents of children with special needs: A manual on parent involvement in educational programming*. Los Angeles: California Regional Resource Center.

Rowell, J. C. 1981. The five rights of parents. *Phi Delta Kappan* 62: 441–43.

Rutherford, R. B., and E. Edgar. 1979. *Teachers and parents: A guide to interaction and cooperation*. Boston: Allyn and Bacon.

Salisbury, C., and I. M. Evans. 1988. Comparison of parental involvement in regular and special education. *Journal of the Association for Persons with Severe Handicaps* 13: 268–72.

Schleifer, M. J., S. D. Klein, and E. D. Griffin. 1978. Parent-professional communication: Practical suggestions. *The Exceptional Parent* 8 (2): f15–f18.

Schopler, E. R., R. J. Reichler, and M. Lansing. 1980. *Individualized assessment and treatment for autistic and developmentally disabled children*. Baltimore: University Park Press.

Scott-Jones, D. 1988. Families as educators: The transition from informal to formal school learning. *Educational Horizons* 66 (2): 66–70.

Seligman, M., and P. A. Seligman. 1980. The professional's dilemma: Learning to work with parents. *The Exceptional Parent* 10 (2): S11–S13.

Shea, T. M., and A. M. Bauer. 1987. *Teaching children and youth with behavior disorders*. Englewood Cliffs, N.J.: Prentice-Hall.

Shigley, R. H. 1980. Parent and professional: Personal views from both perspectives. *The Pointer* 25 (1): 8–11.

Simpson, R. L. 1982. Future training issues. *Exceptional Education Quarterly* 3 (2): 81–88.

Stewart, J. C. 1978. *Counseling parents of exceptional children.* Columbus, Ohio: Charles E. Merrill.

Taccarino, J. R., and M. A. Leonard. 1976. Coping strategies for parents of the mentally retarded. In *Tomorrow's flower,* ed. A. M. Burke. Chicago: Illinois Association for Retarded Citizens.

Taylor, D. 1988. Ethnographic educational evaluation for children, families, and schools. *Theory into Practice* 27 (1): 67–76.

Turnbull, H. R., and A. P. Turnbull. 1982. Assumptions about parental participation: A legislative history. *Exceptional Education Quarterly* 3: 1–8.

Wolfensberger, W. A. 1978. *A multicomponent advocacy protection scheme.* Toronto: Canadian Association for the Mentally Retarded.

CHAPTER FOUR

A Model for Parent-Teacher Collaboration

Ms. S., parent of a six-year-old daughter with moderate mental retardation:

"When we took Lizzie in to be tested, everyone was asking questions: How long did I carry her? Did I take any drugs or drink when I was pregnant? Do we treat her like our other kids? Was she a happy baby? All kinds of questions that made me wonder if they didn't think I did something wrong to have a baby like Lizzie. When they were done and Lizzie went into special education, the first thing the teacher said was, 'We're here to help Lizzie learn everything she can, and to help you do the things you want to do to help Lizzie.' It was nice to know somebody didn't think it was my fault."

Chapter Topics and Objectives

This chapter introduces a model to help education, special education, mental health, and social service professionals work effectively with parents in raising children with exceptionalities. The model, essentially a procedural framework or tool, parallels processes mandated by Public Law 92–142 for individualized education programs and Public Law 99–457 for family involvement plans (see Chapter 3). It, or similar service delivery models, will be an essential component of quality special education service programs in the 1990s and beyond.

The model aims to respond to parents' and children's varied informational, educational, and social-emotional needs, keeping in mind the importance of individualizing the activities designed to do so. It recognizes the importance of teachers and other human service professionals in child raising but assumes that parents are primarily and ultimately responsible for educating and training their children.

The model is essentially a prescriptive-teaching methodology. Activities emphasize exclusively positive, humane child-raising practices and behavior management techniques that recognize each parent and child as an individual with unique abilities, needs, and environmental influences. Aversive interventions are inappropriate in this framework.

The model involves parents, and in some circumstances the child, with the teacher and other professionals in all decision making. It emphasizes cooperation and collaboration—sharing rather than one-way dispensing of information and skills. All channels of communication among parents, children, and teacher are essential and of equal worth in furthering exceptional children's development.

The primary goal of the model is to further, through parent-teacher activities, the optimal development of the exceptional child, as a person, a son or daughter, and a learner. It views parents and teachers as the primary agents of change in the child's life.

Teachers and parents design individualized programs based on assessment data gathered through information-gathering techniques such as those described later in this chapter. Once they have a thorough understanding of parents' and children's needs, teachers can develop appropriate activities. These activities will aim to develop the child's cognitive, affective, and psychomotor abilities, each essential to the child's overall growth and development.

The model is applicable to all children. However, it is especially sensitive to the needs of parents and children confronting problems that lie outside normally anticipated child growth and development processes. It is not designed for treating parents with social-emotional conflicts, psychopathologies, or marital difficulties, however. It is not a form of psychotherapy, as important as such treatment may be for some parents. Teachers and other professionals using the model will find that some parents cannot benefit their child through this or similar programs. In such cases, they must refer to qualified and certified therapists, counselors, or social service professionals. Clearly, too, the effectiveness of the model, as of any model, depends on the interest, willingness, and ability of the parents and teachers participating in the program.

In this chapter, we will:

- Present a model for parent-teacher collaboration.
- Describe communication skills and information-gathering techniques for working with parents.

- Discuss ways of assessing the needs of families with whom we work.

The Model

The family systems model presented in Chapters 1 and 2 and the perspectives on parent-teacher collaboration described in Chapter 3 have several implications for designing programs of parent-teacher collaboration. The model we describe assumes that families are potentially capable and willing to make responsible decisions, that they want the best for their children, and that they frequently are not provided opportunities to acquire the needed information and skills (Cohen et al. 1989). An individualized plan for parents, using a defined model such as that presented here, is needed.

The model we suggest (Shea and Bauer 1987) is consistent with the trend of moving away from parent-involvement to family-focused interventions and empowerment (Winton, 1986). The model's purpose is to help families become better able to solve their problems and meet their needs in ways that permit a sense of family control over programming (Dunst 1987). We recognize the needs of families and concur with Donnellan and Mirenda (1984) that professionals cannot assume that the needs of the child with exceptionalities supercedes all other family needs; and that if interactions with the family are not productive, the family is at fault. We make the following assumptions, as Vincent and associates (1981) have suggested:

- Emotional reactions of families with children with exceptionalities are normal and potentially productive.
- Though families may need professional assistance in managing and educating their children, they are capable of solving problems without professional assistance.
- Professionals must learn to work within the family, and families do not have to change as a consequence of professional assistance.
- Having a child with an exceptionality may not be the most serious problem a family is confronting at a given period of time.
- The family can be the child's best, most committed, and long-term advocate.
- Parents and professionals share concerns for the long-term functioning of the handicapped individual.
- Families want to do what is best for the child.

- Families want to be and should be actively involved in the child's educational program.

Olsen (1988) suggests that because parents are a heterogeneous group, professionals must understand individual parents' current development when working with their child. Service models should consider that parents' needs and services range developmentally from a crisis level, in which it is difficult to address other than the immediate crisis, through a need for information and education, to a need for skill development. Throughout these stages, parents and families require emotional support and support for performing task-oriented activities such as working with the teacher on the child's IEP or interacting with community service agencies' personnel.

In summary, models for parent-teacher collaboration should help families identify their needs, recognize existing family support systems, and help families become independent and compctent problem solvers. In the remainder of this section, we discuss such a model.

The parent-teacher collaboration model (Figure 4.1) includes five phases: (1) intake and assessment, (2) selection of goals and objectives, (3) planning and implementation of activities, (4) evaluation of activities, and (5) review (Shea and Bauer 1987). The flowchart in Figure 4.1 illustrates various decision points in the collaboration process, and the following sections describe each phase in detail.

Phase 1: Intake and Assessment

Ideally, parent-teacher collaboration begins before the child's placement in a special education service program. Collaboration has potentially occurred throughout the prereferral, referral, and diagnostic-evaluation processes. However, in the real world of special education, this early contact is not always used as extensively as possible. Consequently, parent-teacher contact should commence at the first possible opportunity.

Intake and assessment consist of a series of conferences between parents and teacher. These conferences have the following goals:

- To establish a positive interpersonal relationship between parents and teachers
- To ease parents' introduction to and acceptance of parent-teacher collaboration

FIGURE 4.1 • *The Parent-Teacher Collaboration Model*

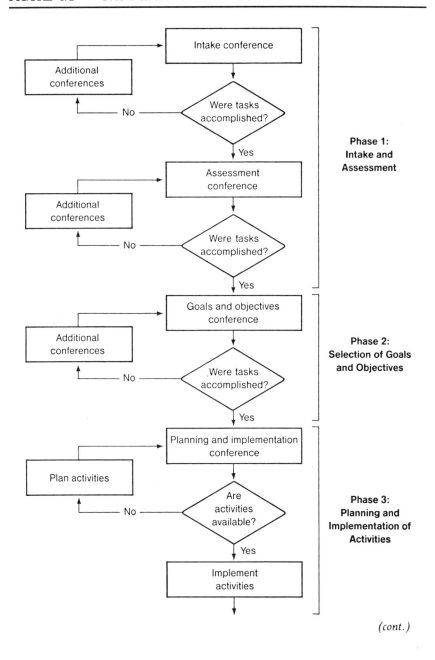

(cont.)

FIGURE 4.1 *Continued*

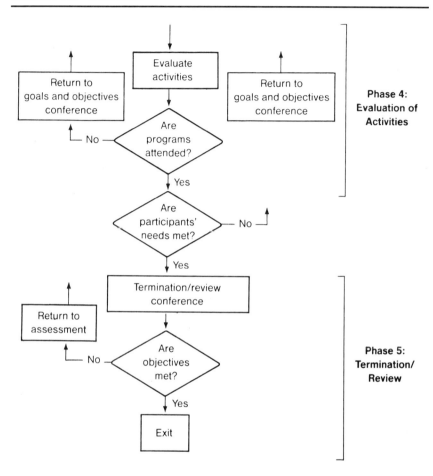

- To share with parents their child's assessment information and describe his or her special and regular education programs
- To ascertain parents' perceptions of their children and their exceptionality, as well as their special needs, prognosis, and educational programs
- To determine parents' needs, desires, interests, and competencies in parenting their children and responding to their special needs.

During the intake conference, the first meeting between parents and teachers, the teacher seeks to establish a positive interpersonal relationship, review and discuss the child's assessment information, and review and discuss the child's regular and/or special educational placement and program. The teacher reviews with the parents the parameters of the child's exceptionality, attempting to ascertain the parents' perception of the child's problems in the process. The intake conference is complete only when parents and teacher agree that they have accomplished the tasks cited above.

Assessment conferences focus primarily on parents' perception of their children and their exceptionality. These conferences help the teacher determine the parents' capacity to attend to their child's problem and to verify their understanding of the information presented to them during the intake conference. Although the conferences rely primarily on interview techniques for assessment, teachers can use various strategies to supplement the interview. During assessment, parents and teacher attend to the following tasks:

- Parents provide their perspective on their child and their assessment of his or her exceptionalities.
- The teacher and parents assess the parents' readiness, interest, willingness, capacity, and need for a parent-teacher program.

Assessment strategies are discussed in detail later in this chapter in the section "Communication and Information-Gathering Techniques."

The assessment is complete when parents and teacher agree that they have sufficient information and understanding to proceed to phase 2 of the model. If they do not have adequate information or if they have not reached consensus, they continue to seek an agreed-upon assessment of the child's status.

Phase 2: Selection of Goals and Objectives

Selecting goals and objectives is one of the most crucial components of a model for parent-teacher collaboration. Dunst and associates (1988) suggest that the failure of most programs is due to a lack of consensus on what is needed or what should be done. Selection of goals and objectives must be a participatory process (Winton, 1986). In phase 2, parents and teacher synthesize the assessment data they accumulated during phase 1 to develop goals for their collaboration program. Phase 2 tasks generally require one or more conferences to clarify the unmet needs of parents and teachers in working with the exceptional child.

The unmet needs identified by parents and teacher translate

into program goals and objectives. Goals are global (or general) targets of the program; they state the desired outcomes of the collaborative activities yet to be determined. Objectives are precise, specific, and limited statements of the desired results of collaborative activity. They state the behavior, knowledge, or skill the parent, child, or teacher will exhibit upon completing an activity; the conditions under which the new behavior will be exhibited; and the criteria for acceptable performance of the new behavior.

Program objectives are essential precursors to planning and implementing activities in phase 3. Parents and teacher should select objectives independent of their knowledge of whether a suitable activity is available. If one is not available, they will later design an appropriate activity to respond to their objective.

Frequently, parents and teachers select more objectives than they can reasonably attain during the time available. Thus, they must organize objectives by priority. It is prudent to include at least one of the parents' and one of the teacher's high-priority objectives among those selected for immediate implementation. Collaboration will break down if either party insists on giving his or her objectives first priority. When parents and professionals have completed phase 2, they can proceed to the next phase.

Phase 3: Planning and Implementation of Activities

Phase 3 includes two steps: planning activities and carrying out the agreed-upon activities. During the activities-planning conferences, parents and teacher translate the objectives of phase 2 into collaborative activities. In many cases, they will find needed activities in the school and community.

Winton (1986) suggests that teachers function as case managers, acquainting families with a wide range of community resources and providing linkage for families as they seek information, service, and support. However, if appropriate programs are not available, parents and teacher will plan a suitable activity or select a suitable alternative from those available.

Parents and teacher will generally select activities such as written and telephone communications, individual parent-teacher conferences, parent-teacher groups, and classroom, school, and community activities (see Chapters 5 through 9). These activities represent a continuum from minimum to maximum collaboration (see Figure 4.2), and parents and teacher will establish in their conferences the most appropriate level of involvement. Thus, the activities selected

FIGURE 4.2 • Continuum of Collaboration

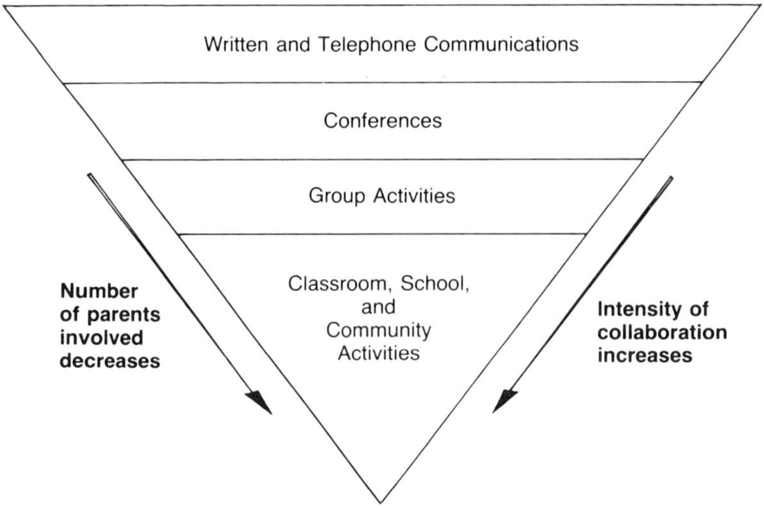

```
            Written and Telephone Communications
                      Conferences
                    Group Activities
                 Classroom, School,
  Number              and                    Intensity of
  of parents        Community                 collaboration
  involved          Activities                increases
  decreases
```

will reflect the intensity of personal involvement required for success, the openness of communication between the parents and the teacher, the degree of personal content in the activity, and the duration and frequency of participation required.

During planning, parents and teacher agree on when, where, and how they will complete each activity. Phase 3 is complete when they implement agreed-upon activities. As parents and teacher proceed through activities, they evaluate their effectiveness.

Phase 4: Evaluation of Activities

In phase 4, parents and teacher evaluate the effectiveness and efficiency of the activities under way. This stage includes both *process* and *content* evaluations that ask two basic questions: Is the prescribed activity available to the right people, and do they participate in it? Is the activity effectively changing the participants' behavior—that is, improving performance, knowledge, or skill?

Parents and teacher evaluate *process* using accountability procedures to answer such questions as the following:

- Is the activity available?
- Is the activity offered as scheduled?
- Are all parties attending the activities?

- Are all parties participating in the activities at the agreed-upon level?

The answers to these questions help both the teacher and parents determine if they are maintaining their part of the agreement. For example, if an activity does not take place as scheduled and both parties had agreed that the teacher was to organize and conduct the activity, the person responsible for the failure is clear. Alternatively, if an activity takes place as scheduled and parents do not attend or do not participate as prescribed, the parents are clearly responsible for the breakdown in the program. By conferring periodically to review the process evaluations, parents and teacher have a mechanism for remedying problems.

The second type of evaluation is *content* evaluation, which responds to the question, "Are the participants learning the knowledge and skills promoted by the activity?" For example, teachers can examine parents participating in a study group on the content of an accompanying text or lectures. Or the teacher can assess competency using a newly learned teaching or behavior management skill by observing changes in the parents' or child's behavior.

Phase 5: Review

The final phase of the parent-teacher collaboration model is the review conference. Generally, collaboration ends only when the parent or teacher leaves the school or community or when the student graduates from school or moves to another program, classroom, or teacher. However, parents and teacher should meet at least annually to review the program plan and modify it if necessary. This step ensures that the program remains responsive to the ever-changing needs of the child, parents, and teacher. The child's annual individualized educational program conference (IEP conference) may be an appropriate and convenient time to conduct the review.

A program development form, such as the one in Figure 4.3, can be an invaluable tool for the teacher as he or she moves through the five phases of the parent-teacher collaboration model. By noting each step of the process as it occurs, teacher and parents have a record of their interactions and mutual decisions. Notes in each column of the form provide data for its use. Teachers can also use the form as a focal point for discussions. (Chapter 12 provides completed examples of the form.)

FIGURE 4.3 • *Program Development Form*

Parents' Names _____ Teacher _____ Date _____

I Assessment	II Goals and Objectives	III Activities	IV Evaluation
A. List the assessment techniques used to obtain the data synthesized in IB.	A. List the goals, by priority, derived from the assessment process and mutually agreed on by parents and teacher.	List the activities designed by parents and teacher to meet the objectives in IIB.	A. Process: List the procedures parents and teacher will use to evaluate the processes for carrying out the activities in III.
B. List the needs mutually agreed upon using the assessment techniques in IA.	B. List the objectives derived from the goals in IIA.		B. Content: List the procedures parents and teachers will use to evaluate the content of the activities in III.

*Caution: The focus of the information to be written in the Program Development Form is on parents' needs, objectives, activities, and so on, not the needs, objectives, and activities of the child, though these are obviously related.

Communication Skills and Information-Gathering Techniques

Mutually respectful communication lies at the heart of the parent-teacher collaboration model. Thus, professionals need special interpersonal skills to work effectively with parents. Some of these skills and techniques are basic to any communication process; others are specific to components of the model. This section outlines the communication skills and special techniques that are the building blocks for effective parent-teacher interactions throughout the five-phase process making up the model. Always, the goal is to help teachers understand parents' and children's needs so that they can support them in developing important coping skills and a positive self-image.

Interpersonal Communication

Communication is a basic human need essential to human existence (Chinn, Winn, and Walters 1978). People communicate to affect others, the environment, and themselves; they send messages in order to obtain a response and thus influence others' behavior. Communication also provides catharsis, relieving tension, frustration, and anxiety, which in turn can lead to self-discovery and self-insight.

Humans communicate at several levels simultaneously; through verbal expressions, or what they say; through body language or nonverbal expression, or how they behave; and through emotional responses, or how they show what they feel. The more congruent these levels of expression, the more meaningful or understandable the messages become to others. To fully interpret others' messages, one must both listen to the words and interpret the accompanying nonverbal components of body language and emotional content.

In an interview, communication is circular and forward moving. An act of communication is not repeatable; it is impossible to "uncommunicate" a message. Through continuing communication, however, people can amend their messages (Webster 1977). By understanding and monitoring three important forms of language—descriptive, inferential, and evaluative—people can reduce the need to amend original messages.

Descriptive language relates information about things the communicator has observed using his or her senses of sight, hearing, taste, touch, and smell. Inferential language describes patterns a person has become aware of through multiple observations. Such language is tentative, qualifying observations with such words as *appears, seems,* and *maybe.*

Evaluative language communicates judgments and conclusions. It "tells about what is going on inside the head of the person making the evaluation. Evaluations can be positive or negative statements because they refer to the speaker's values; such statements will reveal what the speaker considers right or wrong, worthy or unworthy, beautiful or ugly, and so forth" (Webster 1977, 18). Evaluations use forms of the verb *to be* and words like *always, never,* and *must.*

The teacher should be skillful in differentiating between the three forms of language in the messages both sent to and received from parents. He or she should be able to relate objective information to parents about their child (descriptive language), communicate patterns that seem to emerge from observations (inferential language), and formulate conclusions (evaluative language). By the same token, with an awareness of the different levels used by parents, teachers can be more sure of the accuracy of their perceptions of the parents' message.

Numerous barriers exist to effective communiction, however. Webster suggested that human projections can interfere with communication, especially people's perceptions of the messages they receive from others. In an admitted oversimplification, Webster stated that "one projects what one expects to perceive and then proceeds to perceive that which will support his conception; one imagines what one will find in the outer world, sets out to find it, and sometimes does find it" (1977, 6). No stronger statement can be made about the importance of self-insight and self-awareness for teachers wishing to communicate positively and productively with parents. People's perception is selective, reflecting their experiences, associations, and needs.

Humans are expert communicators. They develop self-protective devices, ways or habits of reacting to each other that do not simplify or ease communication. Such habits protect or defend people against making undesirable revelations about themselves or presenting themselves to others unfavorably. Most people understandably want to appear intelligent, thoughtful, and virtuous to others.

People want to avoid being influenced by others against their will. As experienced communicators, they may anticipate what others are going to say and respond to what they expect to hear rather than to what the other person actually says. Most people constantly evaluate, sort, accept, and reject messages as they hear them, consequently changing them in an attempt to assimilate them.

Memory failure is another potential barrier. People's selective memory and forgetfulness can unwittingly distort communication. No matter how cooperative they may want to be, people are often unable to recall information and occurences in an understandable way.

People's place of birth, residence, culture, education, occupation, age, and experience all determine the language they use. Thus, two people may use very different words to describe the same experience. It is easy to see how a teacher's choice of words may ease or inhibit communication with parents. Indeed, teachers' professional jargon and technical terminology may be an enigma to parents, inhibiting communication. Schuck (1979) noted that educators are often unable or unwilling to use jargon-free language. Special educators, moreover, appear to have a particularly large arsenal of technical terms.

In communicating with parents, teachers should use clear language, avoiding or defining specialized terms. Teachers who find themselves in a conference with a parent and another professional who is using jargon can subtly assist the parent by asking the professional to define each acronym or unfamiliar term. This approach saves parents the embarrassment or anxiety of asking and provides them with clearer explanations and information. The use of clear language helps parents, specifically minority parents, by reducing their fear and anxiety during the conference (Marion 1981).

The prudent teacher avoids words and phrases that may give parents false or undesirable impressions of their children or their exceptionality. Many words in the vernacular can anger and alienate others if used inappropriately. Table 4.1 offers examples of inappropriate expressions and possible alternatives.

In a discussion of his work with one particular cultural group (urban Appalachians), Holland (1987) reported on more and less effective styles of parent-teacher communication. In effective communication, teachers assumed an active approach, with persistent follow-up, rather than a more passive approach and isolated attempts at follow-up. Teachers who communicated effectively with parents used personal communication, such as telephone calls, notes, and informal encounters, rather than formal letters and conferences. Effective communicators started early in their relationship with the parents, on an informal basis, rather than formally through a form or letter. The message of effective communicators was, "We need to work together to help your child," rather than "Come in if you want." Teachers who communicated effectively with their parents issued specific, frequent invitations rather than global

TABLE 4.1 • *Sample Word Choices*

Avoid	Use Instead
Must	Should
Is lazy	Can do more with effort
Culturally deprived	Culturally different, diverse
Is a troublemaker	Disturbs class
Is uncooperative	Should learn to work with others
Cheats	Lets others do his or her work
Is below average	Works at his (her) own level
Truant	Absent without permission
Impertinent	Discourteous
Steals	Takes things without permission
Is dirty	Has poor grooming habits
Disinterested	Complacent, not challenged
Is stubborn	Insists on having his (her) own way
Insolent	Outspoken
Wastes time	Could make better use of time
Is sloppy	Could be neater
Is mean	Has difficulty getting along with others
Time and time again	Usually, repeatedly
Dubious	Uncertain
Poor grade or work	Work below his (her) usual standard
Will flunk	Has a chance of passing if . . .

statements such as "Come in any time." They demonstrated flexibility and respect for parents' schedules. Finally, they developed strong rapport and trust with parents.

Cultural sensitivity is essential for effective communication with parents. For example, Asian-American parents may be silent during an interview; attempts by the teacher at open discussion of problems early in a relationship may cause the parents to retreat in an effort to save face. Open discussion may be considered a betrayal of family honor (Chan 1986). Chavkin (1989) reported that African-American families expressed a strong interest in involvement in their children's education yet reported that they felt awkward about approaching school personnel. This was particularly true if they had previous negative experiences with the schools. Hispanic-American families are often isolated from school system personnel due to language barriers, and their children are frequently isolated for the same reason (Hyland 1989).

Listening is an essential part of communication. Teachers who are skilled active listeners state their understanding of what the parents said (and the feelings accompanying the words) and provide feedback for the parents' verification and clarification. Active listening is not a mechanical process of hearing and repeating words. The active listener wants to hear and takes the time to hear what the parents are saying and wants to help them with the problems they face. Teachers who are active listeners accept parents' feelings whether or not they concur with those feelings. Finally, they show faith in parents' capacity to solve their problems with assistance.

Teachers wishing to increase their active listening skills should listen for the basic message in parent's communication and restate to the parents a brief, precise summary of the verbal, nonverbal, and feeling tone of the message as they perceived it. They should be sensitive to parents' verbal or nonverbal cues to their restatement of the initial message and encourage parents to correct inaccurate perceptions.

The Interview

The parent-teacher collaboration model uses an interview as the primary assessment technique. This interview is an information-gathering process and is distinct from a therapeutic interview designed to explore with parents their personal, marital, or social problems.

The parent-teacher interview should help parents develop an undistorted perception of the realities of their child's exceptionality so that they can make rational decisions about the child's education and treatment. Thus, the interview focuses on the child, the child's exceptionality, and the parents' responses to both.

Though a highly useful process, an interview is not an end in itself; it is a means to an end—providing needed assistance to the parents and, ultimately, to the child. Interviewing is an art, a specialized form of communication. For the present discussion, an interview is defined as a structured interaction between individuals (parents and teacher) for the purpose of gathering current and historical information about the parent's concerns and goals with regard to the child with an exceptionality.

According to Kroth and Simpson (1977), one of the most profound realizations an interviewer can have is the interview's tendency to encompass all the complicated aspects of human behavior. Human interactions prove far too varied to submit to a formula approach to interviewing. Teachers can learn to perform the role of interviewer and can learn techniques for getting parents to talk and for obtaining certain types of information; nonetheless, much of the interviewing process remains an art.

Teachers must understand and appreciate both conscious and unconscious human motivation, remaining sensitive to what parents feel as well as what they say. As interviewers, teachers must also recognize that parents do listen and act on their suggestions. Consequently, effective interviewers are aware of the actual and potential impact of their personal experiences, prejudices, attitudes, and training on their communication with the parents and the parents' future action. Conversely, they recognize and appreciate the potential impact the parents' behavior will have on them.

Kroth (1985) pointed out five deterrents to effective communication during an interview:

1. Fatigue. Interviewing is difficult work, requiring considerable energy. Both parent and teacher can tire and become distracted during an interview, particularly if the conference takes place after a day's work.

2. Strong feelings. Strong emotions can prohibit people from perceiving reality clearly, thereby inhibiting communication. Interview participants must recognize and control their feelings to maintain productive communication.

3. Words. The use of emotionally loaded words and phrases can stop or retard communication. A word or phrase used inappropriately may anger or embarrass parents. In addition, the skillful and concerned interviewer knows what topics are inadmissable.

4. Teacher talk. A teacher who talks continuously is not listening to the parents. Parents can only communicate if allowed to do so. Teachers should monitor the amount of time they talk and allow plenty of time for listening. An interview is not the time for lengthy conversation, lectures, and sermons.

5. The environment. A distracting or uncomfortable meeting place limits the possibilities for a productive interview. Parents who are physically and emotionally uncomfortable will end an interview as quickly as possible. Interview locations should be private and comfortable.

The effective parent-teacher collaboration interview requires careful preparation and planning by the teacher, preferably several days before the session. Part of this process is mental preparation—reviewing knowledge about human behavior and remembering the importance of positive communication. The other aspect of planning is to review and analyze all available information of the parents, the child, and the family. Teachers can form judgments of the reliability and validity of the information that will help them direct the interview. Gaps or inconsistencies in the information will guide the teacher in developing questions or topics for the interview agenda. At a practical level, teachers must also determine the parents' primary language, arrange for an interpreter if necessary, and establish an agreed-upon location, hour, and date for the session.

A relaxed, confident parent can more readily share knowledge and feelings with an interviewer. Thus, teachers should make every effort to put the parents at ease at the beginning of an interview. A friendly greeting and handshake, indicating a comfortable chair, or offering refreshments all help break the ice. A few minutes chatting about current events will help the parents relax and gain confidence in their communication skills.

During the interview, teachers have several responsibilities: to listen actively to what parents are saying, to be alert to the parents' central message or messages and seek clarification when necessary, to discern topics the parents do not or cannot discuss, and to observe and interpret the parents' nonverbal messages and feelings. With culturally different parents, teachers must communicate acceptance of the parents' values (Marion 1981).

An active listener avoids interrupting parents when they are making a genuine effort to respond to a question; minority parents in particular are not always afforded the courtesy of being heard. If teachers find it difficult to follow what the parent is saying, they can concentrate on getting the tone and essence of the parents' comments (Marion 1981). On the other hand, teachers may have to redirect the discussion gently when parents depart from the purpose of the interview. Effective interviewers tolerate and encourage appropriate silences for thought and meditation and try to remedy those caused by embarrassment and discomfort.

Questions are an important part of the communication process during the parent-teacher interview. Teachers will generally ask questions for two purposes: (1) to obtain specific, necessary information or to clarify existing information and (2) to redirect the interview when it strays from pertinent topics.

These questions may be closed, requesting a specific item of information, or open-ended, soliciting a detailed response (Webster 1977). The following are examples of closed questions: "What is your full name and address?" "How old is each of your children?" Open-ended questions are of two types, soliciting general information and requesting ideas on a particular topic. Examples of open-ended general questions are "How did your week go?" or "What is your opinion?" The open-ended question on a particular topic is far more specific, such as "How do you feel about John's exceptionality?" or "How do you think we should explore the problems of residential care for Pam?"

Open-ended general questions are often useful at the beginning of the interview. As the interview progresses, open-ended questions on a particular topic can probe parents' perceptions, opinions, and evaluation of a specific issue. Marion (1981) encourages the use of open-ended questions, especially with minority parents, to promote discussion.

Before ending the interview, teachers should review and summarize the discussion with the parents, allowing both parents and teacher to clarify the topics discussed during the session and agree on what has transpired. If additional sessions are desirable, this time is a good one to establish location, date, and hour.

When the parents leave, the teacher should record the information gathered during the interview. This is the time to begin developing an agenda and writing questions for the next session, since the information is still fresh in the teacher's mind.

The Intake Conference. Parents and teachers usually first meet at the individualized education program (IEP) meeting, at which time the child is placed in the teacher's program. This meeting, attended by several school district representatives and parents, generates an educational plan for the child. The intake conference is the first substantive step in a parent-teacher collaboration program and probably the first interview the teacher will conduct with parents. Intake activities frequently require more than a single session, for they must accomplish several purposes:

1. To establish a positive working relationship between parents and teacher
2. To review and discuss diagnostic findings, the child's exceptionality, its parameters, and education prognosis
3. To review and discuss the child's IEP
4. To review and discuss the roles and functions of the special and regular education teachers and other educational personnel, such as the school psychologist, nurse, and paraprofessional, in the child's program
5. To review and discuss the role and function of the parents in the child's education program
6. To introduce the parents to the parent-teacher collaboration and invite their participation.

In some cases, parents and teacher may have accomplished the first two goals before the intake conference—if the teacher has been involved in the diagnosis and placement decision, for example.

Sawyer and Sawyer (1981) suggested that during the first contact, parents often confront teachers with difficult questions and responses. They described several aspects of the initial interview that may be particularly difficult:

- Opening the interview
- Responding to the parents' overprotective behavior toward the child and helping them consider alternative behaviors
- Dealing with parents' feelings of denial and anger
- Using open-ended questions to gain more information about parents' and child's behavior
- Responding to parents' recognition of new responsibilities as the parents of an exceptional child
- Responding to questions about the child's future
- Dealing with silences.

If teachers anticipate these problems and develop strategies to deal with them, they can avoid some discomfort.

Rockowitz and Davidson (1979) viewed the presentation and discussion of diagnostic findings as the first step in developing an effective parent-professional relationship. This part of the intake conference is a two-way flow of information between parents and professional, not a lecture by the teacher. It has four equally important components: the entry pattern, presentation of diagnostic findings, discussion of educational suggestions, and summary. The teacher will have carefully prepared for the presentation by establishing when and where the interview will take place, who will attend, who will act as discussion facilitator, what professional expertise is necessary to explain the findings, and what information will be shared.

The purpose of the first part of the interview, the entry pattern, is to increase parents' comfort in the conference setting and establish rapport. The entry pattern includes an introduction of all people present, a review of the techniques used to obtain the diagnostic findings, a discussion of the parents' perceptions of the child's current functioning, and a statement of the parents' expressed worries and concerns.

The second phase, the presentation of diagnostic findings, includes an overview of the findings, a discussion of parents' reactions to the overview, and a detailed presentation of the findings, specifying the child's strengths and deficits. The presentation of findings should be honest and precise, avoiding unnecessary technical terms and professional jargon and allowing time to discuss parents' reactions to the findings. In this discussion, the teacher should describe the probable effects of the child's exceptionality on performance and explore the overall educational prognosis. In turn, the teacher should encourage parents to discuss possible issues at home that may affect the exceptionality. Teachers should not offer false hope that the child will eventually function fully if, in fact, this probability is limited. Alternatively, they must be sensitive to parents' feelings, avoiding being cruel, blunt, and inconsiderate.

Test results are frequently an issue of concern for parents of culturally diverse children, and minority parents may react strongly to results indicating their child is not functioning at the same level as other chidren. Marion (1981) suggested that the teacher ask minority parents to state their understanding of the information shared to make sure parents understand the results as fully as possible. Marion also suggested that the teacher make a sincere attempt to alleviate any anxiety parents express over possible misuse of test results.

After the diagnosis is discussed, the teacher presents educational suggestions and options. These suggestions should be practical and within reach. Most likely, a discussion of the child's IEP will be appropriate at this point in the interview. Again, teachers should encourage parents to react to their comments.

If the interview takes place in the child's instructional setting, teachers can use show-and-tell methods to present IEP content to parents. They can demonstrate the instructional materials and equipment the child will be using. When they can actually see and use the material, parents gain great understanding of their child's program.

Parents want to know who is responsible for their child. Thus, during the conference, teacher and parents review the professional and paraprofessional personnel who will work with the child and how each will participate in the child's overall program. The teacher may want to prepare a written outline of the functions of each professional to help clarify roles for the parents.

The parents should know the teacher's perceptions of their roles as parents in their child's educational program. The conference can then provide a format for resolving differences in perceptions and negotiating necessary modifications. This discussion of the parents' role is a natural opening for a closing discussion of the parent-teacher collaboration program. Teachers should describe the program and communicate the importance of parents' participation in their child's education. However, they should not imply that parents who cannot or choose not to participate are neglectful of their child.

Parents, preferably both mother and father, and the teacher are the major participants in the intake conference, but special education teachers, regular teachers, school social workers, and psychologist may contribute important information as well. However, the presence of too many professionals during the intake conference may threaten parents who are already anxious about their child and the conference. In some cases, and older sibling, aunt, uncle, grandparent, or other person attends the conference with the parents. The parents may wish to include a friend, interpreter, or advocate. The children may participate as well; many can contribute significantly to decision making about their future education and training.

As in any interview, the teacher must prepare for and plan the intake conference, reviewing the child's cumulative record, individualized education program, recent tests, work samples, and health records. If possible, the teacher should meet or observe the child.

An interview agenda in the form of an informal checklist or series of questions can be useful. Teachers can share the agenda with parents at the beginning of the interview and use it as a focusing device to keep the interview on track and ensure that it covers all key points.

Some teachers prefer to organize the intake conference agenda around a detailed information-gathering guide that structures the conference and ensures that all needed information is obtained. However, a guide may inhibit communication if either parents or teacher become overly concerned with the information-gathering process itself.

Evans, Evans, and Gable (1989) suggest an ecological survey as a guide to discussion with parents. The survey targets important environmental events and conditions affecting a student's behavior and the student's physical, biophysical, and psychosocial environments. In addition, the survey can be used, intermittently, to gather new information as it emerges in discussion with parents. Sample items adapted from the survey are presented in Figure 4.4

The teacher brings to the intake conference all materials needed to attain the interview objectives, including the child's assessment data, recent tests, progress reports, work samples, individualized education program, pertinent texts, workbooks, and worksheets. Providing copies of these materials to parents is useful for family records and also solidifies parents' understanding of their child's exceptionality and the remedial options available.

At the end of the intake conference, the teacher should repeat

FIGURE 4.4 • Sample Ecological Survey Items

Who does the child live with? How long has this been the child's home setting?

What language is spoken in the home?

With reference to your child, what areas seem to be of greatest concern to you?

What expectations do you have for your child?

Does your child enjoy reading? Mathematics? Social studies? Art? Shop?

Does your child adjust well to school?

Does your child play with neighborhood children?

What television programs does your child enjoy watching?

What does your child do when free time is available?

---

the diagnostic findings, restate the parents' comments, and review any plans for future action. This summary assures the teacher that the parents understand the information. The intake conference ends only after parents and teacher agree that they have satisfied the objectives of the interview to their satisfaction.

Assessment Conferences. The assessment conferences are the second substantive step in the parent-teacher collaboration model. Generally encompassing one or two sessions, the assessment process seeks to accomplish two purposes: to assess parents' perceptions of their child, the exceptionality, and its implications; and to assess parents' readiness, interest, capacity, willingness, and need for parent education and training.

The assessment conference helps the teacher evaluate the parents' understanding of the information they received during the intake conference and provides an opportunity to clarify misperceptions or alleviate unrealistic or unfounded fear and guilt. This conference is the time for teachers to identify those parents who cannot benefit from parent-teacher activities or who are averse to participating.

The assessment helps parents and teacher determine the following:

- The parents' needs for information, social-emotional support, services, and training
- The parents' major concerns about their child's present and future
- The areas of their child's functioning that parents would like to change.

Thus, it asks whether the parents have the background and experience to perform activities to benefit themselves and their child. For example, parents who want to change their child's social behavior may be ineffective without training in behavior management techniques. Similarly, parents cannot teach their children language, reading, or motor coordination skills if they lack the training needed to teach these skills.

If parents have only recently learned of their child's exceptionality, they may not be ready to participate in a structured educational program, in which case the teacher may refer them to a counselor or other parents of exceptional children to help them sort out and clarify their feelings. Some parents, though very willing to help their child, may not have the energy or time to participate in an organized program of parent-teacher activities, in which case the teacher should respect the legitimate duties and responsibilities that prohibit their consistent long-term participation.

The parents and teacher are the primary participants in the assessment conferences, with additional participants as appropriate (the child, a parent advocate, or an interpreter, for example). Both parties review the significant information exchanged during the intake conferences before attending the assessment session. In addition, the teacher should prepare materials specific to the assessment interview. The teacher should understand the purpose, administration, and interpretation of the assessment materials to be used, especially commercially available scales, inventories, and questionnaires that may require special explanation or use unfamiliar procedures.

After determining which assessment aids will supplement the interview, the teacher should establish an agenda. Sloman and Webster (1978) suggested a procedure for interviewing parents of children with learning disabilities, for example, that allows teachers to rate parents on five dimensions of parental functioning that affect the child significantly; evaluation, permissiveness of autonomy, mutual affection, hostility, and pressuring. The evaluation scale determines how the parent defines and reacts to the child as a person. Permissiveness of autonomy measures the extent to which parents encourage their child's independence. Mutual affection gauges the warmth of parent-child interactions. Hostility measures the parents' hostility toward the child. And pressuring looks at the emphasis parents place on their child's academic performance.

Sloman and Webster designed their interview technique for use in a study at a summer camp for learning-disabled children. However, teachers will find it useful in a nonresearch environment as well.

The questions are open-ended questions and keyed to the five dimensions noted below (see Figure 4.5). This semistructured approach organizes the information-gathering process and allows the interviewer to gauge the accuracy of his or her intuitive judgments about parents, children, and families.

Assessing the Needs of Families

In the assessment of family needs, Winton (1986) suggests addressing five areas. First, he suggests addressing the characteristics of the child that are relevant to family functioning. Next, the family's need for support, information, and training should be assessed. The third area to be addressed is the nature of interactions between the child and parents. A fourth area of assessment is the parents' perspectives on raising and living with children. Finally, critical events in the family's current life cycle should be discussed. In any assessment, teachers should look at the family's strengths. It is crucial to seek out

---

FIGURE 4.5 • *Interview Questions*

(Evaluation)

1. Are there any activities that you particularly enjoy doing with your child?
2. What do you feel are some of your child's greatest problems?
3. Are there any ways in which you have been able to help him with this?
4. Do you feel that this approach has helped?
5. How did you come to try this?
6. Inquire specifically about areas that have not been covered (physical, social, language, academic).

(Permissiveness of Autonomy)

7. Do you feel that it is important for a child to learn to do things and to manage on his own? Give examples of things your child does on his own. Give examples of things your child does on his own at home. How often during the day do you find yourself helping your child with something?
8. When you think about your child, do you ever feel that he grew up too fast or not fast enough?
9. Does your child give up easily with things he finds difficult to do? Give an example of things he might give up on.
10. Do you feel that your child needs a lot of praise and encouragement? Give examples of situations where you would give him this.

(cont.)

FIGURE 4.5 *Continued*

(Affection)

11. Is your child very affectionate with you?

12. In what way does your child express his affection? Physically? Verbally? How often?

13. Are there any ways in which your child gives you more pleasure than your other children? Or are there any little things about your child that you especially enjoy? Give examples.

14. Are there any ways in which your child is more difficult to enjoy than your other children? Give examples.

(Hostility)

15. When during the day does your child place demands on you?

16. Does your child ever become annoyed when you try to help him with something? Give examples.

17. When do you become most annoyed with your child? How frequently do you end up feeling irritated and angry with your child?

18. When is your child the easiest to manage? When is your child the most difficult to manage?

(Pressuring)

19. Give an example of a recent situation in which your child really wanted to do something that you didn't want him to do. What happened?

20. When during the day do you feel that you place the most demands on your child?

21. Do you have any special rules for your child in your home? Do these apply to your other children as well?

(Hostility)

22. Are there ever situations that are likely to end up with both you and your child feeling angry or frustrated with each other? Give an example.

23. Can you give me a recent example of a situation when you lost your temper with your child? What did your child do? What did you do?

(Affection)

24. How do you usually express your affection for your child? Verbally? Physically? Special privileges or presents?

25. Do you feel you more often show your affection to your child when he has achieved something?

26. Are there ever times when you show your affection for no special reason?

27. Are there any particular situations when you are more apt to show your affection for your child? Give examples.

Source: L. Sloman and C. D. Webster. *Journal of Learning Disabilities* 11 (1978): 74–79. Reprinted by special permission of The Professional Press, Inc.; © The Professional Press, Inc.

how the family handles adversity and how it used imagination and interactions and available supports (Johnston and Zemitzsch 1988).

Bauer (1981) designed two techniques for use with parents. The "Parents' Needs Form" helps the teacher to determine parents' needs and allows parents to indicate their preferences of methods to meet their needs for information, training, counseling, and so on (Figure 4.6). The "Parents' Activities Form" is a checklist of over thirty items of concern to the parents of exceptional children (Figure 4.7). Teachers can add items as necessary. Parents check items of personal interest and then rank them in priority. Both forms are open-ended to encourage parents to elaborate or include additional concerns.

The ecomap (Holman 1983) is another strategy that may be used to gather information about families. Ecomaps originally were used to help social workers in social service departments assess individual family needs. These maps visually portray a family's ecological system, showing the interactions of each member with outside resources such as churches, extended family members, schools,

FIGURE 4.6 • *Parents' Needs Form*

Confidential   Date: _____

Parent's Name _____

Child's Name _____

Introduction:
   Listed below are several statements describing concerns common to the parents of exceptional children. The items may or may not concern you at this time. Please complete only those items that currently concern you.
   The information on this form is used *only* to help plan and implement a parent-teacher involvement program. All information is held in strict confidence.

Directions:
   1. Read each statement carefully.
   2. Circle the number on the 1–5 scale that most closely approximates your current need in each area. Circle *1* to indicate a low priority need and *5* to indicate a high priority need.
   3. Below the 1–5 scale are several statements suggesting ways you may prefer to meet your stated needs. Please check only *two* of the four statements listed below each item.
   4. You may write additional comments in the space provided.

(cont.)

FIGURE 4.6 *Continued*

I. I need the opportunity to discuss my feelings about my exceptional child and myself with someone who understands the problem.

(Circle the appropriate number.)

1	2	3	4	5
Low Priority				High Priority

(Check *only* two statements.)

_____ I prefer to talk to a professional.
_____ I prefer to talk to the parent of an exceptional child.
_____ I prefer to be referred to another agency for counseling.
_____ I prefer to read articles and books discussing the reactions of parents of exceptional children.
_____ I prefer _____.

II. I would like to talk with other parents and families who have exceptional children.

(Circle the appropriate number.)

1	2	3	4	5
Low Priority				High Priority

(Check *only* two statements.)

_____ I prefer to be in a discussion group.
_____ I prefer to participate in social gatherings (picnics, parties, potluck dinners).
_____ I prefer to meet informally.
_____ I prefer to participate in general meetings, workshops, lectures, demonstrations, and other informational gatherings.
_____ I prefer _____.

III. I would like to learn more about my child's exceptionality.

(Circle the appropriate number.)

1	2	3	4	5
Low Priority				High Priority

(Check *only* two statements.)

_____ I prefer to obtain information through reading.
_____ I prefer to observe teachers and other professionals working with my child and then discuss my observations.
_____ I prefer individual parent-teacher conferences.
_____ I prefer a parent-teacher discussion group.
_____ I prefer _____.

(cont.)

FIGURE 4.6 *Continued*

IV. I would like to learn more about how children develop and learn, especially exceptional children.

(Circle the appropriate number.)

1	2	3	4	5
Low Priority				High Priority

(Check *only* two statements.)

_____ I prefer to obtain information through reading.
_____ I prefer to participate in a formal behavior management training course.
_____ I prefer a parent-teacher discussion group.
_____ I prefer individual training in my home by a teacher or other professional.
_____ I prefer to attend meetings at which specialists present information on behavior management.
_____ I prefer _____

VI. I would like to work with a teacher or other professional so that I can use the same instructional methods at home that the school uses.

(Circle the appropriate number.)

1	2	3	4	5
Low Priority				High Priority

(Check *only* two statements.)

_____ I prefer to observe my child in school.
_____ I prefer to attend a training program in observation.
_____ I prefer to attend a course in instructional methods.
_____ I prefer to work with the teacher in my child's classroom.
_____ I prefer in-home training by a teacher or other professional.
_____ I prefer to learn through readings, newsletters, telephone communication, and similar resources.
_____ I prefer _____

VII. I would like _____

(Circle the appropriate number.)

1	2	3	4	5
Low Priority				High Priority

(Write the appropriate statements.)

_____ I prefer _____
_____ I prefer _____

(cont.)

FIGURE 4.6 *Continued*

Comments:

Thank you.

FIGURE 4.7 • *Parents' Activities Form*

Confidential   Date: _____

Parent's Name _____

Child's Name _____

Introduction:
Listed below are thirty-five topics and activities generally believed of interest to the parents of exceptional children. Not all parents are interested in any single item, nor is any parent interested in all the items.

Your response to this questionnaire is used *only* to assist in planning and implementing a parent-teacher involvement program for you. All information is held in strict confidence.

Directions:
1. Read the entire form carefully.
2. In Column A check 15 items of interest to you.
3. In Column B rank 5 of the 15 items you checked in Column A. Number the item of highest priority to you 5, the next highest 4, and so on.
4. You may write additional comments in the space provided.

A	B	
___	___	1. Help my child learn.
___	___	2. Build my child's self-confidence.
___	___	3. Select activities to help my child learn (books, games, toys, projects, experiences).
___	___	4. Teach my child to follow directions.
___	___	5. Help my child enjoy learning.
___	___	6. Assist my child in language development.
___	___	7. Teach my child problem-solving skills.
___	___	8. Fulfill my role as (father) (mother) to my child.
___	___	9. Avoid emotional involvement in my child's emotional outbursts.

(cont.)

FIGURE 4.7 *Continued*

_____ _____	10. Protect my child from getting hurt.
_____ _____	11. Care for my child when he or she is sick or injured.
_____ _____	12. Discipline my child.
_____ _____	13. Deal with my child's misbehavior.
_____ _____	14. Teach my child respect for people and property.
_____ _____	15. Teach my child to express feelings in a socially acceptable manner.
_____ _____	16. Teach my child to show love, affection, and consideration for other family members.
_____ _____	17. Teach my child to live in harmony with the family (television, bedtime, meals, sharing, responsibilities).
_____ _____	18. Develop a positive and productive relationship with my child.
_____ _____	19. Develop my problem-solving skills.

How can I obtain information on the following topics affecting my child:

_____ _____	20. Art activities
_____ _____	21. Creative dramatics
_____ _____	22. Educational games and activities
_____ _____	23. Exercise
_____ _____	24. Health and hygiene
_____ _____	25. Music
_____ _____	26. Nutrition and diet
_____ _____	27. Puppetry
_____ _____	28. Recreation
_____ _____	29. Sleep
_____ _____	30. Toys

Other topics and activities of interest to me are:

_____ _____	31. _____
_____ _____	32. _____

(cont.)

FIGURE 4.7 *Continued*

	33. _____
_____ _____	
_____ _____	34. _____
_____ _____	35. _____

Comments:

Thank you!

---

health care services, friends, and work. The ecomap portrays the nature and flow of the relationships between the family and its members and outside resources. In this way, the ecomap identifies areas of stress and support within the family system as well as areas where individual and family needs are unmet and where untried resources might be available.

To provide the practitioner and the family with a broad understanding of the family's perceptions of its ecological system, Holman suggests involving as many family members as possible in the ecomap development process. To develop an ecomap, the practitioner sits with the family group around a large piece of paper or posterboard and ask nonintrusive questions, such as "Do you have many problems in your family?" and "How do you get along with the family?" In the ecomap, the nuclear family is drawn in a center circle with squares for males and circles of females and with the generational connections usually used in family mapping. Then, the family as a whole and individual members are connected with important extrafamilial systems. Different types of lines are used to illustrate the types of relationships involved; for example, unidirectional relationships are indicated by → or ←; strong positive relationships by _____ ; tenuous relationships by _____ ; and stressful relationships by +++++. An example of an ecomap is presented in Figure 4.8.

Ecomaps provide considerable information on the family's social environment, significant sources of stress, and available used and unused sources of social support. This assessment strategy is valuable during the initial interview because it generates a great amount of information in a brief period of time. The ecomap serves

FIGURE 4.8 · *Ecomap*

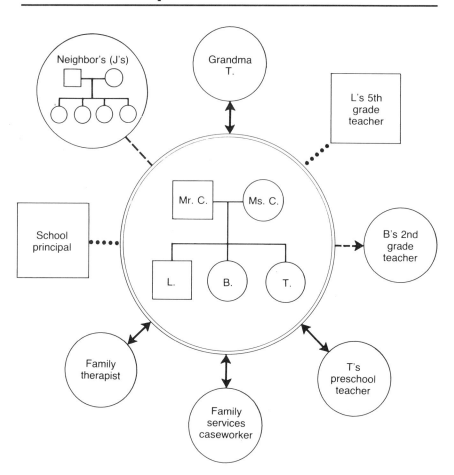

to specify and individualize the strains, conflicts, and available resources within the family system and to generate a comprehensive family history.

Karpel and Strauss (1983) offer an additional family assessment strategy. They suggest that the teacher ask the family to describe each family member's typical weekday and weekend. The teacher, using this nonthreatening information, can develop a sense of the environmental constraints and patterns that must be considered when planning interventions; these patterns may include rising habits and sequences, how meals are conducted, who attends meals, where individuals sit, the comings and goings of members during the day, arrivals home, how evenings and weekends are spent, and the quality and quantity of conversational and general interactions (hostile, silent, inquisitional, cordial, friendly).

Additional Resources

As Clements and Alexander (1975) maintained, the special education teacher is the front-line practitioner, the person primarily responsible for parent services in the school. Experience bears out that teachers initiate most requests to talk with parents and most actively organize services for parents. Nonetheless, special teachers can make excellent use of a wide range of parent, professional, and paraprofessional resources in conducting a parent-teacher program. Prudent use of these resources allows teachers more time and energy to manage or coordinate the program and to concentrate their efforts on those areas in which they have the greatest expertise.

Parents, professionals, and paraprofessionals can provide information and expertise during all phases outlined in the collaboration model. Acting essentially as consultants, they provide direct and indirect services. They may offer direct service in specialized areas, and they can serve as mediators between parents and teachers (Heron and Harris 1982).

It is essential to program success that the teacher conduct an inventory of the skills and potential contributions of those parents, professionals, and paraprofessionals in the school and community willing to assist in the program. The available resource consultants can then be used to the extent feasible.

Teachers should view parents as experts on their children, for they are the people most intimately involved with the child's birth, growth and development, health, behavior, exceptionality, family, home, neighborhood, and other influences on the child. As such, parents are an invaluable resource that cannot be ignored or neglected. Many parents have personal and professional knowledge and skills that can help the teacher, other parents, and children. The teacher should recognize that some parents of exceptional children are professionals and skilled workers in their own right who can contribute significantly to the program. They may have counseling, interviewing, leadership, administrative, organizational, or other skills; they may also have the time and energy to conduct activities for which the special teacher has no training or time.

School district and community professionals are available to both the teacher and parents. Frequently, they work in the exceptional child's school, though their availability will vary. School and community administrators, psychologists, social workers, nurses and physicians, regular teachers, subject matter specialists, communication specialists, guidance counselors, diagnosticians, supervisors, and paraprofessionals all can provide invaluable services and practical or social-emotional support.

Many of the parent collaboration activities described in the remainder of this book require help from resource consultants. Below are examples of the contribution these consultants can make to the parent-teacher program.

- *Regular teachers and subject matter specialists.* These professionals are highly trained in general and specific areas of instruction, teaching methods, and child growth and development. They can contribute significantly to programs for parents of exceptional children who are integrated into regular and specialized instructional programs through diagnosis and treatment of disabilities in reading, mathematics, spelling, writing, and other academic subjects. They can also support art, music, physical education, and other areas of instruction. The communication specialist can advise on the development and remediation of language.
- *Paraprofessionals.* Paraprofessionals are among teachers' most important allies. They can help with many parent-teacher activities, as well as research, prepare, organize, and evaluate them. Many times, the paraprofessional is a professional person and skilled worker in another area and can bring special skills to the classroom. Frequently, too, the paraprofessional is a member of the community, is familiar with the culture and language, knows the parents and children of the community, and understands their living situation.
- *Psychologists, counselors, and diagnosticians.* These professionals offer a broad understanding of personality development and functioning, individual and group counseling skills, and assessment, diagnostic, and observation skills. They can conduct individual or small-group training sessions, offer therapeutic services, and provide information to support assessment, diagnosis, and placement. They can observe and evaluate parent-teacher activities, such as conferences and group meetings, and supply the knowledge and skills that make certain parent-teacher activities possible.
- *Social workers.* Social workers are trained in interviewing, assessment, and counseling skills and can contribute directly to a parent program by referring parents to the teacher, encourag-

ing participation, conducting intake and assessment interviews, counseling individuals and small groups, and connecting parents and children with community and school services. Social workers' knowledge of and relationship with community and school social services is one of their greatest contributions.
- *Administrators.* School administrators and special education directors and supervisors can provide considerable logistical support by granting official permission to start a parent program, setting aside time for the program, supplying facilities, materials, equipment, and so on. They may help draw in parents, as well as school and community consultants, to the program and offer social-emotional support through public recognition of efforts. Administrators can also provide information on special education programs, school organization, administration, placement, available services, and legal issues.
- *Medical professionals.* Nurses and physicians can contribute their expertise on medical diagnostic and treatment services. They are valuable sources of information on medical examinations, diagnostic labels, treatments, medications, diets, and related aspects of caring for exceptional children.

To work effectively in parent-teacher collaboration programs, teachers should consider themselves leaders of a team. As such, they are responsible for involving all appropriate people in program planning and activities, whether they be parent, professional, paraprofessional, or resource consultants.

Summary

This chapter introduces a five-phase model for parent-teacher collaboration that guides teachers through a process of intake and assessment, goal selection, planning and implementation of activities, evaluation, and review. Succeeding sections highlight special skills and techniques essential to effective use of the model.

The chapter discusses criteria for effective interpersonal communication and emphasizes its importance in the parent-teacher collaboration. It highlights the interview as the primary intake and assessment technique used in a parent-teacher program and discusses the use of informal needs and interest assessment techniques to supplement the central interview process. The concluding sections of the chapter describe the use of parents and professionals as resource consultants, specifying the contributions that administrators, psychologists and diagnosticians, social workers, medical professionals, regular teachers and subject matter specialists, and paraprofessionals can make to parent involvement programs.

Exercises and Discussion Topics

1. Read another book or several articles that present a model for parent-teacher collaboration. Write a paper comparing the model in this text with the one you studied, considering each model's definition, purposes, limitations, participants and their contributions, organization, phases or steps, and comprehensiveness.

2. Using a case with which you are familiar or a case study from Appendix A, complete a sample Program Development Form.

3. Discuss with your class the following statement: "People communicate to affect others, the environment, and themselves; they send messages in order to obtain a response and thus influence others' behavior. Communication also provides catharsis, relieving tension, frustration, and anxiety, which in turn can lead to self-discovery and self-insight."

4. Carefully observe a presentation by an individual you consider a great communicator, such as an instructor, employer, television personality, or politician. (You may want to record the presentation if you can obtain permission.) Analyze and evaluate the presentation, considering verbal communication, body language or nonverbal expression, affective tone, and the use of descriptive, inferential, and evaluative language.

5. Discuss in class the following quotation: "One projects what one expects to perceive and then proceeds to perceive that which will support his conception; one imagines what one will find in the outer world, sets out to find it, and sometimes does find it" (Webster 1977, 6).

6. Study the section of the chapter entitled "The Interview." Develop a checklist of interviewing tasks to be accomplished before, during, and after a parent-teacher information-gathering interview.

7. Study the section on the intake conference; then, conduct a conference with the parent of an exceptional child. Have a colleague observe the conference with the parent's permission; later, critique the session together. If a parent is not available for this task, role play a conference with your study group, using a case from Appendix A.

8. Study the section on the assessment conference; then, conduct a conference with the parent of an exceptional child. Have a colleague observe the conference with the parent's permission; later, critique the session together. If a parent is not available for this task, role play a conference with your study group, using a case from Appendix A.

References

Bauer, A. M. 1981. *Program for parents of severely handicapped students: A Plan.* Edwardsville: Southern Illinois University.

Chavkin, N. F. 1989. Debunking the myth about minority parents. *Educational Horizons* 67 (4): 119–23.

Chan, S. 1986. Parents of exceptional Asian children. In *Exceptional Asian children and youth* eds. K. Kitano and P. C. Chinn. Reston, Va.: The Council for Exceptional Children. pp. 36–53.

Chinn, P. C., J. Winn, and R. H. Walters. 1978. *Two way talking with parents of special children: A process of positive communication.* St. Louis: Mosby.

Clements, J. E., and R. N. Alexander. 1975. Parent training: Bringing it all back home. *Focus on Exceptional Children* 5: 1–12.

Cohen, S., J. Agosta, J. Cohen, and R. Warren. 1989. Supporting families of children with severe disabilities. *Journal of the Association for Persons with Severe Handicaps* 14: 155–62.

Donnellan, A. M., and P. Mirenda. 1984. Issues related to professional involvement with families of individuals with autism and other severe handicaps. *Journal of the Association for Persons with Severe Handicaps* 9: 16–25.

Dunst, C. J. 1987 (December). What is effective helping? Paper presented at the biennial meeting of the National Clinical Infants Program Conference, Washington, D.C.

Dunst, C. J., C. M. Trivette, and A. G. Deal. 1988. *Enabling and empowering families.* Cambridge, Mass.: Brookline Books.

Evans, S. S., W. H. Evans, and R. A. Gable. 1989. An ecological survey of student behavior. *Teaching Exceptional Children* 21 (4): 11–15.

Heron, T. E., and K. C. Harris. 1982. *The educational consultant: Helping professionals, parents, and mainstreamed students.* Boston: Allyn and Bacon.

Holland, K. E. 1987. *Parents and teachers: Can home and school literacy boundaries be broken?* Paper presented at the University of Kentucky Conference on Appalachia.

Holman, A. 1983. *Family assessment: Tools and understanding for intervention.* Beverly Hills, Calif.: Sage.

Hyland, C. R. 1989. What we know about the fastest growing minority population: Hispanic Americans. *Educational Horizons* 67 (4): 131–35.

Johnston, J. C., and A. Zemitzsch. 1988. Family power: An intervention beyond the classroom. *Behavioral Disorders* 14: 69–79.

Karpel, M., and E. S. Strauss. 1983. *Family evaluation.* New York: Gardner.

Kroth, R. L. 1985. *Communicating with parents of exceptional children: Improving parent-teacher relationships* 2d ed. Denver: Love.

Kroth, R. L., and R. L. Simpson. 1977. *Parent conferences as a teaching strategy.* Denver: Love.

Marion, R. L. 1981. *Educators, parents, and exceptional children.* Rockville, Md.: Aspen.

Olson, D. G. 1988. A developmental approach to family support: A conceptual framework. *Focal Point* 2 (3): 3–6.

Rockowitz, R. J., and P. W. Davidson. 1979. Discussing diagnostic findings with parents. *Journal of Learning Disabilities* 12 (1): 11–16.

Sawyer, H., and S. H. Sawyer. 1981. A teacher-parent communication training approach. *Exceptional Children* 47: 305–06.

Schuck, J. 1979. The parent-professional partnership: Myth or reality? *Education Unlimited* 1: 26–28.

Shea, T. M., and A. M. Bauer. 1987. Parent involvement: The developmental capital of special education. *Techniques* 1 (1): 1–12.

Sloman, L., and C. D. Webster. 1978. Assessing the parents of the learning disabled child: A semistructured interview procedure. *Journal of Learning Disabilities* 11: 73–79.

Vincent, L. J., S. Laten, C. Salisbury, P. Brown, and D. Baumgart. 1981. Family involvement in the educational process of severely handicapped students: State of the art and directions for the future. In *Quality educational services for the severely handicapped: The federal investment,* eds. B. Wilcox and R. York, Washington, D.C.: U.S. Department of Education, Office of Special Education.

Webster, E. J. 1977. *Counseling with parents of handicapped children: Guidelines for improving communication.* New York: Grune and Stratton.

Winton, P. 1986. Effective strategies for involving families in intervention efforts. *Focus on Exceptional Children* 19 (2): 1–10, 12.

SECTION TWO

Parent-Teacher Collaborative Activities

Chapters 5 through 9 offer examples of collaborative parent-teacher activities and discuss issues appropriate to the model introduced in Chapter 4. Depending on program needs, parents and teachers will be able to use many of these activities directly, may want to modify others, and in some cases, will design alternative activities to fit their needs.

Chapter 5 suggests ways to modify and extend several traditional parent-teacher communications activities—such as daily and periodic reports, notes, notices, newsletters, and telephone communications—for a program for exceptional children. It also introduces technology to support teacher communication.

Chapter 6 discusses ways to approach individual parent-teacher conferences, including problem-solving conferences, behavior management training conferences, and conferences for progress reports. It reviews the individualized education program meeting and home visit as well.

Chapters 7 and 8 look at parent-teacher groups. Chapter 7 reviews those factors essential to organizing small and large parent-teacher groups, such as establishing group objectives, purpose, size, planning, structure, limitations, and leadership. Chapter 8 discusses ways to conduct specific types of groups—informational, communication, problem-solving, discussion, and training groups.

Chapter 9 introduces important parent-teacher home, school, and community activities that encourage parent collaboration as paraprofessionals, instructors, volunteers, and home-based teachers. It discusses parents' roles in classroom, school, and community environments and looks at their responsibility as child advocates.

Teachers' ability to carry out the activities described in this section depend on several factors, including the following:

- *The thoroughness and reliability of the assessment procedures that determine the child's and parents' needs*
- *The time available to parents and teachers to participate in the activities*
- *The teacher's level of expertise and skills to conduct the activities*
- *The resources available.*

Clearly, the assessment process is important because it determines whether parents and teachers have a clear enough understanding of the child's and parents' strengths and weaknesses to design appropriate activities. It also determines whether parents and teachers agree on the activities and can work in concert to the child's benefit.

Both parties must also be realistic about their work loads and available time when selecting activities so that they neither short-change the child nor design overly ambitious activities doomed to failure. Parents cannot devote large amounts of time to the exceptional child at the expense of their spouses, other children, family, employers, church, and community. Similarly, teachers must allocate their time among many children and also act as a husband or wife, parent, housekeeper, employee, and so on. Both parents and teachers must be sensitive to the other's practical limitations.

Teachers must also match the skill level needed for specific activities with the people available. Some activities require few specialized skills; others call for highly specific and specialized competencies. If teachers are not sufficiently expert in the skills needed, they should seek training, enlist the help of an appropriately trained resource person, or develop alternative activities.

Finally, teachers and parents should verify they have the resources they need to collaborate effectively. They must ensure the availability of the needed personnel, materials, equipment, facilities, and funds.

CHAPTER FIVE

Written and Telephone Communication

Mr. Q., father of an eleven-year-old son with behavioral disorders:

"Then there were those phone calls. 'Jay did this today.' 'Jay did that.' 'Jay took something.' 'Jay hit somebody.' Nobody told me what to try for Jay; it was almost like they enjoyed telling me how bad Jay was doing. It was almost like they were tattling on him or something."

Chapter Topics and Objectives

Written and telephone communication can be quick, efficient ways for parents and teachers to keep in touch about the exceptional child's progress. Most written communication and telephone contacts require minimal time and energy of parents and teachers. They do not require much, if any, instruction (Lordeman and Winett 1980). They are generally indirect forms of communication, requiring little personal contact. Thus, they are most appropriate for communicating on relatively impersonal topics.

Though the activities discussed in this chapter—daily and periodic written reports; daily, positive communication notebooks; notes, letters, and notices; newsletters; and telephone communication—require considerably less effort than the activities presented in later chapters, parents and teachers must devote some time and energy to planning them and carrying them out effectively. If properly conducted, written and telephone feedback techniques can transfer important information and support the child's educational progress (Lordeman and Winett 1980).

Teachers must use their professional judgment to determine when and for whom written and telephone techniques are appropriate. Parents' needs for information, ability to understand the message, personalities, time restrictions, and environment will all determine their responsiveness to a specific technique.

It is important to ascertain the willingness and competence of parents to participate in activities requiring reading, writing, and verbal skills. Teachers should determine the primary language of the home and use that language in all written and telephone communication. Many adults lack the academic and verbal skills needed to meaningfully participate in many activities discussed in this chapter. These parents will need more detailed instruction and support in written and telephone activities.

In this chapter, we will:

- Describe daily and periodic written reports.
- Discuss various notes, letters, and notices.
- Discuss telephone contacts.
- Discuss the planning and writing of newsletters.

Written Reports

Daily Reports

The report cards and grades issued periodically by elementary and secondary schools and colleges are assumed to influence students' performance positively, but this effect is probably short-lived. Observations of school and college students suggest that they study more and behave better in the few weeks immediately before and after report cards or grades are due.

More frequent feedback on students' academic and behavioral performance may be more likely to inspire continued positive performance—a proposition that has led several investigators to explore the use of daily report cards with normal and exceptional children at various grade levels (Powell 1980). Daily written reports have several advantages. They are an efficient method of coordinating and monitoring training and, assuming that the teacher obtains the parents' commitment to a daily system, an excellent method of two-way communication.

A daily written report can be as general or as specific as is mutually agreed upon by teacher and parent. With younger children, teachers and parents may agree upon a "smiling face" or "sad face," based upon a global judgment on some prearranged criteria on the child's performance (see Figure 5.1). A more specific daily

112 Section Two • *Parent-Teacher Collaborative Activities*

FIGURE 5.1 • *General Daily Report*

report may include a listing of each of the classroom rules and a summarization of how the student functioned on each of those rules (see Figure 5.2).

Any daily report system should be mutually agreed upon. If the system is used for all students in a classroom, a parent meeting may be useful for discussing the daily reports before implementation. If the system is individualized, a telephone call or conference would be an effective way of negotiating the manner in which the report will be used. Some of the questions and concerns to address when one introduces any daily system include the following:

- What is to be evaluated? Behavior? Academics? Both?
- What are the criteria for each of the ratings used?
- What system will be used to ensure that the report reaches the parents? Will the report be returned initialed? Will the parent call if no report is received? Will any reward be lost if the report is not delivered?
- What rewards or privileges will be associated with the reports?
- How will parents follow through on the reports? Will they provide incentives? Or is the system only to keep parents aware of progress?

FIGURE 5.2 • *Specific Daily Report*

Name:		Date:					
				Periods			
Class Rules	1	2	3	4	5	6	7
1. Complete work.							
2. Keep hands, feet, and objects to self.							
3. Stay in assigned area.							
4. Use appropriate language.							
5. Use equipment safely and carefully.							

Personal Goals:

1.

2.

Comments:

Parent signature: _____

Periodic Reports

The traditional report card has limited value to the parents of children with exceptionalities, whether it uses letter, number, satisfactory-unsatisfactory, or pass-fail grading (Shea and Bauer 1987).

Broad objectives, reflecting parents' interest in their children as people as well as academic achievers, makes the traditional report card an inadequate vehicle for reporting a child's overall development and special strengths. Report cards should lead parents and teachers to action. Thus, it goes beyond simple transmittal of information.

To Granowsky and associates (1977), the traditional report card is "like letting the team in on only one play out of every thirty" (56). They maintain that parents cannot intelligently and constructively follow their child's progress if they receive only three or four reports annually. Rutherford and Edgar (1979) suggested that teachers explain the report card to parents at a conference at the beginning of the school year. At this time, teachers can also spell out for the parents, in writing, their child's instructional or performance objectives in each area of study and the grading system for each.

A report card such as the one in Figure 5.3 can provide valuable information to parents on their child's progress during the preceding marking period. Because of the detailed reporting format, parents can review their child's competence in specific skills, which helps them supplement the child's educational program at home. This evidence of their child's strengths and weaknesses may also encourage parents to seek the teacher's assistance in improving their child's performance of specific tasks.

This progress report format is applicable in many special education programs. The final page is particularly useful, for it allows the teacher to rate achievement and effort in the subject areas while commenting in a more detailed manner as well (see Figure 5.4).

Teachers whose special education programs do not use task analysis report cards can strongly encourage their adoption and, if these efforts fail, prepare informal task analysis forms for enclosure with the child's traditional report card. The progress report selected should reflect the special needs and curriculum of the students. For example, a progress report for emotionally and behaviorally disordered children would emphasize overall appropriate behavior, social adjustments, and personal interaction skills, whereas a progress report for the moderately or severely mentally handicapped would pay little attention to academic subjects and focus on self-help skills,

FIGURE 5.3 • *Overall Evaluation, Pupil Progress Report*

PUPIL PROGRESS REPORT

Student's Name _____

Placement _____

Teacher _____

Principal _____

School _____

(cont.)

FIGURE 5.3 *Continued*

Message to Parents

This report will be sent to you at the end of each nine weeks of school unless it is felt that a conference can better inform you of your child's progress in school.

Please study each area carefully and feel free to discuss this report with your child's teacher. Your interest in and cooperation with the school program are essential parts of your child's education.

The grading system used in this pupil progress report is based upon your child's individual progress at his level of capability.

Grading System

A = Excellent
B = Very Good
C = Average
D = Poor
F = Unsatisfactory

WORK HABITS

	Grading Periods			
	1	2	3	4
Follows directions				
Completes work on time				
Takes care of materials and equipment				
Thinks and works independently				
Asks for help when necessary				
Allows others to work				
Stays in seat				
Talks only with permission				

SOCIAL ADJUSTMENTS

	1	2	3	4
Shows self-control				
Is courteous				
Carries out responsibilities				
Accepts constructive criticism				
Shows respect for authority				
Respects rights of others				
Cooperates in group activities				
Shows good sportsmanship				

(cont.)

FIGURE 5.3 *Continued*

HEALTH AND SAFETY HABITS

Practices good health habits				
Hair is washed and combed				
Is neat and clean				
Obeys safety rules				
Behaves on bus				
Behaves on playground				
Behaves in lunchroom				

ATTENDANCE RECORD	1	2	3	4	Year-End Total
DAYS PRESENT					
DAYS ABSENT					
TIMES TARDY					

PARENT COMMENTS:

1st Quarter

2nd Quarter

3rd Quarter

4th Quarter

PARENT'S SIGNATURE

    1st Quarter _____

    2nd Quarter _____

    3rd Quarter _____

    4th Quarter _____

Source: Courtesy of the administration and staff of the Cahokia Area Joint Agreement, Cahokia, Ill.

FIGURE 5.4 · Sample Subject Area Evaluation, Pupil Progress Report

_____Winter_____ Quarter

NAME John S.

SUBJECT Reading

The ACHIEVEMENT grade reflects your child's progress at his level of learning in each subject area.

The EFFORT grade reflects how hard your child is working within the given subject area.

ACHIEVEMENT C

EFFORT A

Though John's reading skills are currently at the functional level, he has increased his comprehension skills. He is now able to read directions and complete a job application with little help. His use of the newspaper has improved so that he can now locate all parts of the paper and find specific information, such as movie times and prices of items.

John is still reluctant to pursue reading as a leisure activity and needs encouragement to pick up a book during free time. High-interest, low vocabulary books available at the school library may be of help.

Susie Smith

Teacher

independent living and community living skills, leisure skills, and home-living skills.

Daily, Positive Communication Notebook

The passport, or communication notebook, for positive parent-teacher communication (Runge, Walker, and Shea 1975) is an effective technique for starting, increasing, or maintaining systematic parent-professional cooperation. It is an ordinary spiral notebook that the child carries daily—to and from home, to and from classrooms, gym, cafeteria, music room, and so on. Parents, special teachers, regular teachers, teacher aides, physical education instructors, playground monitors, bus drivers, and other people influencing the child's academic and behavioral performance all may write notations in the notebook.

The teacher's first step is to introduce the notebook or passport to the child, emphasizing its positive aspects and explaining that he or she will receive rewards for carrying the passport, presenting it to the teacher and other adults during the day, and showing acceptable academic and behavioral performance. Teachers award points at school for carrying the passport, for appropriate behavior, for academic effort, and for academic accomplishment. Parents award points at home for acceptable behavior, completion of assigned tasks, and completion of home-study assignments. Children who forget or refuse to carry the notebook cannot accumulate points.

At appropriate intervals, children can exchange points for rewards that they have helped select. Parents and teachers agree on the time, place, frequency, amount, level, and kind of reinforcers the child will receive at home and at school.

Teachers introduce parents to the notebook concept and procedures at an orientation session, at which time they respond to parents' questions, concerns, and suggestions and provide instructions for writing in the notebook. Parents also learn how to give points and rewards to their child, and parents and teachers agree on the specific behaviors they wish to help the child change.

Parents and teachers follow certain guidelines in writing notes in the passport:

1. Be brief. (Parents and teachers are busy.)
2. Be positive. (Parents know that their child has problems and need not receive constant negative reminders.)

3. Be honest. (Don't say a child is doing fine if he or she is not. However, write noncommittal comments or request a face-to-face or telephone conference in place of negative notes.)
4. Be responsive. (If the parent or teacher asks for help, respond immediately.)
5. Be informal. (All participants are equals.)
6. Be consistent. (If the passport is the communication system of choice, use it consistently and expect the same from other participants.)
7. Avoid jargon. (Parents may not understand educational jargon, and even professionals may use jargon at cross-purposes.)
8. Be careful. (No one should project personal feelings or the frustrations of a bad day onto the child, parent, or teacher.)

Figure 5.5 offers examples of notes following these guidelines.

Schmalz (1987), using a notebook system with her son, found that teachers had several concerns about the daily system. Teachers reported that they did not have enough time to write in a journal for *every* child. In addition, the teachers suggested that there was not enough to write about daily; the teachers expressed the concern that a description of the daily routine would become boring for parents. Teachers suggested that such a system is useful if a problem exists, but in the everyday workings of a classroom, a weekly newsletter may be as useful.

Notes, Letters, and Notices

Notes, letters, and notices are good ways to notify parents of administrative and record-keeping problems and concerns, schedule changes, special events, holidays, workshops, field trips, attendance, fees, and so on. However, unless used systematically, these techniques have limited value in reinforcing the child's academic performance or social-emotional behavior and are best used as one component of overall parent-teacher communication.

Notes, letters, and notices can provide continuous positive contact if teachers use them appropriately (Magnusson and McCarney 1980). Effective notes are clear, concise, and positive and speak to the parents in their primary language. Rutherford and Edgar (1979) suggested that these notes and letters serve four purposes: to praise the child's general academic performance and behavior; to informally (handwritten) and positively address specific academic and behavior problems; to informally evaluate the child's performance;

FIGURE 5.5 • *Sample Passport Notes*

9:00 AM

TO: Ms. Dolores

   Good day on the bus. Tom sat in his assigned seat and waited his turn to leave the bus. I praised his behavior and gave him two points.

Mr. Parker, Bus Driver

10:30 AM

TO: Ms. Dolores

   During PE today the group played kickball. Tom was well-behaved but had difficulty participating effectively. I awarded him six points and praised his behavior. Can we meet to discuss some means of increasing his participation?

Ms. Minton, Physical Education

2:30 PM

TO: Mr. and Mrs. Hogerty

   As you can see from the notes above, Tom had a good day at school.
   He received 89 percent on his reading test this morning. That's real progress. Please praise him for this accomplishment.
   This evening, Tom is to read pp. 1–5 in his new reading book.
   Even better news! Tom remembered to walk in the hallways today. He is very proud of himself.
   I shall talk to Ms. Minton today about increasing Tom's participation in PE. I'll let you know what we decide at tomorrow night's parent meeting.

Ms. Dolores

9:00 PM

TO: Ms. Dolores

   We praised and rewarded Tom for his hard work on the reading test, the bus, and the hallways. You're right; he feels good about himself today.
   Tom read pp. 1–5 in the new book with his father. The words he had trouble with are underlined.
   We will see you at parent meeting tomorrow night.

Mary Hogerty

and to provide a structured performance evaluation, such as the periodic report cards discussed earlier.

Marion (1979), urging caution in writing to minority parents, offered the following guidelines, which in fact apply to all parents:

- Determine the parents' educational level before sending written communications. By adjusting the language of the message accordingly, teachers increase the likelihood that parents will understand it and perceive it positively.
- Affix Mr. and/or Mrs. to all communications. Minority parents do not widely accept Ms. as a form of address.
- Be positive. Highlight the child's positive attributes before discussing the problem at hand.
- Guard against a condescending or superior tone. Reread the message before sending it to exorcise educational jargon.
- Be brief but clear and precise. Parents often complain that they do not hear about certain problems or hear only part of the story. Messages must clearly convey the teacher's meaning, leaving little room for supposition.
- Offer a clear reason for requesting visits to the school. Parents resent losing time from work or home tasks for unclear reasons.
- If appropriate, include a sign-off portion for the parents. This practice provides a feedback mechanism to assure teachers that parents have received their messages.

Croft (1979) pointed out that persistence pays even when communication appears to be one-way. Though parents may not respond to notes the way the teacher would like, they do gain greater awareness with each note of their child's school program.

Personal letters are one way for teachers to let parents know they perceive them as important to the child's success at school and as vital members of the child's educational team (Granowsky et al. 1977). A letter of introduction mailed to parents at the beginning of each school year is an opportunity for teachers to initiate positive contact and to demonstrate an interest in the child's home life (Magnusson and McCarney 1980). Investigators recommend sending such a welcome letter to each child's parents. The letter should be positive, friendly, and full of hope, emphasizing the parents' importance to the child's educational program and the teacher's desire to help the child (see Figure 5.6). Welcome letters may include the following items:

- A list of the year's scheduled subjects, activities, and events
- An invitation to the parents to visit the school and class

FIGURE 5.6 • *Welcome Letter*

August 20, 199_

Dear _____,

    I am happy to welcome you and your child _____ to Airport School for the 199_-9_ school year. Your child is a member of the Special Education School District resource program. _____ will be in regular class for most academic and special subjects and will receive support services and remedial instruction in the resource program.

    Let me tell you a little bit about myself. I have taught in this school district for nine years. In my first five years, I taught exceptional children in a special classroom. Four years ago I transferred to the resource program. This transfer was in large part a result of new guidelines contained in The Education of All Handicapped Children Act (Public Law 94-142). According to this law, all children are educated in the least restrictive environment possible to meet their individual needs. Your child is most effectively served in the resource program.

    In the near future, I will meet with parents to discuss their children's individualized educational program and to review the goals and objectives established for each child at the end of the last school year. During the conference, we will discuss expectations for your child this year, and I will suggest ways you can help your child at home and in school. I will try to respond to your questions and concerns about your child's educational program at this conference. I will telephone you for an appointment in early September.

    This year, we are implementing a new program in which parents can volunteer in the resource program. This will be an excellent means for us to get to know each other and collaborate in activities to help the children. Also, it will help familiarize you with the child's educational program. We can discuss this exciting project during our conference.

    I look forward to a very rewarding and productive school year with _____. With your support and assistance, I am sure we will make significant progress. Please feel free to contact me at Airport School (555-5534).

                                                 Sincerely yours,

- An invitation to the parents to contribute to the class as an aide, volunteer, or instructor
- The teacher's school and home telephone numbers
- A list of materials the child needs for school
- Suggestions for parents wishing to help the child at home.

Thank you letters are also effective communication devices. Using this format, teachers can express appreciation for parents' contributions to the special education program during the school year (Figure 5.7). They can also offer continued assistance and consultation during the summer months. Kaplan, Kohfeldt, and Sturla (1974) and Kaplan and Hoffman (1981) developed formats for awards, glad notes, and certificates for teachers to duplicate and send home, either as part of a systematic communication program or as periodic rewards (Figures 5.8 and 5.9). Imber, Imber, and Rothstein (1979) developed another positive device, a praise note (Figure 5.10), and studied its effects on the academic performance of three exceptional children. The research design consisted of three phases: (1) baseline, (2) intervention 1 (a teacher-child conference to praise the child and distribute earned-praise notes), and (3) intervention 2 (parent-teacher telephone contact and praise notes). The three children's performance improved significantly during both interventions using praise notes.

It is important that teachers let the children know the content of any notes, letters, or notices that go home. This practice can allay the children's anxiety about possible "bad news" and counteract the traditional negativity that has surrounded parent-teacher written communication.

FIGURE 5.7 • *Thank You Letter*

May 10, 199_

Dear _____,

Thank you for the fine job you've done in supporting our educational team this year. You have been vital to the success of _____'s program. It is a real pleasure to have worked with you. We look forward to future years with you and _____.

It is my sincerest hope that your summer will be a relaxing and enjoyable one. I hope you will have time to enjoy your children.

During the summer, if you have any concerns, please feel free to call me (555-0839). I will provide whatever assistance I can. Enclosed are copies of some "Summer Ideas" you may want to try with your child.

Have a nice summer. See you in the fall.

Sincerely,

124 Section Two • *Parent-Teacher Collaborative Activities*

FIGURE 5.8 • *Behavior and Achievement Award*

Teachers may find it helpful to develop a monthly calendar to be sent home with the students. This calender can prepare parents for upcoming events and keep them aware of classroom activities. A sample calendar is presented in Figure 5.11.

FIGURE 5.9 • *Behavior and Achievement Awards*

A more extensive written communication that teachers may choose to develop and use with their students and parents is a student handbook. In this handbook, the teacher may include any school or classroom policies. A "who to call for what" section can be helpful to parents and prevent phone calls to the teacher that are outside of his or her area, authority, or expertise (such as

FIGURE 5.10 • *Praise Note*

Success – ☺ – Gram

This is an announcement and remembrance of a great deed or accomplishment.

_____ has _____

_____

_____

Congratulations are in order!

Keep up the good work!

Date _____   Signed _____

lunch menus or transportation). A listing of school teachers and the subjects or grades they teach can be helpful to parents. Any further information—specific to the child's disability or general, related to all children in the school—may also be considered for the handbook.

In using written communication with parents, teachers may find it prudent to keep copies and document communication at-

Chapter Five • Written and Telephone Communication **127**

FIGURE 5.11 • *Monthly Calendar*

October 1990

Sunday	Monday	Tuesday	Wednesday	Thursday	Friday	Saturday
1	2	3	4 Jennifer's Birthday	5	6 We're making our own lunch today!	7
8	9	10	11 "Just for Dad's" meeting 7:30	12	13	14
15	16 Trip to Pumpkin Farm	17	18	19 Parent Conference	20 No School	21
22	23 Book Fair 10-1	24 Trip to LIBRARY National Book	25 Children's Library Week. to Your Child!	26 Book Reports Due!	27 Read a	28
29	30	31 HALLOWEEN PARTY: 11:30-11:30				

tempts. In addition, the use of mailing labels may be helpful. Through a filing or listing system, easy access to addresses and names of parents or guardians can be obtained.

Telephone Contacts

A telephone call demonstrates the teacher's personal interest in the parents; and positive, periodic, and consistent telephone contacts can significantly affect the child's school performance. (Alternatively, of course, negative telephone contacts can have a negative effect on parents' and exceptional children's attitudes toward teacher and school.)

Teachers must exercise care in using the telephone to communicate with parents about their child. Telephone contacts are good ways to encourage parents to attend meetings, conferences, and other school events. However, teachers should refrain from burdening an already busy parent with calls about the child's classroom or school behavior problems. It is impossible, in most circumstances, for a parent to control the child's school performance and behavior from home.

Teachers should telephone each parent in the first days of the school year to introduce themselves and demonstrate to parents their genuine concern with the child's welfare. Periodic telephone contacts with parents increase the probability of positive interactions. Positive telephone calls may be used to supplement the periodic report card and other parent-teacher communication techniques.

Some teachers have used recorded telephone messages citing the day's spelling words, for example, and other school activities as an effective, nonthreatening way to increase parent contacts (Chapman and Heward 1982). Answering machines also allow parents to leave messages for the teacher to respond to later in the day. Minner, Prater, and Beane (1989) suggest documenting telephone contacts with parents. A form for this purpose is presented in Figure 5.12.

According to Granowsky and associates (1977), "Many parents are afraid to come to school, and they feel uncomfortable when they do" (54). These authors encourage teachers to reach out to parents

FIGURE 5.12 • *Telephone Documentation Sheets*

Date	Persons Contacted	Reason	Summary

and communicate their wish to know the parents as well as their child. The telephone can be an effective means for beginning this process.

If teachers cannot make home visits, they can conduct telephone miniconferences with the parents. Using this technique, teachers should communicate with parents consistently—for example, biweekly or monthly—to report on student progress, behaviors, and achievements to be reinforced at home. Teachers should plan these telephone miniconferences in advance.

A telephone call from school is extremely threatening to many minority parents, for they have come to expect bad news (Marion 1979). Indeed, most parents probably share this negative perception of telephone calls from school.

Marion (1979) proposed guidelines for minimizing parent-teacher misunderstanding and misperceptions in telephone communications with minority parents; they are in fact applicable with all parents:

1. Address parents as Mr. or Mrs. for two reasons: Minority parents do not always receive the same courtesy and respect as other people. They may also resent or mistrust a professional who seems to want to become too friendly too soon. Common courtesy can make the difference between a good or poor beginning in the parent-teacher relationship.

2. Use a tone of voice that expresses respect and courtesy. Because a phone call from the school usually raises anxiety in many parents, a respectful, polite, calm tone of voice can be reassuring.

3. Discuss some of the child's good points before launching into a report of the problems. This approach will reduce the parent's anxiety, set the tone for conversation, and enhance the parent's perception of the teacher. Parents respond to a helpful person who treats them with kindness and respect and who makes positive comments about their children.

4. Use language the parent understands. Teachers must determine the parents' articulation, response, and level of understanding and adjust their language accordingly as the phone conversation progresses. Teachers should talk at parents' level without being condescending. Most people have built-in antennae that pick up the difference between a patronizing and a respectful attitude.

5. Ask parents to repeat essential parts of the conversation. Teachers should listen and respond appropriately at the parent's level of understanding and communicate empathy if parents have difficulty understanding unfamiliar educational concepts.

Croft (1979) suggested making telephone calls to parents during the evening hours or at times when parents are less likely to be busy. As a rule, calls to parents at work are inadvisable except in an emergency, for many employers frown on employees' accepting personal telephone calls during working hours.

Newsletters

The newsletter is a valuable component of a comprehensive parent-teacher involvement program that can serve several needs. Newsletters can provide information on long- and short-range program plans, explain instructional methods, and report on activities and events (Granowsky et al. 1977). A newsletter may be weekly, biweekly, or monthly, depending on classroom needs, personnel, time, and materials. However, it should be distributed regularly. In all probability, classroom newsletters are as well-received at home as all-school newspapers.

Parents usually read newsletters "on the run" or during a spare minute between activities. Thus, newsletters should not exceed four to six typewritten pages, should be written in common language, and should be positive and personal.

Teachers can supplement their contributions to the newsletter by soliciting contributions from other professionals, parents, and children. Children's and parents' contributions increase the newsletter's readership because parents enjoy this type of personal material. Every child in a class should contribute an article or drawing to the newsletter sometime during the year.

Parents may be willing to help prepare and distribute newsletters—often writing articles, typing manuscripts, or duplicating. Teachers can send newsletters home with the children, distribute them at parent meetings, or mail them.

Diversity makes for interesting and inviting newsletters. By developing an annual plan for newsletter content, teachers can ensure that they include relevant items at key points during the year. They might include any or all of the following items, for example:

- An explanation or description of class activities
- General news from classroom and school
- Announcements (future activities, materials and equipment needed, resource people needed, holidays, birthdays, celebrations, workshops)

- Suggestions for reading and viewing (new and significant books, current articles, motivational and inspirational literature, news articles, movies, lectures, and television and radio presentations)
- Abstracts and summaries of articles and books
- Learning activities for parents and children to do at home
- Recreational activities and games for parents and children
- Recognition of volunteers and other classroom contributors
- Introduction of community resource people and groups serving parents and exceptional children
- Program descriptions, including personnel working with the children, functions of resource personnel, class schedules, school calendars, materials and equipment, class organization, and behavior management techniques
- Children's drawings, poems, and stories
- A question-and-answer column
- Want ads for volunteers, equipment, materials, and suggestions.

The Carbondale Special Education Cooperative in Carbondale, Illinois, produces "The Co-op Connection" for parents, friends, and supporters of a program serving children and youth who are severely and profoundly mentally handicapped and multiply handicapped (Figure 5.13). The young people live in a residential environment and seldom see their parents, siblings, and relatives. Consequently, the newsletter is an important vehicle for highlighting the residents, their activities, and their progress. It also introduces the co-op faculty and staff to parents and others interested in the program in an informal, visually attractive, and cheerful format.

"Kiddie Kapers" is a monthly newsletter for parents of children with exceptionalities attending a public preschool program (Figure 5.14). This newsletter highlights classroom learning activities, as well as introducing activities parent and child can do at home. The newsletter is informational: "We want to tell you," "We are learning," "We need," and so on. Newsletter sections aim for brevity and clarity in an attractive format.

Summary

This chapter describes several techniques for parent-teacher collaboration that depend on written and telephone communication: daily and periodic report cards; positive parent-teacher communication notebooks; notes, letters, and notices; telephone communi-

132 Section Two • *Parent-Teacher Collaborative Activities*

FIGURE 5.13 • *Sample Newsletter: "The Co-op Connection"*

CARBONDALE SPECIAL EDUCATION COOPERATIVE Carbondale, Illinois April, 1980

What happened to spring? Temperatures have been in the 90s this week and everyone is talking about splash parties, picnics, and other summer activities. The Co-op's wading pool has been unpacked and cleaned up. One afternoon a number of our children dunked their feet in and splashed up a storm!

We welcome two new students to C.S.E.C.:

    Joan is in Sue's class and

    Mike is in Louise's class.

Mrs. Smith also has two new teacher aides, Elizabeth Riley and Dan Train. We are all glad to have them with us.

DID YOU KNOW. . . .

. . .that Jill, our secretary, was the guest of honor at a "Spring Sing"

    during National Secretary's Week?

. . .that Dr. Johnson of the SIU Department of Music has volunteered

    to provide music therapy for our students twice weekly since 1976?

    She is really APPRECIATED. Thank you.

ARTS AND CRAFTS

The change of season always brings a change of artwork displays. A trip down the hall features trees in full blossom, (blossoms of pop-corn, that is), fluffy white clouds made of soapsuds with brightly colored tissue paper kites. Another wall has kites flying every which way with shiny cellophone tails. Spring cannot be complete without lovely "pudding painted" flowers! Gardens are popping up all over.

(cont.)

FIGURE 5.13 *Continued*

NEWS FLASHES!

Vincent plays the drum in music class all by himself!

Joe puts his shirt on and takes it off with very little help!

Betty is learning to use her new communications board! (Her pet mouse, Felix, (or is it Felicia) is enjoyed by all her friends.)

Andrew side-steps along the handrail independently and walks holding an adult's hand on one side and the handrail on the other side!

Dwayne drinks from a cup independently!

Jenny matches identical objects!

Sarah holds her own cup and needs just a little help to scoop her food at lunch time!

Mona's toileting program has been very successful. She has had 12 accident free days!

Mickey is putting circles into a shape box independently!

Timothy really gets around taking small steps in his walker and goes just about any place he wants in his classroom!

John is the V.I.P. of the month in the Intermediate I room. He has become a very outgoing young man. Frequently, John may be seen heading for the candy jar in the secretary's office. He is also learning to climb the stairs.

Mary Ann is making great strides in self-feeding.

Eileen enjoys sitting in a teacher aide's lap. It is nice to see her relaxed and enjoying herself.

Kathleen looks forward to strumming the autoharp and playing the tambourine during music.

SPEAKING OF KITES. . . .

The first annual kite flying contest was held on April 23rd. Each room made a kite and eagerly anticipated its launching. Tension was high! Would it fly! How long would it stay up! Which one would go the highest!

It was a beautiful day with a slight breeze. Everyone gathered in the field behind the Co-op. The time has finally come to see everyone's kite in the air - or so we thought!

(cont.)

The pre-schoolers had a very pretty little kite and won the award for longest flying kite. It stayed up for 23 seconds.

The primary room's kite was a big red and white striped bird. It was the highest flying reaching an altitude of about 12 feet (if you stretch it a bit).

Every kite flying contest has a dragon and our dragon was judged the funniest kite of the day! It tried to fly but its power source fell down.

The prettiest kite was made by the people in the Intermediate I classroom. It looked like a stained glass windmill.

A double kite which was awarded the prize for most original kite was entered by the Intermediate II class. It also made every effort to fly but couldn't quite make it.

Despite the fallen kites, everyone had a high flying good time!

THANK-YOU!

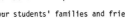

Many visitors have been to the Co-op since the threat of bad weather has passed. As always we are pleased to see our students' families and friends.

(cont.)

FIGURE 5.13 *Continued*

Mr. and Mrs. William Smith
Mrs. William Jones
Mr. & Mrs. William Davis
Mr. and Mrs. Kurt Swoboda
Mrs. Janice Lang

Phone calls are always welcome. Recently we have heard from Mrs. Marcus and Mrs. Mines.

Some of our children have recently gone home for a visit.

Mickey
Elizabeth
Barbara
JoAnn

JUST FOR FUN

Our children have participated in a number of special activities in addition to the kite flying contest!

Two of our talented aides organized a super afternoon at the Co-op. Our very own clown entertained with stunts and acrobatics. She is none other than Paula (Her mother was a "real circus clown"!) Gwen assisted her by leading a sing-a-long, an event considered to be a favorite by students and staff.

Paula and Gwen also planned a spring dance for everyone. A great time was had by all! The activity therapists cooperated by providing refreshments. Thank you!

Some of the teachers and one of the nurses have had four-legged visitors at school. Most of the children enjoy feeling the soft fur of kittens, puppies, and dogs. It's fun to watch them, too!

(cont.)

FIGURE 5.13 *Continued*

A trip to the stables is planned for this Spring. We also hope to have some baby farm animals visit the schoolyard.

Our traditional picnic will take place during the last week of school. It will be a super special picnic this year at "Touch of Nature," the Southern Illinois University's outdoor laboratory and camp for the handicapped located on Little Grassy Lake. Some of the exciting activities which are planned are a pontoon boat ride, sand play, a nature hike, and cook-out. We might even fly a kite!

SPLASH!

We have a new swimming program every Friday at the YMCA. Our group started out with five children from various rooms and has expanded to include three more.

The eight children have been responding to the water very well. Mary seems to have acquired the name "fish" after displaying her ability to kick and move her arms with very little support. Naomi finally found the bottom of the pool and is now standing while holding on to the side. Enos has been working with one of our new volunteers and has finally <u>lost</u> the bottom. He is floating very nicely with support. Joshua is "warming up" more easily each session and has kicked one of the nerf balls several times in the water. Drew is our rowdy in the bunch! Besides managing to drench himself he also likes to splash everyone that comes near. Dora is kicking and moving her arms in a very progressive manner. Pamela made her debut in the water a couple of weeks ago and holds great potential in moving her arms with more control. Laura is scheduled to come this week and we eagerly anticipate her participation.

(cont.)

FIGURE 5.13 *Continued*

A special thanks goes out to all the joint efforts put forth in helping to make the swimming program the success that it is:

>The staff from Styrest, staff from the school, our volunteers, and especially Mr. Miller who originally said, "yes" to the whole idea!

SPECIAL PROJECT

The entire staff of the Co-op salutes Joel for an ENORMOUS project filled with love, devotion, creativity, and time. A dream has come true due to Joel's talent and interest in the seed of an idea. He nurtured that seed and helped it develop. What is it? It is a stimulus controlled learning center large enough for two people to comfortably work inside. All sights, sounds, and smells are under complete control. More information will be included in next year's first issue of the Co-op Connection. Until then, thanks, Joel.

SCHOOL'S OUT

Another school year is about to end. It seems as though it just started. We have seen progress in our students and growth in our staff. It has been out pleasure to have had a small part in developing each child's potential and providing love and security so vital for growth.

Source: Courtesy of Carbondale Special Education Cooperative.

138 Section Two • *Parent-Teacher Collaborative Activities*

FIGURE 5.14 • *Sample Newsletter: "Kiddie Kapers"*

We want to tell you:

that January is an especially busy month here at school. By this time in the school year, parents are usually noticing many signs of maturation and growth in their children. Please remember to talk with your child about what he is doing here at school. It is not uncommon for children to refuse to talk immediately when they get home. However, most children will share later when they have had a chance to unwind or relax. If your child refuses or is not able to tell you about his school experiences, let me know so that we can make up some type of notebook.

We are learning:

these new words:

Fall	Spring
New Year	Summer
Seasons	Winter
Snow	

We need:

you. Please plan on coming to visit school if you have not done so already.

We want to thank:

our room mothers, Mrs. Dale and Mrs. Hill for coordinating another fantastic party. They said that they couldn't have done it without the help of all of you.

We want you to remember:

January 19th - No School. Teacher Institute.
January 29th - No. P.M. Session. Teacher Conferences.

Source: Courtesy of V. DeGiacinto.

cation; and newsletters. These techniques require a minimum amount of parent-teacher time and energy and are most appropriate for transmitting information. Thus, they communicate primarily *to* parents, providing only limited opportunities to communicate *with* them.

The techniques are most effective as components of a comprehensive parent-teacher collaboration program. They are valuable for initiating interaction, bridging the gap between parents and teachers, and supporting ongoing activities. The chapter suggests the

Chapter Five • Written and Telephone Communication 139

best use of each communication method, provides guidelines for productive use of the techniques, and offers samples of each.

The next four chapters present techniques suited for communicating *with* parents. Chapter 6 discusses the most frequently used of these techniques, the parent-teacher conference.

Exercises and Discussion Topics

1. Design and carry out a daily report card system for one or more children in your class (or for a child described in Appendix A). Train parents and children in the system.

2. Design and carry out a notebook system of communication with one or more children in your class (or for those described in Appendix A). Train the children, parents, and other professionals and paraprofessionals to use the notebook, implement the system, and evalutate it.

3. Using the material in this chapter, develop a checklist for the content of an introductory letter to parents. Write one or more examples of an introductory letter for the parents of the children in your class (or for parents of those in Appendix A). Ask several colleagues or parents to critique the letter, and rewrite it based on their critiques.

4. Write several notes to parents to accomplish the following objectives:
    a. To praise the child for appropriate behavior
    b. To praise the child for superior academic performance
    c. To alert parents to potential academic difficulties
    d. To tell parents about a behavior problem
    e. To invite the parents to a conference.

Ask several colleagues or parents to critique the notes, and rewrite them to reflect their comments.

5. Call several parents of children in your class on the telephone (or role play telephone calls using the cases in Appendix A) to convey the messages listed in Exercise 4.

6. Plan a monthly newsletter for your class (or a hypothetical class) for distribution ten times a year (September to June). After establishing the content for each of the ten newsletters, develop a format and prepare at least two samples.

References

Chapman, J. E., and W. L. Heward. 1982. Improving parent-teacher communication through recorded telephone messages. *Exceptional Children* 49 (1): 79–82.

Croft, D. J. 1979. *Parents and teachers: A resource book for home, school, and community relations.* Belmont, Calif.: Wadsworth.

Granowsky, A., A. Hackett, A. Hoffman, J. Keller, F. Lamkin, J. Morrison, M. Rabbit, M. Schumate, E. Schurr, E. Stranix, and J. Woods. 1977. How to put parents on your classroom team. *Instructor* Nov: 54–62.

Imber, S., R. Imber, and C. Rothstein. 1979. Modifying independent work habits: An effective teacher-parent communication program. *Exceptional Children* 46 (3): 218–21.

Kaplan, P.G., and A.G. Hoffman. 1981. *It's absolutely groovy.* Denver: Love.

Kaplan, P.G., J. Kohfeldt, and K. Sturla. 1974. *It's positively fun: Techniques for managing learning environments.* Denver: Love.

Lordeman, A.M., and R.A. Winett. 1980. The effects of written feedback to parents and a call-in service on student homework submission. *Education and Treatment of Children* 3 (1): 33–44.

Magnusson, C. J., and S. B. McCarney. 1980. School-home communication. *The Pointer* 25 (1): 23–27.

Marion, R. 1979. Minority parent involvement in the IEP process: A systematic model approach. *Focus on Exceptional Children* 10 (8): 1–15.

Minner, S., G. Prater, and A. Beane. 1989. Alternative methods of communicating with parents. *Academic Therapy* 24: 619–24.

Powell, T. H. 1980. Improving home-school communication: Sharing daily reports. *The Exceptional Parent* 10 (5): S24–S26.

Runge, A., J. Walker, and T. M. Shea. 1975. A passport to positive parent-teacher communication. *Teaching Exceptional Children* 7 (3): 91–92.

Rutherford, R. B., Jr., and E. Edgar. 1979. *Teachers and parents: A guide to interaction and cooperation.* Abr.ed. Boston: Allyn and Bacon.

Shea, T. M., and A. M. Bauer. 1987. *Teaching children and youth with behavior disorders.* 2d ed. Englewood Cliffs, N.J.: Prentice-Hall.

Schmalz, N. 1987. School-home notebook: How to find out what your child did all day. *The Exceptional Parent* 17 (6): 18–19, 21–22.

Thorman, J.H. 1979. A supplement to the report card. *Education and Treatment of Children* 2 (1): 65–70.

CHAPTER SIX

Parent-Teacher Conferences

Ms. J., parent of an eleven-year-old son with mild mental retardation:

"I was just raised by my mother, and when I was going to school I didn't have parents to go to school with me to talk with the teachers if I was having problems or whatever. Since I didn't have it, my children are going to have it. So, I go to school, I talk to the teachers, I meet with the teachers. I keep up to date with everything that's going on here on a day-to-day basis. If they have a problem, we sit together and we talk it through, where I didn't have that when I was growing up. My mother, she raised nine kids herself, so I didn't have that. But my children are going to have it."

Chapter Topics and Objectives

The parent-teacher conference is "an individualized, personalized meeting between two or three significant persons in the child's life with the purpose of accelerating his or her growth" (Kroth and Simpson 1977, 2). This chapter discusses the types of conferences most likely to be useful to teachers of children with exceptionalities: progress report, problem-solving, and behavior management training conferences. In addition, it discusses the individualized education program meeting mandated by Public Law 94-142 as a special type of conference. Home visits, the three-way conference, and coping with negative reactions are discussed.

The quality of the communication between parents and teacher in a conference is key (Kroth and Simpson 1977). Just as positive communication can help improve the child's performance, so can negative interactions cause performance to deteriorate (Truax and

Wargo 1966). Consequently, it is important to structure every conference to encourage a positive exchange.

Individual conferences are one part of a comprehensive parent-teacher collaboration program. They require more planning, preparation, and personal involvement than do written and telephone communication. However, because communication is face to face, the probability of miscommunication decreases. The content of the parent-teacher conference is more personal than that of traditional written and telephone communications. Both parents and teacher must devote time and energy to planning, scheduling, attending, and evaluating each conference.

In this chapter, we will:

- Describe progress report conferences.
- Discuss problem-solving conferences.
- Make suggestions regarding training conferences.
- Discuss IEP conferences.
- Discuss home visits and three-way conferences.
- Discuss methods for coping with negative reactions during conferences.

Progress Report Conferences

The progress report conference supplements traditional reporting procedures, such as the report card, providing an opportunity for personal interactions and open communication (Björklund and Burger 1987). The conference is an opportunity for parents and teachers to exchange information about the child's school and home activities. It is an occasion to involve parents in helping to plan and carry out their child's program. Based on systematic evaluation of the child and information from the parents, the conference can guide the teacher in modifying the child's program. Ultimately, the progress report conference is a forum for sharing skills and information to benefit the child.

When teachers contact parents to schedule progress report conferences, they should explain the purpose of the conference and possibly give the parents a written agenda. These steps help reduce the parents' anxiety about attending the session.

Since the conference serves as a verbal report card, the agenda centers on the child and the program, not on the parents' or teacher's personal, social, emotional, or marital problems (as important as they may be to the parent or teacher). Björklund and Burger

(1987) suggest assuring the parents of this focus by sending home a progress summary prior to the conference.

In many cases, the conference is a show-and-tell session. The teacher presents and discusses the child's work and the instructional materials used in the educational program. Many parents welcome an invitation to try out instructional materials and equipment used by their child.

Activities related to the progress report conference can be grouped as before, during, and after the conference. Preparation is as important as, if not more important than, the actual conduct of the conference. An outline to assist in this preparation is provided in Table 6.1. Teachers should write a jargon-free report before the

TABLE 6.1 • *Outline for Preconference Report*

A. Social behavior (in the classroom, during recess, on field trips, on the bus)
   1. Self-control (in large and small groups, during activities)
   2. Affective behavior (enthusiasm, leadership, followership, responsibility, reactions to rewards and contingencies)
   3. Group participation
   4. Social conventions (manners, courtesy, respect for others and their property)
B. Communication
   1. Conversational and verbal skills
   2. Written communication skills
   3. Listening (responsiveness, following directions, stories, music)
   4. Language (receptive language, expressive language, development, verbal communication of experiences, appropriate use of language in context)
   5. Speech
C. Skills and information
   1. Personal information
   2. Basic concepts (colors, shapes, letters, numbers, size, etc.)
   3. Reading
   4. Written communication (fluency, spelling)
   5. Arithmetic and computation
   6. Social studies (current events)
   7. Expressive arts (art, music, movement)
   8. Sensory-motor skills
   9. Learning styles
D. Self-care, practical, and work skills
   1. Use of school tools (paper, pencil, scissors, paste)
   2. School chores and duties
   3. Bathroom and personal hygiene
   4. Body use (awareness, climbing, walking, running, motor planning)
   5. Study skills

---

session evaluating the child's educational program and progress. They give the parents a copy at the beginning of the conference for their home records, for future reference, or for the convenience of an absent parent, if necessary.

Price and Marsh (1985) suggest that in addition to preparing a progress summary and agenda, the teacher needs to plan the format for the progress report conference. The teacher should plan the site of the conference, providing a comfortable, informal, and private setting. Elksnin and Elksnin (1989) suggest that since parents and teacher are collaborators, a more neutral setting, such as the school library or conference room, would be more appropriate than the classroom. Materials should be ready and orderly, so that the show-and-tell nature of the meeting can proceed smoothly.

During the meeting, Roberds-Baxter (1984) suggests, the teacher should communicate that he or she is confident and at ease while conducting the meeting. Parents should feel wanted and necessary. Roberds-Baxter recommends relaxation exercises to reduce physical tension before the meeting. Time should be allowed to get acquainted with the parents before initiating weighty discussions.

The teacher guides the actual conference, systematically reviewing the report and encouraging and responding to the parents' questions and comments. Because parents' questions and comments reflect their most pressing concerns, teachers should take care to respond fully and reassuringly. They should also see that they obtain the information they need from parents.

After making parents comfortable at the beginning of a session, teachers clarify the time available for conferring. The conference tone is positive: The teacher accentuates the positive and encourages the parents to do likewise. Thus, rather than saying, "Tommy does not recognize fourteen letters of the alphabet," the teacher says, "Tommy recognizes twelve letters of the alphabet; this is three new letters since we last conferred." Instead of "Jean is out of her seat without permission sixteen times a day," the teacher says, "We are seeing some progress in Jean's in-seat behavior. Last month when we conferred, I reported that she left her seat twenty times per day. Now she's out of her seat about fifteen times per day. That's an improvement." Teachers should review and accent the areas of functioning in which the child demonstrates skill, competency, and progress. This approach provides a balanced view of the child as a learner rather than as an exceptional child only.

Except for the initial conference, the teacher focuses on the child's progress since the last scheduled session. However, once each year, parents and teachers may find it valuable to review the child's progress since the beginning of the year or since the implementation of a specific educational program.

If the teacher sees that parents wish to and can increase their involvement in their child's educational program, he or she can encourage them to do so at this time, although it is not an immediate objective of the progress report conference. However, the teacher has the duty to ensure that such parent involvement is helpful to the child, which it generally is.

Parents and teacher may want to take notes during the conference, but the teacher should make sure that all participants are comfortable with note taking and drop it if necessary. Immediately after the conference, the teacher writes a conference summary to attach to the report and file in the child's folder. This summary includes questions the teacher wishes to raise with the parents at the next conference.

Several activities should take place following the progress report conference. Björklund and Burger (1987) suggest that immediately after the parents leave, the teacher should write a careful record of the conference, including suggestions that were made and questions that were raised. An informal note to the parents referring to the conference or an evaluation form asking for suggestions about the conference format demonstrates openness on the part of the teacher. Elksnin and Elksnin (1989) suggest debriefing the student if he or she was not present at the conference. Additional tasks discussed at the conference and time lines for completing these tasks should be developed (Price and Marsh 1985).

Teachers can help parents to participate fully in the conferencing process in a variety of ways. Providing parents with a handout offering tips on activities for before, during, and after the conference is one way (Figure 6.1).

They may provide the parents with specific questions that are selected to facilitate their participation. The questions may be helpful in defining terms, getting more descriptive information, and determining the implications of the information the teacher is providing (Nye, Westling, and Laten 1986). A parent questionnaire, which may increase the effectiveness of the conference, may be completed by the parents. Sample items from such a questionnaire are presented in Figure 6.2.

Problem-Solving Conferences

Conferences to plan and carry out solutions to academic or behavior problems are often useful to both parents and teachers. The

FIGURE 6.1 • *Parent Handout for Conference Preparation*

Before the conference:

1. Make arrangements for your other children, if necessary. The conference is for you and your child's teacher; small children can be distracting and take time away from the discussion.
2. Jot down any questions you may have for the teacher, such as:
   • Is my child working to the best of his (her) ability?
   • How is he (she) progressing in reading, math, handwriting, and other subjects?
   • Does he (she) get along well with teachers, children?
   • Does he (she) follow classroom rules?
   • What is his (her) attitude in class?
   • How do you handle (specific behaviors)?
   • What do the tests say about his (her) ability?
3. Talk to your child about the conference. Ask if he or she wants you to ask any questions or voice any concerns.
4. Collect any records or information that may help the teacher. Try to anticipate questions and prepare answers.

At the conference:

1. Please be on time and stay only for your scheduled time. You may schedule another conference if you do not cover all the necessary information in the allotted time.
2. Discuss only the child at issue. Try not to stray off the subject. Do not bring up your other children's problems.
3. Ask any questions about your child's education. Advocate for your child. Know your child's and your rights.
4. Volunteer information that may help the teacher plan programming for your child.
5. Feel free to take notes to review later.

After the conference: Feel free to contact your child's teacher for further clarification.

successful problem-solving conference considers in detail the environment in which the problem is taking place, the nature of the problem, conference preplanning, conference timing, the required data and information, the needs of parents' and teachers' for reinforcement, and the provisions for training parents to help solve the problem (Kroth 1985; Elksnin and Elksnin 1989).

Parents and teacher must recognize that a child may have a problem in one environment but not in another. Thus, they must

FIGURE 6.2 • *Parent Conference Preparation Questionnaire Items*

1. What school activities does your child describe or discuss most often?
2. What seems to be your child's favorite school subject?
3. Does your child talk about school friends?
4. Does your child complete homework assignments independently?
5. What is your child's greatest strength?
6. What concerns you most about your child?

---

determine if the problem is primarily at school, at home, in the neighborhood, or in several places. Similarly, they should avoid projecting their personal and social problems or behaviors onto the child and should determine if the problem rests with the child or with the parent or teacher.

Elksnin and Elksnin (1989) suggest the use of the Heron and Harris (1987) consultation model as a format for problem-solving conferences. They suggest that more than one conference is usually needed to work through the following eight steps of the process:

1. *Entry.* During entry, rapport is established. Talking informally relaxes both parents and teacher before they initiate discussion of more controversial or disturbing topics.
2. *Gathering additional information about the issue.* Though data was gathered before the conference began, additional information will probably be needed. Parents and teacher need to discuss their perceptions related to the issue.
3. *Defining the problem.* This step is probably the most critical step. Without a clear definition, solutions may be difficult to generate. Parents and teacher may not share a perception of the problem.
4. *Determining solutions through brainstorming.* Problem definition impacts on the generation of potential solutions.
5. *Stating objectives.* The objectives may include defining the target behavior, the conditions for the behavior, and criteria for acceptable performance.
6. *Implementing a jointly agreed-upon plan.* If the plan is modified or abandoned, both the parents and teacher must agree.
7. *Evaluating the plan collaboratively.* In addition to discussing whether or not the objectives were met, parents and teacher should identify the variables that may have contributed to progress.

8. *Termination.* Termination occurs when both parents and teacher agree that problem solving is no longer needed.

Clearly, the problem-solving process is a collaborative activity among parents, teacher, and child, who may participate during planning as well as in carrying out solutions. Regularly scheduled conferences are the best way to develop this relationship. Crisis conferences, when feelings run high, are less likely to be productive; an ill-timed conference can create tension between parents and teacher that interferes with effective problem solving.

Rutherford and Edgar (1979) have proposed a general problem-solving process applicable to several theoretical problem-solving models. They have discussed parent-teacher problem-solving conferences using applied behavior analysis, interpersonal communication, and assertiveness strategies. Their model and the prerequisite skills for its effective implementation can guide teachers and parents in their problem-solving activities (Table 6.2).

Applied behavior analysis systematically approaches observing and analyzing behaviors where they occur. Specific behavior change strategies are used to increase or decrease selected behaviors. Interpersonal communication stresses effective communication skills as an intervention procedure. Assertiveness strategies stress helping people better control their destinies while learning to feel better about themselves.

Training Conferences

Training conferences teach parents how to design, carry out, and evaluate home and home-school behavior management interventions. Blackard and Barsch (1982) suggested that professionals underestimate parents' teaching abilities and lack confidence in parents as teachers of their own children. However, the literature amply documents that training in the principles and practices of behavior management helps parents change their children's behavior.

This section discusses the parent-teacher conference as the appropriate instructional setting for this training. Preferably, both parents should attend the training sessions to ensure that they use the same management interventions at home with consistency. With the teacher using the same techniques at school, the child has the security of consistent expectations throughout the day.

The teacher, as a conference leader and parent educator, should aim for a positive tone that communicates personal interest, enthu-

TABLE 6.2 • *A Problem-Solving Model*

Problem-Solving Model	Skills
Defining the problem	Applied behavior analysis: Pinpointing observable, measurable behaviors; recording; charting
	Communication: Expressing ownership and "I" messages; listening actively
	Assertiveness: Recognizing irritation; defining territorial issues
Developing the solution	Applied behavior analysis: Analyzing the antecedents and consequences of the behavior
	Communication: Employing bilateral decision making to determine solutions and develop a written contract
	Assertiveness: Stating needs; defending against weapons; drawing up written contract
Implementing the solution	Applied behavior analysis: Aiming for consistent application of procedures
	Communication: Allowing ample time for understanding the problem
	Assertiveness: Testing the contract
Evaluating the results	Applied behavior analysis: Conducting an ongoing assessment; charting; maintaining; generalizing
	Communication: Using "I" messages to discuss whether the problem is resolved
	Assertiveness: Renegotiating agreements if there is displeasure.

Source: Rutherford and Edgar 1979, 198. Reprinted with permission.

siasm, knowledge, and faith that the training will pay off in a happier, more competent child. The training program must be specific, starting with problems significant to the parents. The more the teacher enlivens the conferences with real-life examples speaking to the parents' needs, the more useful it will be.

Adhering to structured conference procedures in the early stages of parent training also helps both teachers and parents feel secure and develop faith in the potential effectiveness of their cooperative efforts. As parent and teacher become more comfortable, the teacher can relax the structure somewhat. Several behavior management training techniques are available for teachers to match with their instructional purposes and the parents' level of knowledge and skill. Beginning teachers will find them useful in establishing a framework for their work with parents; as they gain more experience, they can adapt them to fit specific circumstances.

Walker and Shea (1987) suggested a psychosituational assessment interview designed by Bersoff and Grieger (1971) as an effective behavior modification interviewing technique. Teachers can use the interview to analyze unacceptable behaviors, uncover their antecedents, and examine the consequences that elicit, reinforce, and sustain them. This information guides parents and teachers in their decisions to use specific behavior management interventions.

Bersoff's and Grieger's interview departs from the predominant assumption that personality needs and traits predispose people to respond in certain ways; operating on this assumption, professionals try to fix the individual rather than the setting in which the behavior occurs. Alternatively, Bersoff and Grieger proposed that behavior results from the individual's inability to respond in certain ways in certain situations rather than from inherent needs and traits. Thus, their model views behavior as a consequence of prior learning and the situation or environment.

A psychosituational assessment interview is designed to help teachers determine to what extent the environment reinforces the exceptional child's behavior and to what extent changes in the environment may alter the behavior. Thus, it focuses on three major aspects of any behavior problem: the child's behavior, including its antecedents and consequences (for example, the responses of parents, siblings, and others); the environmental variables surrounding the behavior, including the presence of significant others; and the parents' attitudes and expectations. Thus, the interview should accomplish four tasks: defining the target behavior(s), explicating specific situations in which the behavior occurs, uncovering the contingencies that seemingly sustain the behavior, and detecting any irrational ideas that stand in the way of understanding, accepting, and modifying the behavior.

To define the target behavior, the interviewer gathers information on its frequency, its intensity, and its duration. Looking at the problem within this framework not only helps narrow it down to manageable proportions but also helps parents check their perceptions of the behavior and focus on its most important aspects. Next, obtaining information about the specific situations in which the behavior occurs is important to clarify links that may lead to a solution.

Third, by exploring the antecedents and consequences of the behavior, parents and teacher can become aware of the role they play in the problem. Finally, by looking at parents' possibly irrational and unrealistic ideas about their child, teachers may learn of unwarranted short- or long-term expectations burdening the child or causing inappropriate responses to specific behaviors. The following irrational ideas commonly emerge during the interview:

- The notion that the child is infallible and has wide-ranging competence. When parents expect their child to be competent in all respects, they may view inefficient functioning in one or two areas as general failure.
- The idea that the child should meet certain absolute, unsupportable, or unreasonable standards. Parents often express this belief in "ought" and "should" statements: "He should be able to sit longer," or "He ought to know better."
- A belief that anger is the most helpful response to the child's misbehavior. This feeling may cause parents to feel guilty and anxious, thereby interfering with positive parent-child interactions.
- The belief that the exceptional child is blameworthy and should be punished for misdeeds.

The psychosituational assessment interview may be a single session or a series of sessions. One or two sessions may be sufficient to design an intervention for a single behavior. However, the interview technique is most effective in an ongoing series of behavior management training conferences.

During the assessment interview, the teacher has several objectives:

    1. Establish rapport with the parents. Sample questions: How was your day? How is your child today?
    2. Obtain the parents' description of the behaviors concerning them, including their frequency, intensity, and duration. Sample questions: What exactly does the child do that you find unacceptable or annoying? What exactly does he do that makes you say he is hyperactive, nonresponsive, or disobedient? In the course of an hour, how often is he hyperactive, nonresponsive, or disobedient?
    3. Obtain the parents' description of the situations and environments in which the behavior occurs and the people present when the behavior occurs. Sample questions: Where does this behavior occur? In the house? In the yard? On the playground? In a store? Does it occur when the child is working on a particular project? With a particular group? While watching TV? When getting ready to go to bed? When getting up in the morning? Who is present when the behavior occurs? Mother? Father? Brothers? Sisters? Playmates? Visitors?

4. Explore the contingencies that may stimulate and sustain the behavior. Sample questions: What happens just before the behavior occurs? What happens just after the behavior occurs? What do you usually do when the child behaves in this way? How do other people indicate to the child that the behavior is unacceptable?

5. Attempt to determine the ratio of positive to negative interactions between the child and the parents. Sample questions: Is your relationship with the child usually pleasant or unpleasant? Do you usually praise his accomplishments? Do you think you praise his successes as much as you reprimand his failures, or do you think you do one more than the other?

6. Explore the parents' methods of behavior control. Sample questions: Do you punish the behavior? How do you punish inappropriate behavior? Who administers the punishment? Do you always use this method of punishment? What other methods do you use?

7. Determine how aware parents are of the way they communicate praise or punishment and its effect on the child's behavior. Sample questions: Can the child tell when you are angry? How? Can he tell when you want him to stop doing something?

8. Explore how parents communicate their expectations to their child. Sample questions: How clearly do you spell out the rules you expect the child to follow? Does he know what you expect him to do?

9. Detect irrational and unrealistic ideas that make it difficult for the parents to understand, accept, or modify the child's behavior. Restate these irrational ideas but avoid reinforcing them. Sample questions: What do you feel is the reason for the behavior? Do you think the behavior can be changed?

10. Conclude the interview by restating the unacceptable behavior and clarifying the desirable behavior.

At the end of the interview, the teacher may suggest that the parents keep a log of their child's unacceptable behavior (Figure 6.3). The teacher should complete the top portion of the form, describing the target behavior in behavioral terminology. The parents write the day or date of the target behavior's first occurrence each day in the far left column. They then note the time the behavior begins and ends each time it occurs. If the behavior ends quickly, they note the time only in the "Begins" column. Each time the target behavior occurs, parents also note its antecedents (what happened immediately before the behavior) and the consequences (what happened immediately after the behavior) in the designated columns. In the "Applied Interventions" column, they note what they or someone

FIGURE 6.3 • *Behavior Log Form*

Target behavior _____

Observer's name _____ Child observed _____

Day or Date	Time		Antecedents	Consequences	Applied Interventions	Comments
	Begins	Ends				

else did to change the child's behavior. In the "Comments" column, parents note any additional observations. (See supplementary materials, pp. 169–174.)

Parents return the completed log at the next conference, usually scheduled at the end of the psychosituational interview, at which point the teacher analyzes and discusses the information with them. Graphing the data can be helpful in such discussions. The next step is to plan and put into effect a behavior management intervention.

Individualized Education Program Meetings

The *individualized education program* (IEP) mandated by Public Law 94-142 is central to providing effective education and related services to exceptional children. Public Law 94-142 reaffirmed the legitimate and essential role of parents in the education of their exceptional children, requiring that parents be active participants in the development, approval, and evaluation of their children's individualized education program. Specifically, parents participate with professionals in the assessment, planning, approval, placement, and evaluation processes. They may also participate actively in implementing their children's education program and related services.

The IEP meeting is the vehicle that brings parents and professionals together in a formal setting to plan the exceptional child's program. Meetings typically involve the following participants:

- An administrator of the local school district or special education district who can ensure the availability of necessary resources (staff, programs, funds)
- The teacher primarily responsible for the exceptional child's education, who is qualified to assess the skills, educational programs, and related services the child needs
- The child, if parents and professionals consider it appropriate
- The parents, who are ultimately responsible for the child's welfare and who possess a wealth of information and experience pertinent to the meeting
- Others with important information and expertise, subject to parents' and professionals' approval.

Scanlon, Arick, and Phelps (1980) found that in practice, only the special education teacher and mother attended 75 percent of the meetings they analyzed. When other people did attend, their roles were perceived as more important, and they may be more influential in decision making than the parents and special teachers.

Gilliam and Coleman (1981) found that parents were perceived as low in actual contribution and influence in IEP meetings. Psychologists were most influential in the diagnostic portion of the meetings, the special educator in planning and implementation of the program, the special education director in placement decisions, and the special education supervisor in assuring due process. Parents tended to be passive, serving as listeners and "consenters." Vaughn, Bos, Harrell, and Lasky (1988) report similar results. Parents asked few questions, made few comments, and yet reported satisfaction with the IEP process.

The IEP written at the meeting is the program agreed on by the participants. It describes the provisions of certain specific services. McAfee and Vergason (1979) suggested that current legislation is weaker than it could be because the IEP is not a contractual agreement between parents and professionals. Currently, the professional alone is responsible for initiating and fulfilling the terms of the IEP. McAfee and Vergason suggested that if the IEP became a contract outlining professionals' and parents' responsibilities, parent-teacher cooperation would be more effective and thus improve the child's education and related services program.

Both the IEP concept and the IEP meeting are unfamiliar to the vast majority of parents, especially parents who have just learned about their children's exceptionality. Thus, to avoid inefficient use of time at the meeting, the teacher should prepare the parents. Several authors have suggested that parents receive the following preparation for the IEP meeting (Lusthaus and Lusthaus 1979; Bauer 1981):

- Adequate notice of the meeting
- An opportunity to review the child's educational records with a competent professional familiar with the information
- A meeting agenda stating the session objectives, discussion topics, and questions to be addressed to the parents
- A list of the people to attend the meeting and descriptions of their positions and functions
- Information on obtaining an independent or supplemental assessment of their child if they so desire
- Information on who may accompany them to the meeting (the child, an attorney, an interpreter)
- A list of the materials they may wish to bring.

Before the IEP meeting, parents should talk to their children about their feelings about school, the teacher, and peers. They may also wish to ask their child whether they want to attend the meeting. Gillespie and Turnbull (1983) suggested that parents and teacher consider three factors before inviting a child to participate in the meeting: Will the child understand the language used in the conference, and will he or she be able to communicate preferences and interests? How comfortable will the child feel, and how will he or she react to possible disagreements during the conference? Will the child understand the purpose of the conference and the possible benefit of his or her attendance?

Uninitiated parents may benefit from talking with other parents of exceptional children who have participated in IEP meetings. They may also wish to observe their children in the classroom and discuss the child and his or her educational performance with the teacher. If a change in placement is under consideration, parents should visit the potential classroom and confer with the teacher.

Parents should prepare a list of the questions they wish to ask at the meeting. They should also clarify their personal short-term and long-term expectations for their child. This type of preparation is time-consuming and, on occasion, frustrating for parents inexperienced in exceptionality and special education. However, the more thorough their preparation, the greater the chance is that the meeting will result in a responsive program.

Goldstein and Turnbull (1982) found that two actions are especially effective in encouraging parents to participate. The first is sending questions home to the parent, followed by a phone call for clarification. The second is including the school counselor in the conference as a parent advocate. These two strategies increased fathers' attendance at the conference and increased the parents' participation during the meeting.

During the meeting, parents should feel free to make comments, ask questions, and offer recommendations. Thus, teachers should be approachable, listen to parents' ideas, and communicate a sense of unity in working for the child. Teachers should also be flexible, adaptable, responsive to parents' needs, and sensitive to each parent's uniqueness (Swick, Flake-Hobson, and Raymond 1980). Professionals are responsible for seeing that the education and related service program respond directly to the child's assessed needs and that the child is to be placed in the least restrictive environment in which he or she can be effectively educated. Parents must be sure they have a complete understanding of their child's educational program and related services, including who is to provide the agreed-upon services.

Shevin (1983) stated that too often professionals focus more on obtaining parents' signatures on the appropriate line by the correct date than on encouraging them to participate fully in decision making for their children. He described four typical levels of parent participation at IEP meetings. The first level is that of uninformed consent, in which parents agree to the IEP without sufficient information on the risks, implications, and alternatives. In this situation, the teacher may outline IEP goals, ask parents if they have any questions, request that they sign the IEP, and take the signature as consent. Professionals typically present only positive possible outcomes in such cases, omitting programming alternatives.

Shevin's second level is uninformed participation, whereby parents are requested to identify goals for the teacher to implement but the parents are provided with no information on which to base their decisions. The third level is informed consent. Here, parents fully understand the rationale behind the program, its potential benefits and risks, and available programming alternatives, but are not really full participants because the professionals view them as "informed lay persons" who can either consent or not.

Shevin's final level of participation is informed participation, which involves parents in identifying educational priorities, developing instructional strategies, and reviewing and modifying goals. This level of interaction develops continuity between home and school in the child's program, provides parents with information about resources and alternatives, and yields more appropriate and feasible goals than lesser degrees of participation. It also guarantees the child strong advocates, the parents, on his or her educational team.

To ensure parent involvement in the goal-setting process, the teacher should identify and clarify the parents' personal values with regard to their goals; discuss with the parents alternative approaches to attain the goals; set priorities among the agreed-upon alternative approaches; explore both available and potential resources; and decide on time lines for achieving and evaluating progress toward the goals.

The IEP meeting can be a valuable learning experience for parents. They learn a great deal about their child, special education and related services, placements, professionals, and themselves. In addition, they learn the answers to these questions (Lusthaus and Lusthaus 1979):

- What are the professionals' views of the child's special needs?
- How do they define the child's strengths and weaknesses?

- What do they consider the child's current level of performance?
- What are the possible placements for the child?
- What potential problems exist in each placement? What solutions exist to these problems?
- What potential benefits does each placement offer?
- What do meeting participants think is the best placement for the child?
- If the placement is new, when will it begin and how long will it last? How will the transition take place?
- What are the goals for the child in this placement?
- Who will determine if the goals are attained? How and when?
- What related services (speech therapy, for example) will the child receive in this placement? When will each service begin and how long will it last? How will meeting participants evaluate the usefulness of these services?
- What percentage of time will the child spend in special education and what percentage in regular education?
- Who in the school is responsible for the child's progress?
- How and when will the effectiveness of the placement and the program be evaluated?
- How do the professionals think the parents can help in the child's educational program?
- Who in the school system is responsible for communicating the child's progress to parents? How and when will progress reports take place?
- To whom should the parent convey concerns about the child's education?

At the end of the meeting, parents should either receive or arrange to receive a copy of the child's individualized education program.

Morgan (1982) provided the following guidelines for parental involvement in the IEP process:

- Parents should participate in the process as much as they want to and are able to.
- Schools should deal with parents on a program level rather than a legal level.
- Professionals should not view parent participation as an intrusion but as a help in controlling arbitrary evaluation, placement, and instruction.

Parents should remain calm, cool, and collected during the IEP meeting to preserve the spirit of cooperation. However, they should not allow professionals to intimidate them and dominate the meeting or to do all the planning and assume responsibility for all services. Nor should parents settle for inadequate or inappropriate services for their child. Clearly, parents' responsibilities do not end with the meeting, for they should monitor implementation of the child's educational program as well, continuing to meet with and otherwise communicate with those responsible for service to the child.

Home Visits

Home visits by teachers are increasingly common. Indeed, many elementary and secondary school teachers are discovering that annual home visits are an expected part of their jobs. The practice is standard in many special education and preschool programs.

Boards of education and school administrative personnel are demonstrating greater willingness to adjust school schedules to accommodate home visits. A few schools provide time for teachers to prepare, conduct, and evaluate home visits, sometimes employing substitute teachers or dismissing classes to permit visits during school time. Some school districts provide transportation, pay mileage, or offer escorts to teachers making home visits.

A home visit helps the teacher get to know the child's family, environment, and culture better in order to serve both child and parents more effectively. A conference at home is an occasion for the teacher to meet the other members of the child's educational team and become acquainted with the child's learning context. Teachers can use home visits for several purposes: information gathering, reporting the child's school performance, problem solving, preliminary discussions for the formal IEP meeting, and parent training.

Because the home conference takes place in the child's natural environment, the teacher's careful observation can often answer questions about the child's behavior and academic achievement, particularly the quality of the interactions between the child and other people in the household. In the home setting, the teacher can express concerns about the child directly in a face-to-face discussion; because the parents are in a familiar and secure environment during the home conference, they are more willing to express concerns about the child, teacher, and school (Rutherford and Edgar 1979).

Children usually enjoy teacher visits. Young children in particular see a visit by the teacher as a very special and exciting occasion. Children are eager to have the teacher meet their parents and brothers and sisters, see their bedrooms, and share the delight of personal treasures. They like to tell their friends and classmates about the visit, for it makes them feel important (Croft 1979). Before the conference itself begins, parent and teacher must decide whether the child should participate.

Parents' reactions vary. Some parents are very pleased by the visit and welcome the teacher into their homes; others are reluctant to permit a visit. A few become annoyed and angry at this attempt to invade their privacy. Those families who do not accept a visit may cite illness or death in the family, a previous appointment, an emergency, the demands of work, or other reasons. Some parents will never feel free to tell the teacher their reason. However, the teacher should accept the parents' stated reason. Time and patience may eventually make the parents more receptive to the idea.

If parents are reluctant to participate in a home conference, Croft (1979) suggested five things a teacher could do:

1. Become acquainted with the parents on neutral territory, such as a park, a coffee shop, a community center, or a church.
2. Establish a positive relationship before requesting a home visit.
3. Discuss the purposes and advantages of a home visit.
4. Enlist the assistance of a third party respected by the parents, such as a friend, neighbor, or minister.
5. Focus the proposed visit on a subject of special interest to the parents.

A teacher should never make an unannounced visit to a child's home. An advance telephone call or note can establish a time convenient for parents (preferably both parents) and teacher.

When teachers schedule a visit, they should tell parents the purpose of the conference and let them know if they must prepare or have specific information or questions ready for the discussion. Teachers should let parents know approximately how long the visit will last and be careful not to overstay their welcome. They should recognize when it is time to end the conference and then do so promptly and politely.

At the beginning of a visit, teachers should talk informally with parents and child for a few minutes to establish a friendly tone and reduce parents' anxiety. At all times, teachers must remember that they are guests and avoid judging affairs and conditions in the home. A home conference is not an inspection tour. Parents will have greater confidence in the teacher if they know the content of the discussion will be confidential as well. Marion (1979) urged teachers to dress properly and conduct themselves with dignity in the child's home. Many minority group families view teachers as extremely important people in the community, deserving of honor and respect, unless they prove otherwise.

Home visits do have disadvantages. They are time-consuming and often inconvenient for both parents and teachers. Both parties must prepare for the visit. However, the many advantages of meeting on the child's home ground generally outweigh the disadvantages.

Special Issues

The Student's Participation

Interest in three-way conferences—including parents, teacher, and child—has grown in recent years. This trend reflects parents' renewed participation in their child's formal education, the growing recognition of the child as an active participant in the educational planning process, and recent legislation mandating parent involvement in decision making for their children's individualized education programs.

Children benefit in several ways from three-way conferences:

- They become aware that their parents and teacher are interested in their welfare and see them work cooperatively.
- They hear firsthand the teacher's and parents' evaluation of their performance.
- They feel involved in efforts toward personal achievements.
- They sharpen their perceptions of parents' and teachers' problems and concerns.
- They develop a task-oriented view of improving performance.

Children excluded from the parent-teacher conference are less likely to learn responsibility for personal behavior and achievement; parents and teacher tend to assume total responsibility for the child's learning. Excluded children also become curious about what the parents and teacher are saying about them in the conference and become anxious unnecessarily. Children receive information about the conference either secondhand from their parents or teacher or not at all. When they do receive information, it may misrepresent or distort the discussion, or they may misinterpret it. Such miscommunication can cause conflict among the three parties.

Occasionally, parents resist including their child in the conference. Their reluctance may stem from various reasons:

- They expect the child's presence to inhibit their behavior.
- They fear their child will expose private family information during the conference.
- They are unsure they can express themselves positively with their child present.
- They fear their child's anxiety will be too high if he or she has to participate in a personal evaluation.

Teachers can discuss such concerns with parents before including the child in the conference. They should never include the child over parents' objections, however.

Parents benefit from their children's presence in a three-way conference:

- They sharpen their understanding of the problems concerning their children and the teacher.
- They become aware of their children and the teacher as individuals and see how they relate to each other.
- They develop greater understanding of their role in their children's development.

Three-way conferences help teachers in their work in several ways:

- They gain greater understanding of the parents' and children's problems and concerns.
- They get a feeling for how parents and children interact.
- They have everyone together at one time to simplify planning and communication.

Three-way conferences appear to be most appropriate for progress reports and behavior management program-planning sessions (McAleer 1978). Like all conferences, the three-way conference requires careful planning, preparation, and organization. The teacher must select a manageable conference goal and collect the information needed to discuss it. As always, the teacher's observations and recommendations should be positive. Moreover, the teacher should involve both the parents and the child in the discussion, actively listening to their messages and responding appropriately. According to Carberry (1975), the teacher's empathy, nonpossessive warmth, and genuineness are essential ingredients of a successful three-way conference. Freeman (1975) suggested that three-way conferences incorporate formal contracting procedures as a means of recording agreed-upon academic and behavior goals and providing impetus for all parties to fulfill their obligations.

Negative Reactions to Conferencing

Parents' reactions to conference requests depend on their personalities and life conditions, the child's exceptionality, their awareness of and experience with the exceptionality, their past experiences in conferences with school personnel, and the quality and circumstances of the request. According to Losen and Diament (1978), some parents become angry when invited to a parent-teacher conference, often for one of the following reasons:

- They received little warning from the teacher of their child's academic or behavioral difficulty.
- Previous information led them to believe their child's problem was either resolved or caused by another child or the teacher.
- Past experiences with the school, either in their own childhoods or in their attempts to seek help for their child, have been negative.
- They have a negative attitude toward the school or education in general.
- They cannot attend fully to their child's problem because of personal or family circumstances.

Teachers must respond appropriately to parents' anger, avoiding meeting anger with anger, if they are to encourage positive and productive communication. Prudent teachers acknowledge the parents' anger and express concern, perhaps suggesting a meeting in the immediate future to discuss the parents' feelings. In addition, teachers can assure parents they will personally investigate their concerns before meeting with them.

The key to working effectively with angry parents is to focus on the present. It is avoiding unproductive discussions of past errors and attempting to focus parents' attention on what can be done *now* and in the *future* to help the child (Wallbrown and Meadows 1979). "Active listening" skills are particularly important; teachers should encourage parents to talk out their anger by using open-ended questions, neutral responses, and brief pauses (Table 6.3).

TABLE 6-3 • Conferring with Angry Parents

Do	Don't
Listen	Argue
Write down what they say	Defend or become defensive
When they slow down, ask them what else is bothering them	Promise things you can't produce
Exhaust their list of complaints	Own problems that belong to others
Ask them to clarify complaints that are too general	Raise your voice
Show them the list of complaints and ask if it is complete	Belittle or minimize the problem
Ask for suggestions for solving the problem	
Write down suggestions	
As much as possible, mirror their body posture	
As they speak louder, speak softer	

Source: Courtesy of R. Kroth, Institute for Parent Involvement, University of New Mexico (1979).

In addition to meeting with angry parents, the professional must confer with other difficult parents, such as self-centered parents, passive-resistive parents, overwhelmed parents, and denying parents (Carberry 1975; Losen and Diament 1978). Self-centered parents perceive the world only as it affects them and their well-being and comfort. Teachers must help these parents see their children as separate from them. When conferencing with self-centered parents, professionals can emphasize their children's individuality, highlighting strengths and weaknesses, for example.

Passive-resistive parents can be difficult in conferences for they reject any and all recommendations. They might state that a neighbor or friend already tried the recommended technique without success. The best approach with such parents is to involve them in all planning, using their recommendations whenever possible.

Some parents are overwhelmed by personal, marital, and family problems and are unable to attend to the child's problem. In such cases, the teacher can listen to the parents' difficulties, reschedule the conference if possible, and refer the parents to a trained professional.

Teachers must also learn to communicate with parents who are unable to keep a confidence by discouraging gossip about other children and parents, guarding information and impressions the parents could use against others. In conferences, teachers should politely but firmly keep the parents' attention on their child and their role as parents.

Some parents deny that their child has a problem, adopting a unique perspective that convinces them they are right. In such cases, teachers should avoid arguing with the parents, instead raising their awareness by inviting them to observe their child in the classroom and review tests, assignments, and other evidence of actual performance.

More frequently than most teachers wish to admit, they work with punitive, abusive, and neglectful parents. It is difficult to avoid alienation from these parents, for psychological or physical child abuse raises teachers' feelings of anger and righteous indignation. Nonetheless, direct expression of these feelings is harmful to the child and the parent. Teachers who can control their anger are in a better position to help parents recognize the harmfulness of their behavior and encourage them to seek professional counseling. Many punitive parents have never learned to control their children in nonabusive ways; most likely they were abused as children. Punitive parents often suffer from severe pathologies that impede rational thinking and behavior.

In the United States, many people, through no fault of their own, lack the education, training, money, and other resources to provide for their children. Teachers must recognize that neglectful parents may have little choice but to neglect their children. These parents' primary need is practical help and guidance from the teacher.

Summary

This chapter presents several formats for effective parent-teacher conferences: progress report, problem-solving, behavior management, and IEP conferences. The discussion focuses on the prerequisites for a successful conference in each case and details procedures that can help teachers plan and conduct the conferences. The chapter reviews the individualized education program meeting as a special type of conference and outlines parents' and teachers' roles. In addition, it discusses the advantages of home visits, which have become more common in recent years. Final sections of the chapter look at two conferencing issues: including the child in three-way conferences and coping with parents' anger and other negative reactions to conferences.

A major theme of the chapter is the importance of conferencing skills in the special education teacher's arsenal. Teachers need interpersonal skills as well as administrative and organizational skills to get maximum benefit from the conference.

Exercises and Discussion Topics

1. Plan, conduct, and evaluate a series of three progress report conferences. You may confer with the parent of an exceptional child you know or use a case in Appendix A.

2. With the members of your study group, discuss the "dos and don'ts" for teachers conducting a progress report conference. Do you agree or disagree with the recommendations? Why? Can you add to the list?

3. Plan, conduct, and evaluate a series of three problem-solving conferences. Apply one of the following models: behavior modification, communication, assertiveness. You may confer with the parents of an exceptional child you know or use a case in Appendix A.

4. Plan, conduct, and evaluate a series of six behavioral management training conferences. Train the parents of an exceptional child you know or use one of the cases in Appendix A.

5. Conduct a psychosituational assessment interview with the parent of an exceptional child or role play the interview by using a case in Appendix A. With the parent's permission, ask a colleague familiar with the interviewing method to observe the interview and critique your performance.

6. To familiarize yourself with the Behavior Log Form, use it for one week to record a personal behavior of a relatively high frequency. Graph your results. Explain the results to a colleague. Plan an intervention to change your behavior.

7. Plan, conduct, and evaluate a home visit. You may visit the parents of an exceptional child you know or role play a visit by using a case in Appendix A.

8. Research the advantages and disadvantages of the three-way conference for child, parent, and teacher. Discuss or present your findings with the members of your study group.

9. Plan, conduct, and evaluate a three-way conference. You may confer with a parent and child you know or role play the conference by using a case in Appendix A.

10. Carefully study the sections of this chapter on the IEP meeting, the sections on rights and responsibilities in Chapter 3, and the rules and regulations governing the IEP in your state, commonwealth, or province. Interview a special education teacher, a parent,

an administrator, and/or a psychologist about the role of IEP committee members. Ask them to discuss with you their and others' roles "ideally" and "in reality."

11. Plan, conduct, and evaluate an IEP meeting. You may confer with a committee familiar to you or role play meetings by using a case in Appendix A.

12. Conduct a discussion of the following topics in your study group:
- Negative reactions I have had as an interviewee
- Negative reactions I have had as an interviewer
- My role in my own and others' negative reactions.

References

Bauer, A. M. 1981. *Program for parents of severely handicapped students—A plan.* Edwardsville: Southern Illinois University.
Bersoff, D. N., and R. M. Grieger, II. 1971. An interview model for the psychosituational assessment of children's behavior. *American Journal of Orthopsychiatry* 41: 483–93.
Björklund, G., and C. Burger. 1987. Making conferences work for parents, teachers, and children. *Young Children* 42 (2): 26–31.
Blackard, M. K., and E. T. Barsch. 1982. Parents' and professionals' perceptions of the handicapped child's impact on the family. *Journal of the Association for the Severely Handicapped* 7: 62–69.
Carberry, H. H. 1975. Parent-teacher conferences. *Today's Education* Jan./Feb., 67–69.
Croft, D. J. 1979. *Parents and teachers: A resource book for home, school, and community relations.* Belmont, Calif.: Wadsworth.
Elksnin, L. K., and N. Elksnin. 1989. Collaborative consultation: Improving parent-teacher communication. *Academic Therapy* 24: 261–269.
Freeman, J. 1975. Three-way conferencing. *Teacher* 93 (4): 40–42.
Gillespie, E. B., and A. P. Turnbull. 1983. It's my IEP! Involving students in the planning process. *Teaching Exceptional Children* 16 (1): 26–29.
Gilliam, J. E., and M. C. Coleman. 1981. Who influences IEP committee decisions? *Exceptional Children* 47: 642–44.
Goldstein, S., and A. P. Turnbull. 1982. Strategies to increase parent participation in IEP conferences. *Exceptional Children* 48: 360–61.
Heron, T. E., and K. C. Harris. 1987. *The educational consultant* 2d ed. Austin, Tex.: Pro-ed.
Kroth, R. L. 1985. *Communicating with parents of exceptional children: Improving parent-teacher relationships.* Denver: Love.
Kroth, R. L., and R. L. Simpson. 1977. *Parent conferences: A teaching strategy.* Denver: Love.

Losen, S. M., and B. Diament. 1978. *Parent conferences in the schools: Procedures for developing effective partnership.* Boston: Allyn and Bacon.

Lusthaus, C., and E. Lusthaus. 1979. When is a child ready for mainstreaming? *The Exceptional Parent* 9 (5): R2–R4.

McAfee, J. K., and G. A. Vergason. 1979. Parent involvement in the process of special education: Establishing the new partnership. *Focus on Exceptional Children* 11 (2): 1–15.

McAleer, I. M. 1978. The parent, teacher, and child as conference partners. *Teaching Exceptional Children* 10 (4): 103–05.

Marion, R. 1979. Minority parent involvement in the IEP process: A systematic model approach. *Focus on Exceptional Children* 10 (8): 1–15.

Morgan, D. P. 1982. Parental participation in the IEP process: Does it enhance appropriate education? *Exceptional Education Quarterly* 3 (2): 33–40.

Nye, J., K. Westing, and S. Laten. 1986. Communication skills for parents. *Exceptional Children* 17: 274–78.

Price, B. J., and G. E. Marsh. 1985 Practical suggestions for planning and conducting parent conference. *Teaching Exceptional Children* 17 (4): 74–78.

Roberds-Baxter, S. 1984. The parent connection: Enhancing the affective component of parent conferences. *Teaching Exceptional Children* 17 (1): 55–58.

Rutherford, R. B., Jr., and E. Edgar. 1979. *Teachers and parents: A guide to interaction and cooperation.* Abr. ed. Boston: Allyn and Bacon.

Scanlon, C. A., J. Arick, and N. Phelps. 1981. Participation in the development of the IEP: Parents' perspective. *Exceptional Children* 47 (5): 373–74.

Shea, T. M., W. R. Whiteside, E. G. Beetner, and D. L. Lindsey. 1974. *Microteaching module: Psychosituational interview.* Edwardsville: Southern Illinois University.

Shevin, M. 1983. Meaningful parental involvement in long-range educational planning for disabled children. *Education and Training of the Mentally Retarded* 18: 17–21.

Swick, K. J., C. Flake-Hobson, and G. Raymond. 1980. The first step—Establishing parent-teacher communication in the IEP conference. *Teaching Exceptional Children* 12 (4): 144–45.

University of New Mexico, Institute for Parent Involvement. 1979. *Tips for teachers conferencing with angry parents—Dealing with aggression.*

Vaughn, S., C. S. Bos, J. E. Harrell, and B. A. Lasky. 1988. Parent participation in the initial IEP conference: Ten years after mandated involvement. *Journal of Learning Disabilities* 21 (2): 82–89.

Walker, J. E., and T. M. Shea. 1988. *Behavior management: A practical approach for educators.* 4th ed. Columbus, Ohio: Charles E. Merrill.

Wallbrown, F. H., and F. B. Meadows. 1979. Working with angry parents. *The Directive Teacher* 2 (2): 10, 29.

Chapter Supplement

Protocol Psychosituational Interview One*

Mr. S. arrives at the conference alone because his wife "wasn't feeling well" and did not wish to attend.

Teacher: Good afternoon, Mr. S.
Mr. S.: Hello Mrs. M. How are you?
T.: Fine, thank you. Glad to meet you. Sit down, please, I am Mark's special education teacher this year, and I'd like to ask you some questions about Mark. Let's see. He's nine years old and he's presently in Mrs. Lee's class, that's third grade.
Mr. S.: Yes.
T.: Mrs. Lee has told me that he does rather well in some of his subjects; he's particularly good in math. He enjoys that very much. He has a little bit of difficulty with reading and writing, however. And she says that she has some problems with his leaving his seat frequently. He's rather active in the classroom.
Mr. S.: Yeah, she's not the only one that has problems with him.
T.: I see.
Mr. S.: He's a bad boy. We have trouble with him at home all the time.
T.: Oh, you do.
Mr. S.: Yeah, I'm . . . well, I know Mrs. Lee too because my wife tells me that Mrs. Lee calls and the principal calls about him and sending him home from school all the time. My wife should be here today. She really spends most of the time with Mark, but she didn't want to come, she wasn't

*Source: Shea, Whiteside, Beetner, and Lindsey 1974.

	feeling very good. I drive a truck and am on the road most of the time. I don't see much of him.
T.:	It was very nice of you to come today.
Mr. S.:	Well . . . thank you.
T.:	I'd like to ask you some more questions about Mark's behavior at home. You said that he seems to . . . you have some trouble with him, too. Would you explain that to me a little?
Mr. S.:	He fights all the time. He's just always getting in fights, and like I said, I'm gone a lot but my wife tells me that she has trouble with him all the time. Fights with his brothers and every once in a while he fights with the neighbors. He's just always getting into trouble—that seems to be about it.
T.:	Fighting seems to be the biggest problem.
Mr. S.:	Oh, yeah, he fights all the time—always in trouble.
T.:	Could you give me an example of how one of these fights occurs.
Mr. S.:	Well, my wife was telling me last night that he and the older boy were playing Chinese checkers and he lost. Mark lost and Bill picked up a handful of . . . not Bill, but Mark picked up a handful of marbles and threw them at Bill and went at him with his fists.
T.:	He became so agitated by losing that he started a fight.
Mr. S.:	He can't lose. He just goes . . . losing, he fights—that's just automatic, one, two. He just can't stand to lose. As long as he's winning, he gets along fine.
T.:	Are there any cases you can tell me about when he wins—how he acts?
Mr. S.:	Well, I take the boys fishing in the spring and in the summer.
T.:	That's nice.
Mr. S.:	Oh yeah, I like to fish. Actually it's comforting and it's lots of fun. We enjoy it being out, and usually Mark, when he goes with us, he catches most of the fish.
T.:	Oh, really.
Mr. S.:	Oh yeah, and yeah he has a good time then, bragging around and measuring, comparing the size of his fish and the other boys' fish and boasting about it. Yeah, he likes that.
T.:	He doesn't seem to fight much when you go fishing, does he.
Mr. S.:	Well, it all depends now if one of the other boys catches a

Chapter Six • Parent Teacher Conferences

	bigger fish, or more fish, then he'll fight. He'll go at them, he'll hit them, holler at them—yeah, he can't stand to lose.
T.:	But if he's winning and especially when he's fishing, he must enjoy that . . . to go with you.
Mr. S.:	Yeah, he likes to go fishing. We have a good time.
T.:	Do you ever go with him by yourself?
Mr. S.:	We all go fishing. I tried to get my wife to go, but she doesn't care much for fishing. She doesn't like to bait the hook; you know how women are.
T.:	Oh yes. So fishing is one thing that Mark really enjoys, especially when he's winning, and then he's pretty good at it from what you say.
Mr. S.:	That's right.
T.:	He must have had some good training. Let's talk about the fighting that goes on at home. Could you tell me a little bit more about it? You said that if losing is involved, then he seems to fight.
Mr. S.:	Yeah, that's right.
T.:	One example was with the Chinese checkers and his older brother. Could you give me any other examples of . . . ?
Mr. S.:	Yeah, if he thinks one of the other kids gets more ice cream, like his younger brother, he'll poke him and start a fight. You know. It's really bad. My wife says that she's on him all the time at home and she has to spank him or send him out of the house or send him up to bed and it keeps going on. He's really a bad boy at home.
T.:	And you say he fights all the time. It probably seems like it's all the time because it's rather upsetting.
Mr. S.:	She's always complaining about it.
T.:	Yeah. Do you have any idea of how often exactly this happens? Once a night, twice a night, once a week?
Mr. S.:	Well, it may be two or three times a week.
T.:	Two or three times a week?
Mr. S.:	Yeah, about two or three times a week. Mainly because he wins the other two or three days.
T.:	Oh, I see.
Mr. S.:	Yeah, he's pretty good.
T.:	On the winning days, he's really not that much of a problem.
Mr. S.:	No problem. As long as he's winning, he gets along with everyone really well.
T.:	Let's talk about these fights a little. You mentioned that

	he gets into almost real fisticuffs. Do you mean that he actually punches?
Mr. S.:	Not almost. He really does. Punches. And he keeps punching until the kid gives up.
T.:	That's how the fight usually is settled?
Mr. S.:	That's how it's settled unless one of the adults steps in and stops it.
T.:	By one of the adults, I assume you mean yourself or your wife.
Mr. S.:	My wife is home most of the time; she does this. When I'm home, I'm watching television, and if he starts a ruckus, I get in there and grab him and shake him and I stop it right away. I don't let anything go on. I stop it unless it's a tight inning, and then I may wait until the action's over and then I stop it. But it doesn't stop until I stop it.
T.:	You mentioned shaking him to stop it.
Mr. S.:	Yeah, I shake him.
T.:	Does that seem to work?
Mr. S.:	Well, you know, shake them till their teeth rattle; that straightens them out. That's what my daddy always said.
T.:	Do you use any other forms of punishment besides shaking?
Mr. S.:	Well, if that doesn't work, yeah. Sure, I spank them when I feel that I should, and sometimes I just send them out of the house.
T.:	How long do these fights last? Just until . . . someone gives up? Maybe a minute, two, five minutes?
Mr. S.:	If an adult is not there, sometimes they'll go on five or ten minutes, fifteen minutes. If an adult is there, of course the adult stops it. Or an older kid can stop it, but they usually like to watch the fight.
T.:	Do you think what you're doing—this shaking and spanking—has changed his behavior any? Has it stopped the fighting?
Mr. S.:	It stops it then.
T.:	It stops it for that time?
Mr. S.:	Yeah.
T.:	When he loses, he fights, and when he fights, it's physical. It's dangerous to the other person.
Mr. S.:	Sometimes he yells and just hollers and screams at the other kids. One time he hit his older brother with a chair because he was losing the fight. And I mean he really gets violent. He really wants to win.

Chapter Six • Parent Teacher Conferences 173

T.: These fights, even though they are violent, last sometimes less than five minutes, sometimes up to fifteen minutes?
Mr. S.: Yeah, that's about right.
T.: And they seem to happen two or three times a week?
Mr. S.: Yeah, that's about right.
T.: But it seems like otherwise, the other four or five days a week, he's really pretty agreeable and easy to get along with. Things seem to go all right as long as he's winning.
Mr. S.: As long as things are going his way and nobody steps on him or steps on his toes, he's all right.
T.: Fine. Most of the time you're dealing with Mark, is it a pleasant interaction or are there problems? Let's say, for the most part.
Mr. S.: See, I'm not home very much, and when I'm at home I like to do what I like to do. I like to watch television and sports and so forth, and you know of course we do go fishing in the spring and summer and then we get along fine, and you know, unless of course someone catches more fish than he catches. But when I'm home I like to watch television. I really don't pay that much attention to the kids. But my wife says that, you know, some days he can be very nice, but most of the time he's a bad, rotten kid.
T.: Well, I think maybe we should start to work on this fighting behavior. Maybe I could help you with some suggestions.
Mr. S.: Well, I'll tell you we'd appreciate anything you could suggest.
T.: Well, one thing I think would be a good idea is if you and your wife could keep what we call a log. We train our teachers to keep this. All you do is write down each day what day it is and whether or not there was a fight. Then what time the fight occurred and what the behavior was just before the fight happened and how it was resolved. So an example of this, which was done by another parent, would show that, say, Monday there was a fight, Tuesday nothing, Wednesday nothing, but Thursday there were two fights. If you and your wife together would keep this kind of log . . .
Mr. S.: Well, I know what a log is; that's what I do because I'm a truck driver. We keep a log, and I can show my wife how to do it, but I can't guarantee she'll do it . . . but I can show her how and . . .
T.: That would be very helpful.
Mr. S.: Yeah, fine.

T.:	I think that you can probably explain it better than I could.
Mr. S.:	Probably so, right.
T.:	Then maybe in three weeks we'll make another appointment for an interview and you and your wife can come together.
Mr. S.:	Well, I'm not sure that I'll be able to make it 'cause I'm on the road, but I think if my wife has something to talk about and hold onto, why she'll probably be willing to come and chat with you.
T.:	Let's see if we can't arrange it for the three of us.
Mr. S.:	All right.
T.:	I'll do it at your convenience.
Mr. S.:	Okay, right.
T.:	And if you will bring in the log for the next three weeks of behavior. How many times he fights. We won't worry about anything else, just the fighting behavior. Until that time, I'd also like you maybe to take some time with Mark alone and let me know how it works out when you deal with him individually, apart from his brothers. Just once in a while. I realize that you're very busy, but that may give us some insights.
Mr. S.:	Kinda father-son talks.
T.:	That kind of thing; that might work out well.
Mr. S.:	I'll try that.

Protocol Psychosituational Interview Two

Mrs. G., a Hispanic-American parent, is accompanied to the conference by her nineteen-year-old daughter, Rosa, who serves as interpreter, and her three-year-old daughter, Luisa.

Teacher:	Hello, Mrs. G., Rosa. Hi, Luisa. Don't you look happy today!
Rosa:	Hi.
T.:	Thanks for coming, Mrs. G. And thank you, Rosa, for coming again to help us out. I really appreciate it.
Rosa:	No problem.
T.:	Would you like me to get some puzzles or picture books for the baby, Mrs. G.?
Mrs. G.:	No. She'll be a good girl.
T.:	I'm happy to say that since we last talked, Raffie is becom-

	ing more and more independent. His self-help skills are really improving.
Mrs. G.:	Raffie is a good boy. He tries.
Rosa:	What kind of things has he learned to do?
T.:	He's getting away from using the spoon for all foods, and is using his fork more neatly and without us reminding him.
Mrs. G.:	He's eating lunch with a fork?
T.:	Yes. He still sometimes pushes the food onto the fork with his fingers, but he's getting much neater and trying to use his fork when he should.
Rosa:	Do you think we should start giving him a fork at home?
T.:	That would be great. I think he's ready to generalize his skill.
Rosa:	Generalize?
T.:	Yes, that's what we call it when a student takes something he learned in school and begins to apply it in other places, like home
Mrs. G.:	What is generalize?
	(Rosa explains in Spanish.)
T.:	Is Raffie doing better with his meals at home, too?
Mrs. G.:	He does okay, except when my husband is on him.
Rosa:	Yes, he seems to do better when my dad's not around.
T.:	What happens? Can you tell me about a time when he had a problem when his father was around?
Rosa:	Well, like at dinner. Dad's really noticed that Raffie is now doing more and more things by himself. He wants him to do more, to be more like other kids. So he asks him to do things he can't do, and then Raffie blows it, and then Dad gets mad.
T.:	What kind of things does he ask him to do?
Rosa:	Well, like last night, Raffie asked for more milk. Dad was really impressed, the way he said please and all. So Mama got him more milk.
Mrs. G.:	He said "More milk, please" so clear! I got him more milk right away, but my husband said, "See he can do things for himself. He can get his own milk. Let him pour his own."
T.:	Did Raffie get the milk and pour it into his glass?
Rosa:	Sure, in the glass, on himself, and all over the table, too.
T.:	Then what happened?
Mrs. G.:	My husband, he got mad. Not yelling mad, just mad. He left the table and went out on the steps.

Rosa:	It's like, before Raffie started doing things by himself, and Mama just sort of took care of him, Dad could handle that. But now Raffie's starting to do things by himself, and gets out with the other kids and talks for himself, Dad's having a harder time figuring out what to do.
T.:	He seems to be proud of Raffie's accomplishments.
Mrs. G.:	He's happy Raphael is talking and doing by himself.
Rosa:	Yeah, but he thinks that because Raffie is doing better, he should be able to do a lot more than he can. It's like, now Raffie isn't going to be a baby forever, so he should start acting his age.
T.:	How do you feel about the progress Raffie's made, Mrs. G.?
Mrs. G.:	He's working hard. It's hard now, he wants to do "by myself." Before, I always got him on the bus on time. Now you say let him dress himself and feed himself breakfast. I have to wake him up at six-thirty!
Rosa:	He's doing these things by himself, but like it's almost easier to do them for him.
T.:	So, we seem to be at an awkward time with Raffie. He's showing you at home the things that he's learned at school, but he's not doing them proficiently enough to really help out.
Mrs. G.:	Again?
	(Rosa and Mrs. G. converse briefly in Spanish.)
Rosa:	So what do we do?
T.:	I think one thing we might try, in helping Mr. G. with Raffie, is to make sure that I let him know what things Raffie is able to do by himself and the things he just isn't quite ready for.
Mrs. G.:	My husband won't come to school. As long as Raphael is with those slow kids, he won't come to school.
T.:	I'll make up a list of the things Raffie can do by himself. Do you think your husband would look at it?
	(Rosa and Mrs. G. converse in Spanish.)
Rosa:	You'd write up a list?
T.:	Right.
Rosa:	And address it to my Dad? He doesn't like secondhand notes.
T.:	Fine.
	(Rosa and Mrs. G. converse in Spanish.)
Rosa:	We'll give it a shot. Just make sure that you don't say anything about Raffie being retarded. Just say how good he's doing and what he can do now.

T.:	Do you think I could give Mr. G. a telephone call?
Mrs. G.:	Don't call him at work. He can't talk on the phone at work.
Rosa:	That might be okay. Just don't say you're a special ed teacher or anything. And tell him how good Raffie's doing.
T.:	Fine. The other problem, the one about his doing things by himself, but more slowly, is something we can work on together if you'd like.
Rosa:	Great! It takes him ages to dress, and he gets mad if anybody tries to help.
T.:	We'll begin to keep track of how long it takes him to do things. Could you time him at home?
Mrs. G.:	Time him?
	(Rosa and Mrs. G. converse briefly in Spanish.)
Rosa:	We don't have a timer or anything.
T.:	Could you keep track on the clock?
Rosa:	Sure, we can watch the clock.
T.:	Okay. When we meet next week, do you think you could bring in a list of the amounts of time that dressing and breakfast are taking?
Rosa:	Sure.
T.:	When we have that information, we can begin to look at ways to decrease the time Raffie requires to dress and eat breakfast.
Mrs. G.:	You mean speed him up?
T.:	Yes, we'll try it.
Mrs. G.:	Good. You speed him up.
Rosa:	I think Ms. F. means *we'll* speed him up—all of us, right?
T.:	Right, Rosa.

CHAPTER SEVEN

Group Activities

> Mr. L., father of a fourteen-year-old son with learning disabilities:
>
> *"I went to the meetings at first. I was trying to figure out what was going on with Roy. I read everything they gave me, went to talks, sat around and discussed. Then I didn't go so much. It seemed like there were really two groups working at every meeting: one or two old-timers who'd been through it all, and a bunch of new people who were looking for answers. I wasn't going to treat my kid as that different, and make a career of being a dad of a kid with learning problems."*

Chapter Topics and Objectives

Teachers frequently use group activities to foster parent-teacher collaboration. Carefully designed group activities can have significant value for the participants, with ultimate benefit to the exceptional child. When organizing group activities, teachers should have a clear idea of their purpose and plan the size and structure accordingly. This chapter discusses general issues of planning and conducting large and small parent-teacher involvement groups as an introduction to the discussion of specific types of groups in Chapter 8.

Parent-teacher group activities require more planning and preparation and often greater personal involvement by parents and teachers than do written and telephone communications or parent-teacher conferences. Personal involvement varies with group purpose. For example, a group designed to provide social-emotional support to parents requires a greater personal investment than does a group designed to transmit information to parents. Time and energy requirements are considerable, for successful groups require planning, preparation, and scheduling, as well as participation in and evaluation of group activities.

In this chapter, we will:

- Explore the effects of group size on participation.
- Discuss planning and leading large-group activities.
- Describe planning and leading small-group activities.

Group Size

Parents and teachers meet together in group settings for three basic purposes: to transfer information; to teach and learn instructional, behavior management, or interpersonal communication techniques; and to give and receive social-emotional support. Whatever its primary purpose, however, every group will to some extent include all three elements.

Both large or small groups are effective forums for transmitting information. However, a small group is preferable for exchanging personal or highly specific information. Small groups are also well-suited for providing social-emotional support. Either a small group or a large group can effectively provide training and instruction as long as the larger group offers a small instructor-to-member ratio.

Group processes and procedures vary with the purpose of the group as well. Structured processes are most appropriate for instruction and information exchange. Less structured processes, those that encourage interpersonal communication, are most appropriate for a support group.

Participants in large groups tend to be passive recipients of information and instruction, for the limited amount of time available to each individual and the complexity of communication networks restrict active participation. Small groups, on the other hand, allow discussion, cooperative problem solving, and expression of feelings.

By necessity, control of large-group activities rests with a few people or one person. Frequently, a few people plan, organize, and conduct activities for the entire membership. Without this concentration of control, a large group may disintegrate. Small groups permit and encourage shared control among members.

The large group has several advantages and disadvantages. It allows teachers to transmit information quickly and easily to a relatively large number of people; however, the depth and specificity of the information is generally limited. Quiet, shy people may be more likely to attend large-group meetings than small-group gatherings because pressures to participate are limited. Thus, large-group meetings may get information to people who would otherwise not receive it.

The large group is also an excellent means of motivating people to seek additional information, training, or assistance in small groups or individual conferences. A dynamic speaker, dramatic audiovisual presentation, panel discussion, product or technique demonstration, or informal mingling before and after the meeting may all pique attendee's interest in further participation.

A major disadvantage of the large-group format is its inability to respond to the needs of individual attendees. It is usually difficult to respond in depth to questions and comments. Another disadvantage is potential difficulty finding an adequate facility or scheduling dates and times acceptable to all participants.

The major advantage of the small group is its suitability for addressing participants' specific concerns. The informality and cohesiveness of small groups encourage interpersonal communication and allow flexibility in selecting locations and times.

On the negative side, small-group activities require extensive planning and can be time-consuming. Small groups often find it difficult to obtain speakers because presenters are reluctant to devote time to a small audience. Perhaps the greatest danger is the formation of subgroups and cliques within small groups, which may work at cross-purposes to the majority of the members. Cohesiveness among members is an essential ingredient of small-group success (Karnes and Zehrback 1972).

When is a group small? When is it large? Small-group size may range from three people, the parents and teacher, to perhaps twenty people. However, the parent-teacher ratio may be more important than the number of group members; small-group processes appear most effective in groups maintaining a six-to-one parent-teacher ratio. Any group that exceeds a twelve-to-one parent-teacher ratio is really a large group. Group size depends on the group's purpose, the leader's strengths, and most important, the members' wishes and needs (Table 7.1).

This chapter and Chapter 8 focus on parent-teacher group activities but many community organizations offer opportunities for parents in large and small groups. The Association for Children and Adults with Learning Disabilities offers groups helpful to parents of exceptional children, as do the National Association for Retarded Citizens, the Down Syndrome Congress, the National Society for Children and Adults with Autism, the Spina Bifida Association of America, the Parent Advocacy Coalition of Educational Rights, and others. These organizations offer parents information, training, and

TABLE 7.1 • *Large- and Small-Group Characteristics*

	Large Groups	Small Groups
Depth of information	General	Specific
Demands of participation	Limited	Extensive
Purpose	General informational and instructional	Specific informational, instructional, and social-emotional
Potential for interpersonal communication	Limited	Frequent

support through large- and small-group activities. A listing of organizations and agencies offering services to the parents of children with special needs is presented in Appendix B.

Large-Group Activities

Planning

Careful, systematic planning is the key to a successful parent-teacher large-group meeting or series of meetings (Croft 1979). Kroth (1985) suggested organizing a parent advisory committee—as representative of the population of potential participants as possible—to work with teachers in planning and publicizing group activities. The advisory committee would plan and conduct three or four large-group meetings during a school year. Planning begins the moment parents and teachers sit down with pencil and paper to determine the meeting's purpose. Kroth itemized the following committee objectives:

- To identify potential members and assess their needs and interests
- To establish general and specific meeting objectives
- To design or select methods of attaining the group's objectives
- To determine criteria and measurements for ascertaining the meeting's effectiveness.

The committee conducts a needs assessment before the group organizes formally or begins programming. Several approaches are possible: a survey questionnaire, an extensively publicized orientation meeting for potential participants, or preliminary small-group sessions for representatives of potential constituencies. The assessment process continues throughout a series of meetings. Meeting organizers can set aside time at the end of each session to discuss members' interests for future meetings.

The assessment will lead to group objectives. Planners should state objectives clearly, establishing what members will be able to do or will have gained at the end of the group. For example, at the conclusion of the meeting, parents will have knowledge of the federal and state laws governing educational services for exceptional children.

Group activities are "the highways and signposts" the members travel to reach the objectives (Croft 1979). Activities may include lectures, discussions, social events, visits, film viewings, reading assignments, workshops, work projects, and so on. After the meetings, the advisory committee may use tests, checklists, rating scales, attendance rates, opinion surveys, or other means to evaluate the program's effectiveness and to modify it or plan additional programs.

To be effective, a parent advisory committee must have sufficient freedom to accomplish its objectives. Teachers and other professionals should resist the impulse to dominate the committee. Once the committee is operational, the teacher serves as an adviser.

As a rule, three or four well-attended and well-received large-group meetings per year are more desirable than eight or nine monthly meetings that are hurriedly planned, poorly attended, and focused on topics irrelevant to participants. The committee is wise to schedule only enough meetings to attain the group's objectives.

Guidelines for Conducting Large-Group Meetings

Planning and preparation are of little value if the meeting is at an inconvenient time, poorly publicized, inaccessible, disorganized, or inhospitable. Several authors have suggested guidelines for conducting an effective large-group meeting (Karnes and Zehrbach 1972; Kroth 1985).

Participants should receive proper notification of the meeting via bulletins, newsletters, written invitations, or person-to-person or telephone communication. The first invitation should go out three or four weeks before the meeting to allow people to plan their schedules. A follow-up telephone call or note three or four days before the meeting is a helpful reminder. Teachers should take care that meeting invitations truly invite parents to attend and avoid a coercive tone.

Meetings should begin and end on time. If a business session is necessary, it should be brief; it should also be at the end of the meeting if the discussion is not relevant to most attendees. Meeting organizers should avoid soliciting fees and funds at the meeting unless absolutely necessary or pressuring members of the audience to sign up for committees.

Meeting sites should be appropriate for the group's purpose and size, with furniture suitable for adults (no children's desks or bleachers). The meeting location should also be accessible to those wishing to attend, including handicapped children and adults. If transportation is not readily available, meeting organizers can organize car pools. The committee should consider transportation issues when they issue invitations.

Planners may want to provide child care services near the meeting room to draw parents reluctant to hire babysitters. (It is often impossible to find a qualified babysitter for children with exceptionalities, and babysitters are in short supply on school days.) Volunteer high school and college students can provide child care services at the meeting facility.

All communication during meetings must emphasize the fact that parents and teachers are equals. Teachers and presenters should use commonly understood language, avoid technical terms and jargon, and define unfamiliar terms as necessary. The program should be well-thought-out so that it speaks directly to the audience's needs. Audiovisual aides and demonstrations often help underscore the message of the program in attention-getting ways.

To establish an informal, friendly atmosphere, teachers should greet parents as they arrive at the meeting room door. This greeting should be personal, including a positive comment about the parents and their child and recognizing the parents' efforts to come and their potential contributions. Teachers should invite parents to complete name tags and may want to give them a written agenda and pencil and paper for notes.

After the formal program, time should be available for questions and discussion. By requesting written questions, the meeting leader can encourage shy members of the audience to contribute. Recognition of everyone who helped with the evening's activities is a good way to close the meeting. This time is also good for soliciting immediate feedback on the meeting, using an evaluation form that is easy to understand and complete (Figure 7.1). Meeting organizers should plan a time for informal socializing and refreshments after the meeting. (Parents and teachers may share responsibility for refreshments.)

FIGURE 7.1 • *Meeting Evaluation Form*

Date: _____

Meeting Subject: _____

Please circle the responses that best reflect your feelings about this meeting.

1. The subject was: Not relevant   Somewhat   Relevant   Very relevant
                                           relevant

2. The information   Somewhat
   was: Not useful   useful   Useful   Very useful

3. The manner of
   presentation was: Poor   Fair   Good   Very good

4. Audio visual
   materials and
   handouts were: Poor   Fair   Good   Very good

5. Would you like more information on the subject?   Yes   No

6. Comments:

Thanks! By letting us know how you feel, we can better meet your needs.

                              Your Advisory Committee

Revitalizing a Disintegrating Large Group

Hamilton and Koorland (1988) explored three broad reasons for nonattendance at parent meetings: (1) not meeting parents' needs, (2) attitudes toward school and schooling, and (3) meeting times. In their study, four items within these categories demonstrated a significant difference between parents who attended and those who did not. Nonattending parents indicated that they found it difficult to discuss their children's problems, were unable to find transportation, had a perception that the school was overly concerned about paperwork, and were not interested in the content of the meetings. The need for child care was of great concern to the parents. When teachers are confronted with lack of attendance, action must be taken.

Smith (Olson et al. 1976) successfully reactivated a group by taking the following steps:

1. Sending a notice to all parents about the problem
2. Inviting parents to vote whether to continue or discontinue the group
3. Asking parents to indicate the contributions they are willing to make if the majority of parents voted to continue the group
4. After an affirmative vote, reorganizing the group in line with parents' wishes and establishing a council composed of parents, teachers, and an administrator
5. Asking the council to write limited organizational guidelines authorizing five working committees: community relations, learning materials, construction and repair, fund raising, and classroom helpers
6. Appointing parents chairpersons of all committees
7. Conducting meetings only when called by the council or required by an emergency.

As a result of this revitalization, the working committees, functioning with relative independence, accomplished many necessary tasks, and many parents became involved in activities meaningful to them and beneficial to their children.

Small-Group Activities

Planning

Small-group programs can be effective for a variety of informational, instructional, and social-emotional purposes. However, planners should be aware that small groups are sometimes inappropriate ways to meet parents' needs. Kelly (1974) cited the following cases in which small group activities are inappropriate:

- If the child's problem is unique and the parents are unable or unwilling to discuss it in a group setting
- If a group setting inhibits the parents' behavior and ability to communicate
- If the child's problem is a sympton of the parents' personal or marital problems

- If the probable solution to the child's problem is highly specific and inappropriate for other group members.

Once they have established that small-group activities are indeed desirable, parents and teachers must consider many of the same factors they would consider for large-group meetings: goals and objectives, the physical setting, meeting time, length and frequency of meetings, group size, program, attendance, materials and equipment, refreshments, leader or facilitator qualifications and preparation time, transportation, and child care services (Dinkmeyer and McKay 1976). For small groups, determination of group size, selection of the leader, program sequence, and physical comfort can be especially important, however, for they will determine the climate for sharing ideas.

Facilities that are either too large or too small are not conducive to free-flowing communication among members, for example. The facility should also be free of artificial physical barriers—such as fixed seats, bleachers, and desks and chairs—that may inhibit face-to-face communication. Quiet and privacy are important, for a group cannot function effectively with interruptions by traffic sounds, activities in adjoining rooms, or people passing through the meeting room.

Generally, evenings are the best times to find both mother and father free to attend meetings. Nonworking parents of school-age children may find it convenient to attend a meeting during the school day, and some parents of preschool children can attend meetings during the day as well if child care services are available.

Parents and teachers generally have busy schedules and can seldom devote more than an hour or two a week to a parent-teacher group meeting. However, the length of a meeting should reflect its content. A session to instruct parents in a behavior management or communication technique will be as long as the content demands; it is often easier to reorganize the instructional content into briefer lessons than to reorganize the schedules of a group of individuals, however. Once the session length is established, the leader should announce and discuss any exceptions in advance.

Frequency also reflects the group purpose and the members' schedules. As a rule, small groups should meet no more than once a week and no less than once a month.

The prudent planner determines the maximum allowable size of the group before organizing it. If the number of interested parents exceeds the limit, leaders must either cut off enrollment or form another group. The group purpose, the competencies of the leader or leaders, and the parents' characteristics all determine the best size. Recruiting parents of similar interests, backgrounds, and concerns will enhance group cohesiveness. Members should be parents of children with similar developmental levels and exceptionalities (Webster 1977).

Planning lesson sequence is an important part of preparing for training, instructional, and information groups. Group leaders should distribute outlines, agendas, instructional materials, and texts to participants to alert them to the course content and the cumulative nature of the materials. In many cases, group planners must submit purchase orders and rental requisitions for instructional materials and equipment several weeks before the first meeting. If the teacher lacks the qualifications or time to lead the group, he or she must seek others who are competent to assume or share leadership responsibilities.

Refreshment plans must take place ahead of time also; frequently, members share this responsibility. Well-planned transportation and child care services will encourage group attendance.

The program planner must determine if attendance is to be mandatory or voluntary. When the program content is cumulative, attendance should be mandatory, unless the leader has time to offer individual instruction to absentees. Programs dependent on group interaction and the exchange of feelings will also be more cohesive if attendance is mandatory.

Structure

Webster emphasized the importance of structure and limits in parent-teacher small-group activity programs: "While everyone enjoys participating in spontaneous events from time to time, it would be anxiety producing if everything in their lives were unplanned, unstructured, and unlimited" (1977, 49). Thus, structure helps both parties function purposefully. Webster suggested a verbal contract between parents and teachers as one way to establish an agreed-upon structure. The teacher opens the discussion of the contract, but all parties are responsible for negotiating its content and reaching consensus. Any verbal or written contract should be brief and concise, establishing meeting times, group purpose, participants, and activities. No party should enter into a program with a hidden agenda; thus, discussion of the group's purpose should be open, straightforward, and free of jargon. In discussing who will participate in the group, parents and teachers should decide whether they will work alone, with other parents and teachers, with the child, or with "experts." Finally, all parties should clarify expectations for the meetings themselves, clarifying meeting content and determining whether note taking, reading assignments, role-playing activities, and home assignments will be part of the program.

Meeting Effectiveness

Karnes and Zehrbach (1972) suggested the following guidelines for conducting effective small-group meetings:

1. *Meeting content.* Content should relate directly or indirectly to the concerns expressed by the parent members. It should be challenging yet at a level that everyone can understand and assimilate.
2. *Planning and operation.* As the group matures, members should share responsibilities for planning and conducting meetings.
3. *Member preparation.* All members, including the leader, should prepare for the meeting by reading articles and chapters in books, listening to tapes, viewing films and videotapes, and digesting information in other ways.
4. *Members' needs.* Meetings should respond to the members' individual social, emotional, and intellectual needs.
5. *Atmosphere.* Meetings should take place in a relaxed, informal atmosphere. However, the atmosphere should further meeting goals, with all members observing social conventions.
6. *Meeting date and time.* Meetings should take place on agreed-upon dates and times. They should begin and end on time. A session should seldom, if ever, exceed two hours.
7. *Teachers' roles.* Teachers should participate in and facilitate but not dominate the meeting. They must avoid condescension and be alert to the needs of parents who have outgrown the group, suggesting a more appropriate group or an alternative activity in such cases. Teachers should remain alert to the members' changing social-emotional needs and offer them support and guidance as needed.
8. *Member support.* Members should have opportunities to help new members, and reluctant participants become involved in group activities. This practice strengthens the group's cohesiveness.

Leadership Techniques

Small-group leaders or facilitators have many responsibilities before, during, and after the meeting. These responsibilities include preparing themselves through study, preparing the setting and necessary materials, establishing the session tone, facilitating the group's activities, resolving problems within the group, and evaluating the meeting.

Small-group leaders can select from a range of directive to nondirective techniques (Kroth 1985). Directive techniques, which assume parents need help to make effective decisions about their children with exceptionalities, are generally most appropriate in information and training meetings. Nondirective techniques are more appropriate in small groups designed to provide social-emotional support to parents. The nondirective leader is primarily responsible for setting an atmosphere conducive to discussion. Nondirective techniques assume parents are capable of free choice about themselves and their children and will make effective decisions if given the opportunity.

Leading the Meeting. During the small-group meeting, the leader's central function is to keep the group on the topic and progressing in an orderly fashion through the problem-solving, discussion, or training process. To accomplish this task, the leader must have several special skills (Hymes 1974; Dinkmeyer and McKay 1974, 1976; Shea and Bauer 1987).

At the opening of the meeting, the leader reminds the members of the meeting purpose, perhaps linking the topic at hand to previously discussed topics. A skilled leader will also link the meeting content to members' stated concerns and interests. If the session is one of a series of meetings on a central theme, the leader reviews the group's progress so far and praises participants for their accomplishments.

Next, the leader highlights the specific objectives of the meeting as clearly and precisely as possible. As necessary, he or she reviews the procedures and practices governing the meeting.

After these introductory comments, the leader issues an open invitation for members to begin the discussion. Buzz sessions, round-robins, and brainstorming activities are helpful ways to stimulate discussion, especially among shy and quiet members.

During the discussion, the leader restates or represents participants' comments and opinions, avoiding negative judgments, and relates them to other members' comments. Dinkmeyer and McKay (1974) called this function *universalizing.* When questioning and commenting, the leader should use plural pronouns (*we*, *us*) to convey to members that he or she is speaking for and with the group.

The leader points out similarities and differences among participants' comments and helps redirect statements or questions to other group members. The leader should avoid dominating the group by personally responding to all comments. Closed and open questions help keep the discussion moving. The leader asks closed questions to obtain specific information and open questions to facilitate the discussion (see Chapter 4).

Throughout the meeting, the leader gives the members feedback and encouragement. He or she reinforces the group as a whole and individual members for their participation and for their support of others. If the discussion bogs down, the leader encourages members to persist in their efforts to solve the problem under consideration.

Dinkmeyer and McKay suggested that the leader obtain from the members a commitment to apply what they learned in the meeting. The leader encourages participants and helps them develop an action plan, periodically seeking feedback on their commitment to act.

Occasionally during the meeting, and especially at the conclusion of the meeting, the leader summarizes progress and, if necessary, restructures the discussion. This procedure keeps the group focused on its task. In the end-of-session summary, the leader relates the present discussion to previous and future discussions.

Some leaders must make a concerted effort to remain silent when other members are struggling with a problem. The effective leader does not become anxious when silences occur. Such times are necessary for members to receive, integrate, and evaluate information and to formulate opinions, phrase questions, or prepare comments.

Problems of Leadership. No small group functions smoothly all the time. Participants vary in personality, interests, attitudes, knowledge, experience, feelings, understanding, and social skills. They also express themselves in many ways—some productive, some counterproductive. The leader must recognize and redirect negative behaviors that hurt individuals or impede the group's functioning. Dinkmeyer and McKay (1976) described the following common problem behaviors and suggested appropriate leader responses.

- *Behavior:* Monopolizing the discussion. *Response:* Intervene and redirect the group's attention to the topic; in extreme cases, ignore the monopolizer's inappropriate comments.

- *Behavior:* Challenging the leader's authority. *Response:* Be serious but casual in responding to the challenger; avoid defensive responses.
- *Behavior:* Talking too much or perseverating on a topic. *Response:* Interrupt the discussion and state clearly but courteously that the discussion of the topic is over and a new topic is now under consideration.
- *Behavior:* Resisting change. *Response:* Be patient and encourage the resisters to accept change.
- *Behavior:* Seeking a magical solution to the child's exceptionality. *Response:* Encourage interaction between the miracle-seeking parent and the parent who has experienced the difficult, frustrating, and time-consuming work of raising a child with an exceptionality.
- *Behavior:* Rationalizing and intellectualizing problems. *Response:* Call attention to the intellectualizing and encourage parents to carry out an action program.
- *Behavior:* Enjoying and passively accepting problems. *Response:* Assist and encourage such parents to take command of their problems.
- *Behavior:* Stating exceptionality is normal. *Response:* Offer factual information about normal child growth and development and the problems and characteristics of the exceptionality.

In addition to problems introduced by individual members, the leader may confront group problems. Progress may come to a standstill, for example, or members may become bored, frustrated, and distracted. The leader should be alert to such problems and act immediately to restructure activities to draw the group back to its original purpose and objectives.

Summary

This chapter explores the structure of parent-teacher group activities. It discusses the advantages and disadvantages of large and small groups and their effective applications. Large groups are most appropriate for transmitting information efficiently; small groups are better-suited to providing social-emotional support or intensive training. The chapter offers guidelines for conducting large- and small-group meetings, describes methods for revitalizing a disintegrating large group, and highlights leadership techniques for small groups.

Chapter 8 discusses several specific parent-teacher group programs in detail, including informative, communication, problem-solving, discussion, and training groups.

Exercises and Discussion Topics

1. Research and write a brief paper on the relationship between a group's purpose and its size, processes, procedures, and leadership techniques.

2. Develop a checklist for planning, conducting, and evaluating a large group.

3. Develop a needs assessment instrument for a parent-teacher group for use with your special class or a hypothetical class.

4. Discuss in your study group or class the composition, objectives, functions, and operations of an advisory committee for a parent-teacher group.

5. Discuss in your study group or class the guidelines for conducting large-group meetings.

6. Develop a checklist for planning, conducting, and evaluating a small group.

7. Research and write a brief paper on small-group leadership.

8. Lead a study group discussion of a topic selected by your instructor. Discuss your leadership effectiveness with your instructor and members of your group.

9. Conduct a panel discussion in your study group or class on "The Trials and Tribulations of Group Leadership." Each person on the panel should research the topic before the discussion.

References

Croft, D. J. 1979. *Parents and teachers: A resource book for home, school, and community relations.* Belmont, Calif.: Wadsworth.

Dinkmeyer, D., and G. D. McKay. 1974. Leading effective parent study groups. *Elementary School Guidance and Counseling* 9 (2): 108–15.

Dinkmeyer, D., and G. D. McKay. 1976. *Systematic training for effective parenting: Leader's manual.* Circle Pines, Minn.: American Guidance Service.

Hamilton, K., and M. A. Koorland. 1988. Factors effecting program attendance by parents of exceptional secondary students. *Teaching Behaviorally Disordered Youth* 4: 16–19.

Hymes, J. L., Jr. 1974. *Effective home-school relations.* Sierra Madre, Calif.: Southern California Association for the Education of Young Children.

Karnes, M. B., and R. R. Zehrbach. 1972. Flexibility in getting parents involved in the school. *Teaching Exceptional Children* 5 (1):6–19.

Kelley, E. J. 1974. *Parent-teacher interaction: A special educational perspective.* Seattle: Special Child Publications.

Kroth, R. L. 1985. *Communicating with parents of exceptional children: Improving parent-teacher relationships.* 2d ed. Denver: Love.

Olson, S. A., E. Gaines, J. H. Wilson, N. Volstad, and P. A. Smith. 1976. Reinforce that home-school link. *Instructor* 86 (2):112–14, 119, 166.

Shea, T. M., and A. M. Bauer. 1987. *Teaching children and youth with behavior disorders.* Englewood Cliffs, N. J.: Prentice-Hall.

Webster, E. J. 1977. *Counseling with parents of handicapped children: Guidelines for improving communications.* New York: Grune and Stratton.

CHAPTER EIGHT

Group Meeting Models

Ms. S., parent of a preschooler with multiple handicaps:

"At one of the meetings at Reggie's school, I sat next to this other mom. The meeting was during the school day, and afterwards we both went to the rooms to pick up our kids. I met her again in the hall, and her little girl had a wheelchair as complicated as Reggie's. She said, 'Are you going right home? Why don't we take these kids out for ice cream? We deserve a treat.' And I asked her, 'With the kids in their chairs?' And she said, 'Mine's too big to carry, and I know a place we can get in and move tables around.' I didn't say anything, but I guess she saw me looking at Reggie's chair and her little girl's chair, so she said, 'Hey, let 'em look. Nobody's going to give two of us grief.' So we went, that time, and every other time we had a meeting. It was easier when there were two of us to handle the stares and the 'silent treatment.'"

Chapter Topics and Objectives

Teachers with skills in planning, conducting, and evaluating large and small parent-teacher collaboration groups can select specific parent-teacher group models to fulfill their purposes. This chapter presents models for informative group meetings and for communication, problem-solving, discussion, and training groups. No single model will respond to all parents' needs. Consequently, teachers must use professional judgment in matching group processes to parents' needs, strengths, personal characteristics, and cultures.

In this chapter, we will:

- Explore the use of informational meetings.
- Describe examples of communication groups.
- Discuss problem-solving groups.

- Describe discussion groups.
- Discuss training groups.

Informational Meetings

Informational meetings are useful for communicating general information to large groups of parents. Though the topics for these meetings may be generated by means of a parents' needs assessment procedure, the meetings are usually teacher-planned and -implemented.

Topics that may be of interest to parents include the following:

- Laws, rules, and guidelines regarding the education of preschoolers and other students with disabilities
- Health and medical care and insurance
- Estate planning
- Tax information for persons with disabilities or persons with dependents who are disabled
- Community resources—that is, available resources and how to locate and use them
- Special education services.

Evaluation of large-group meetings is essential and can provide additional information regarding topics for future meetings. Evaluation forms should include such items as "Would you like additional information on this topic?" and "What other topics would you like to have presented at meetings?" These and similar questions stimulate parent interest.

Among the most common informational meetings are orientation meetings, open house, and parent-child parallel programs.

Orientation Meetings

An orientation meeting for parents whose children are new to the school or program is supportive for parents and helps the teacher establish rapport and open communication. An orientation meeting includes introductions to program personnel, a tour of the facility, and general information about program goals and objectives. An agenda for an orientation meeting and a portion of a handout given to the parents at the meeting are presented in Figures 8.1 and 8.2.

FIGURE 8.1 · *Orientation Meeting Agenda*

AGENDA
ORIENTATION NIGHT
Wildwood Elementary School
Special Education Program

I. Introductions
   A. Building Principal, Michael R. Nolan
   B. Faculty
      Teachers, Ellen M. Lynch, Maryellen Smith, Jay Obaey
      Paraprofessionals, George Jessup, Bee Hope
   C. Support Service Personnel
      School Secretary, Charlotte Wilbur
      Physical Education Teacher, Michael Wang
      Communication Specialtist, Suzanne Fernandez-Barr
      Occupational Therapist, Liz Harriot
      School Nurse, Lorraine Hymes, R.N.
II. Distribution of student/parent handbook
III. "Who to call for what" (see handout)
IV. Building tour, ending in your child's classroom
V. Refreshments

FIGURE 8.2 · *Sample Handout*

WILDWOOD ELEMENTARY SCHOOL

TELEPHONE 555-4367

WHO TO CALL FOR INFORMATION ABOUT

• Your child's program	Classroom teacher
• Lunch fees and bills	Ms. Wilbur
• Your child's absence	Ms. Wilbur
• Immunization, illnesses, medication, contagious diseases	Ms. Hymes
• Bus scheduling	Mr. Dooley, Transportation: 555-4937
• Alternative lunch menus	Mr. Wilcox, Food Management: 555-9874

Open Houses

Open houses are less formal group programs designed to enhance communication among parents and teachers. The open house is an annual event in most special education programs. Generally held in the fall, the open house is an excellent opportunity to introduce parents to the parent-teacher collaboration program. It is helpful if other professionals and paraprofessionals associated with the program attend the open house to describe their roles in the program.

The open house is an opportunity to display students' academic work, artwork, texts, workbooks, and other instructional materials. The special education teacher may wish to describe the classroom program briefly, including subject matter, psychomotor and physical education activities, and affective education programs. Parents will probably be interested in the behavior management techniques applied in the program as well. The teacher should invite parents' questions and comments.

Mitchell (1989) suggests a variety of strategies to increase attendance at open house. She suggests that teachers mention open house to parents early in the school year, perhaps in their first communication with the parents. Involving the class in preparation and planning for the open house and having students discuss which work to display and how to decorate the classroom increase their enthusiasm, which they transmit to their parents. Students may design and make the notices or invitations to be sent home. Mitchell suggests planning activities that involve the parents in the open house as participants rather than passive recipients. In addition, she urges teachers to have a meeting conclusion planned, with thanks to those who attended and assisted with the program and an explanation of activities for continued communication.

Hietsch (1986) suggested a variation on the traditional open house to increase attendance and participation of fathers and significant other males in the students' lives. When teachers plan a father's day, she suggests they provide adequate notice so that the parents may make arrangements at work. Reminder letters and telephone calls will increase attendance. When fathers arrive for the meeting, teachers must know their names and some commonalities among them to increase their level of personal comfort. Involving the students in greeting their fathers and serving as hosts may increase attendance. A program specifically for fathers may be appropriate because fathers frequently have concerns and issues that differ from mothers, due primarily to their family role. Fathers have personal resources they can share with other fathers in the form of personal experiences and solutions to common problems (Meyer et al. 1985).

Parent-Student Parallel Programs

The issue of child care during parent activities can be solved in an innovative way through the use of parent-student parallel programs. Baker and McCurry (1984) describe such a program, which they used effectively with low-income and Hispanic parents. During a half-day minicamp for their children, parents attended training sessions on helping their children in preacademics, self-help, language, play, and motor skills. In addition to group presentations, each parent was assigned to one trainer and received consultation on tailoring teaching and behavior management programs and planning home activities. Parents were also included in the minicamp activity schedule, which enabled them to practice their newly acquired skills. Parents began by observing the staff, then each taught other parents' children, and finally, each taught their own child. Individual video recordings were taken to provide parents with feedback. Parent self-reports were positive, and significant gains in knowledge of behavioral principles and the ability to apply these principles in teaching were reported.

Shea (1977) published a detailed description of an evening/weekend camp program. Evening/weekend camps, conducted in school or community recreation centers, involve exceptional children and their siblings in activities designed to improve psychomotor, leisure, social-personal, academic, and study skills. University special education trainees lead the activities under the supervision of special education teachers.

While the children are busy with their activities, parents participate in small-group meetings with a school social worker and psychologist. These meetings emphasize social-emotional support and problem solving.

Communication Groups

Two commercial programs are discussed in this section to represent the communication group approach to helping parents of children with exceptionalities. These programs—Parent Effectiveness Training (PET) and Systematic Training for Effective Parenting (STEP)—offer complete systems of instruction.

Parent Effectiveness Training

Parent Effectiveness Training (Gordon 1970) is designed to teach parents the communication skills they need to raise responsible children. Parents of any child—young or adolescent, normal or exceptional—can benefit from the PET course.

The program includes twenty-four hours of instruction in eight sessions of three hours. A trained instructor works with classes of twenty to thirty parents. Parents pay an instructional fee and purchase PET texts and workbooks.

Instructional methods include lectures, role playing, and discussion. Parents study the topics active listening, changing behavior by modifying the environment, conflict resolution, changing personal behavior, and interacting with other individuals who parent your child.

In an article on the need to design training programs responsive to the trainees, Gilliam (1975) cautioned teachers on the use of Parent Effectiveness Training with all parents. He suggested that the cost, reading and study requirements, and complexity of PET may make it most appropriate for parents who are professionals (physicians, teachers, managers) and less appropriate, without modification, for others, particularly nonliterate groups.

Systematic Training for Effective Parenting

Systematic Training for Effective Parenting (Dinkmeyer and McKay 1976) is an educational program to help parents raise responsible children and feel more adequate and satisfied as parents. Because of changes in society and in parenting practices, Dinkmeyer and McKay believe today's parents need training to be effective. Society has evolved from autocratic parenting practices to practices based on mutual respect between parent and child, equality, and individual rights and responsibilities. Many present-day parents were raised in an autocratic manner and lack understanding and experience in democratic parenting practices. STEP teaches parents the knowledge and skills needed to be a democratic parent.

Dinkmeyer and McKay do not recommend STEP for parents of troubled children, for it is not a form of therapy. However, Kroth and Kroth (1976) stated that STEP is valuable to parents of exceptional children because it helps improve communication skills among family members.

STEP is designed for use in small study groups of ten to twelve parents plus the group leader. The group meets for nine sessions of one and a half to two hours. Because the material is cumulative, attendance is mandatory.

STEP is a highly structured program of instruction. A leader's manual provides specific directions for each lesson. The STEP kit includes an invitational brochure and audiotape to publicize the program. Lesson materials, published in English and Spanish, include a leader's manual, parents' handbook, five audiotapes, six discussion guide cards, nine posters, and ten charts. In the group setting, parents share concerns and provide each other mutual support. They grow in self-awareness and awareness of their parenting effectiveness, learning they are not necessarily the cause of the child's difficulties. STEP teaches parents to communicate constructively with their children and how to reinforce acceptable behaviors and not reinforce unacceptable behaviors.

The STEP leader may be trained in psychology, social work, counseling, education, or another helping profession. A lay person willing to study the STEP materials may serve as group leader. The leader conducts each lesson guided by the STEP manual but must have the skills to facilitate discussion and set the tone or atmosphere for the group.

The leader's manual discusses the rationale for the program and instructs leaders on how to organize and conduct the program, how to lead the group, and so on. Clear and concise descriptions of nine lessons provide detail on materials, objectives, procedures, use of instructional aids, discussion topics, class exercise, home assignments, and reading assignments.

STEP's developers state that it is effective with any interested parent and can be taught by both lay and professional instructors. However, STEP is a complex program requiring considerable organizational and leadership skills. Thus, an instructor probably needs background and experience in child development, parenting, and the helping professions to effectively answer parents' questions and concerns. In addition, participating parents need skills in observation, discussion, and reading and writing to benefit from the program. Parents lacking these skills may not find it satisfactory. Other parents will be unable to participate because they cannot pay the fee.

James and Etheridge (1978) evaluated the use of the STEP program with families who lived in the inner city and found that after initial meetings, enrollment dropped significantly. They suggested that initial sessions were not sufficiently directed to parents' specific concerns. They concluded that "prepackaged" programs such as STEP may not be appropriate for all parents and that it is more practical for trainers to design their own program to fit parents' needs.

Problem-Solving Groups

According to Kelly (1974), parent-teacher problem solving is most effective when organized around a central theme that focuses members on the group's primary purpose of helping the child with an exceptionality. This focusing device helps counter the tendency to stray into discussions of inappropriate topics, such as personal and marital problems.

Teachers should evaluate their personal capacities and competencies to lead parent problem-solving groups, for these groups require counseling skills unlike those teachers usually learn (Kelly 1974). Teachers lacking the competencies and confidence to counsel parents should enlist the services of an appropriately trained school counselor, social worker, or psychologist as group leader. The teacher retains the responsibility of helping the facilitator and members and should nonetheless participate actively in the group.

Rutherford and Edgar (1979) developed a problem-solving process model that provides logical and sequential procedures generally applicable to most problems, conceptual frameworks, and intervention strategies (see Chapter 6 also). The four-step process provides a structure for facilitating group activities.

1. Defining the problem
2. Developing probable solutions
3. Implementing a solution
4. Evaluating the results.

In the first step, the group identifies the problem and specifies its parameters, determining the people, times, and settings related to the problem and reaching consensus on the desired outcome of the problem-solving process. At this stage, the group considers who owns the problem: the child, the parent, the teachers, or a combination of these people.

The second step, developing probable solutions, calls for the group to prepare a plan for solving the problem. Group members consider the who, what, where, when, how, and how many of the proposed solution, paying special attention to parents' and teachers' roles.

The third step is to carry out the proposed solution in line with the group's agreed-upon plan. During this stage, parents and teachers, as well as the child, need reinforcement for their efforts and successes. Changing a child's behavior may require that parents and teachers change their personal behavior. Frequently, a positive change in the child's behavior is sufficiently rewarding to sustain their efforts. However, when change is slow, parents and teachers become frustrated and discouraged and may discontinue their efforts. Avoiding this consequence may necessitate an external reinforcement program, whereby parents and teachers reinforce each other through periodic conferences, notes, or telephone calls.

The final step in the problem-solving process, evaluation, is a continuous process that takes place throughout implementation of the solution. The group assesses the impact of the intervention on the problem and assesses the efficiency and consistency of parents' and teachers' efforts. Collecting and graphing observation data on frequency, percentage, or duration of the behavior help in evaluating the solution's effectiveness. Observations can ascertain the efficiency and consistency of interventions. The parents and teacher may want to observe each other's efforts and discuss their observations.

Discussion Groups

Shea (1978) described a model for parent-teacher discussion groups. These discussion groups have three objectives:

1. To communicate practical information to parents
2. To help parents solve problems related to their child
3. To provide a setting for parents to exchange support and understanding.

Shea's groups are parent-centered groups that focus on an agreed-upon information topic and on parents' immediate practical concerns and problems. The first part of each session is devoted to a ten-minute presentation by the teacher or a parent of a topic announced at the previous session. Thus, members have had an opportunity to read or, simply, think about the subject before the meeting. After the presentation, group members discuss the topic and relate it to their concerns and circumstances. The group can select discussion topics from a text on parenting, child development, behavior management, or exceptionality.

Groups generally contain ten to twelve parents and one or two teachers. It is best if both mothers and fathers attend. Regular attendance is encouraged but not mandatory. Attendance increases if child care service is available. Teachers may want to organize a few members of the group into a subgroup responsible for reminding members of the next meeting. Car pools can help ensure that everyone who wishes can attend meetings.

Schools usually have a conference room available for group meetings. Conducting meetings in members' homes is generally undesirable for several reasons: preparing for the meeting can easily upset family harmony, parents lose the opportunity to get out for a few hours, and some parents consider their homes, furnishings, or neighborhoods inadequate.

Classrooms are also inappropriate for meetings unless adult-sized furnishings are available and artificial barriers can be removed. All sessions should begin and end at the agreed-upon time. The leader is unwise to remain after meetings for private discussions with individuals or small groups of parents. These activities should take place at another time.

Initially, the teacher functions as a directive leader. However, as the group progresses and cohesiveness grows, the teacher's role may change from direct leader to member and resource person. To fulfill their functions, the members ideally initiate discussion, give and request information, give and request evaluation, restate and give examples of their perceptions of others' statements, confront and reality-test suggested solutions, and clarify, synthesize, and summarize. However, many nonfunctional behaviors are likely to occur during group discussions as well, such as aggression, competition, confession, sympathy seeking, horsing around, withdrawal, domination, and negation. These behaviors, though unrelated to the task at hand, are often necessary to maintain group cohesiveness and affirm the integrity of individual members. They can also provide needed tension release after intense discussion. However, leaders cannot allow such behaviors to interfere with the group's productiveness.

According to Shea (1978), an effective group will have the following characteristics, which help create a positive atmosphere:

- Parents enjoy attending meetings.
- Group members are warm, accepting, and cordial toward each other.
- The group is a nonthreateninng environment in which each member feels free to express his or her problems and concerns.
- Members attend meetings regularly, arrive on time, and are prepared for presentation and discussions.
- Learning is a cooperative activity to which all members contribute.

- Members view learning as the group's reason for existence and accept that learning requires effort.
- All members participate actively in the discussion.
- Members share leadership functions; no one dominates activities.
- The exploration of topics is thorough and well-paced so that all members feel satisfied.
- Members accept evaluation as an essential component of group activity.

In another example of discussion groups, Johnston and Zemitzsch (1988) described an evening parent/teacher group that emphasized family strengths. Through multiple phone calls and mailings, parents were repeatedly invited to attend. The discussion group was led by both the school social worker and the school psychologist. Meetings were held in students' classrooms so that their educational programs were conspicuous. Issues that emerged in discussion were parenting skills, action and support for school programming, and expanding communication between home and school. A parent phone network resulted from the meetings. A reception and awards night was provided for parents with consistent attendance.

Supper meetings have also been used for discussion groups (Hallenbeck and Beernink 1989). During these meetings, parents may discuss a film, videotape, or cassette presentation; hear a guest speaker; watch a program featuring student projects; or have a panel discussion. If the topics seem beneficial to students, they can be invited to the meetings.

Parent discussion groups may evolve into support groups. Phillips (1985) suggests that the key to an effective support group is a strong leader who facilitates the group. Members may be recruited through direct invitation, presentation of the idea at PTA or faculty meetings, or invitation letters from student services personnel or school psychologists. Phillips recommends that in managing the group, teachers begin each group meeting with a warm-up activity that includes positive statements or questions. A year-long agenda may assist the group in maintaining membership. The leader should continually redirect discussion back to the group, rather than answering an individual. Phillips cautions that support groups are not substitutes for counseling and that the leader should avoid serving as mediator or problem solver. An essential ingredient in an informal, relaxed atmosphere, with an honest, nonjudgmental approach. A hot-line system for members to utilize in crisis situations may provide additional support to families.

Training Groups

The professional literature covers a wide range of training programs for parents. This section highlights several of these programs, which represent the range and character of those available.

A Practical Approach to Parent Training

Walker and Shea (1988) presented a behavior modification training program for parents in their text *Behavior Modification: A Practical Approach for Educators*. The program has two primary objectives: to train parents in the theory and application of behavior modification principles and practices and to help parents systematically modify selected behaviors of their children. Although not a primary objective of the program, the opportunity to receive support and understanding from the teacher and other parents is often an additional benefit for many parents. The program proceeds in three phases.

Preparation Phase. The teacher interviews each parent or couple one or more times before the training begins to determine the parents' needs, interests, and readiness to participate in a formal training program and to identify at least one child behavior the parents wish to change. These interview sessions are an excellent time for the teacher to discuss the program objectives, organization, and requirements and to invite the parents' participation.

Instructional Phase. The instructional phase of the parent training program includes eight weekly sessions. The one-and-one-half-hour sessions break into two forty-minute segments and a ten-minute recess.

In the first forty-minute segment, the teacher offers brief formal presentations on the principles and practices of behavior modification and then opens the segment to a question-and-answer session, group discussion, and practice exercises and activities. The ten-minute break is an opportunity for informal discussion, perhaps over coffee, tea, milk, soft drinks, and snacks furnished by the parent educator and the parents.

The second forty-minute segment focuses on planning, implementing, and evaluating the parents' behavioral intervention programs. Interventions aim to change the behaviors the parents selected during the preparation interviews. During this second segment, parents report on their interventions, and the other members question, discuss, and make suggestions for improving the interventions. The teacher has the responsibility for keeping the discussion positive and helpful throughout this segment.

Group membership is limited to twelve to fourteen people, plus the teacher. Teachers of the children under discussion can become group members. As in most parent collaboration activities, participation by both parents is desirable.

Regular attendance is important because of the cumulative nature of the material. Parents unable to attend a particular session should receive an update from the teacher; however, absences should be discouraged for the sake of group cohesiveness and the teacher's time.

The teacher functions as both instructor and group facilitator. However, the teacher can offer opportunities for parents to make instructional presentations. And the teacher's function as group facilitator should diminish as the instructional phase of the program progresses and individual parents begin to assert leadership.

Occasionally, a team of two teachers presents the training program, a format that is particularly effective if one acts as instructor and the other as facilitator. Of course, success in team teaching assumes personal-professional compatibility as well as fundamental agreement on the subject matter and instructional methods.

Any person who is knowledgeable about behavior modification, child behavior, and group leadership can serve as instructor-facilitator. Thus, regular and special education teachers, college instructors, counselors, psychologists, nurses, social workers, and other helping professionals are good candidates.

Instructional materials include the Walker and Shea text and worksheets. Each participant should have a copy of the text, which suggests instructional aids for each lesson.

The training program includes eight sessions:

Session 1	An introduction to behavior modification
Session 2	The consequences of behavior
Session 3	Potentially effective reinforcers
Sessions 4–5	Strategies to increase behavior
Sessions 6–7	Strategies to decrease behavior
Session 8	Ethical and effective applications

The text presents detailed lesson plans that specify goals, content, instructional methods, group and individual activities, instructional resources and aids, evaluation techniques, and home assignments. (See Figure 8.3 for a sample lesson.)

Follow-up Phase. Teachers should maintain contact with parents after the eight-week training program. Walker and Shea suggest that the teacher develop a follow-up plan, maintaining periodic contact with the group and with individual parents to reinforce their efforts and help them plan and implement additional interventions. Individual interviews, telephone conversations, and monthly group meetings are several follow-up methods. This periodic reinforcement increases the probability that the skills learned during the training program will not fall into disuse.

Training for the IEP Process

The vast majority of parents of children with exceptionalities would profit greatly from training in the IEP process. Katz and

---

FIGURE 8.3 • *Sample Lesson Plan*

LESSON 1: AN INTRODUCTION TO BEHAVIOR MODIFICATION

Goals

1. To familiarize students with the models of causation of human behavior and with the behavior change process
2. To enable parents to exemplify each of the principles of behavior modification
3. To enable parents to complete two or more target behavior selection checklists correctly
4. To enable parents to accurately observe and record a target behavior

Content

1. Models of causation of human behavior
2. Principles of behavior modification
3. Overview of the behavior change process
4. Selecting target behaviors
5. Observing and recording target behaviors

Instructional Methods

1. Lecture
2. Discussion
3. Demonstration

(cont.)

FIGURE 8.3 *Continued*

---

4. Completion of a target behavior selection checklist
5. Recording the target behavior rate or frequency

Activities

1. Segment A (40 minutes)
   a. Introduction of the parent educator(s) and individual parents
   b. Overview of the course organization and content
   c. Brief lecture on theories of causation of human behavior
   d. Brief overview of the behavior change process
   e. Lecture on the principles of behavior modification; each participant requested to cite a personal example of each principle (may be written)
   f. (1) Examples of target behaviors and explanation of the target behavior selection process;

      (2) Demonstration of how to complete a target behavior selection checklist;

      (3) Each participant requested to select a target behavior selection checklist.
   g. Procedures for observing and recording target behaviors presented, exemplified, and discussed
2. Break (10 minutes)
3. Segment B (40 minutes)
   a. Target Behavior 1 (home behavior)
      (1) Each participant (or mother and father) presents to the group the target behavior selected during the psychosituational assessment interview of the course preparation phase. Participants also present and discuss the data that they recorded on the behavior log form.
      (2) Each participant completes a target behavior selection checklist on Target Behavior 1.
      (3) Each participant transfers the data on the behavior log form to an appropriate tally form.

Resources

1. Segment A
   a. Parent educator and individual participants
   b. Chapter Six: Preparation phase of program and lesson titles
   c. Chapter One: Models of human behavior
   d. Chapter Three: Entire chapter

(cont.)

FIGURE 8.3 *Continued*

   e. Chapter Two: Principles of reinforcement
   f. Chapter Three: Selecting a target behavior
      Target behavior selection checklist
   g. Chapter Three: Collecting and recording baseline data
2. Break
3. Segment B
   a. Target Behavior 1
      (1) Behavior log form
      (2) Target behavior selection checklist
      (3) Chapter Three: Collecting and recording baseline data

Evaluation

1. Quiz on or written examples of the principles of reinforcement
2. Completed behavior log form, target behavior selection checklist, and tally form

Home Assignments

1. Observe and record baseline data on Target Behavior I
2. Read
   a. Chapter Two: Consequences of behavior; schedules of reinforcement
   b. Chapter Three: Collecting and recording baseline data

Source: Walker and Shea 1988, 245–46. Reprinted with permission.

colleagues (1980) designed an adult education course to help parents improve their effectiveness in the IEP meeting. The course includes three two-hour training modules, or lessons. However, Katz and associates indicated that other formats, such as three miniworkshops or a one-day workshop, could be equally effective. One strength of the program is its wide applicability, for participants require only limited reading, writing, and verbal skills.

The first module, "Parents' Role and Rights Under Public Law 94-142" provides information on the history, purpose, and components of the law. In addition, it reviews due process procedures and explains how to find the local special education agency responsible for services for exceptional children.

The second module explores the parents' role in evaluating and observing their exceptional children. After a brief review of the first lesson, the group leader conducts a discussion to help parents share common experiences with and feelings about their exceptional children and their families' adjustments. Next, the group leader describes the assessment and evaluation methods used by the school's professional staff, including cumulative records, formal and informal tests, psychological evaluations, and classroom observations. At the end of the second lesson, parents receive worksheets and instructions to help them observe their child's strengths and needs more objectively and systematically. The parents record their observations on the worksheets for the next session.

The final module prepares the parent for the meeting itself. After reviewing their "homework," parents discuss with the group the goals they have established for their children. Also during this lesson, the group leader shows parents how to organize a file of all the information they have about their children. The instructor suggests several ways for parents to prepare for and participate in the IEP meeting. Finally, in the third module, the group conducts a simulated IEP meeting to practice skills.

Training in Transition Issues. Haline and Halvorsen (1989) suggested the use of a minicourse to assist parents in the transition of their children from more restrictive to less restrictive educational settings. Topics included in the minicourse were the concept of integration, methods for supporting the child through the transition process, program quality, and success/failure and advantages/disadvantages. Through presentations, visitation, observation, and parent-to-parent teaming, these issues were explored in depth. A similar minicourse for parents experiencing the transition of their children from preschool to public school and from school to work may provide parents with needed information and support.

Stress Management for Parents. Singler, Irvin, and Hawkins (1988) suggested a training program in stress management for parents of students with severe handicaps. Through eight classes, parents were taught self-monitoring, progressive muscle relaxation, applying relaxation techniques as an active coping skill, and cognitive reframing of stressful events. As a result of the classes, parents demonstrated improvement in measures of depression and anxiety.

Summary

This chapter concludes the discussion of parent-teacher collaboration groups by reviewing several models for informational communication, problem-solving, discussion, and training groups. Working in groups requires parents' and teachers' time, energy, and commitment beyond those demanded by written, telephone, and conferencing activities. The models described in this chapter are teacher resources to be adapted to group purpose and the unique needs of the parent participants. The next chapter presents several classroom, school, home, and community parent-teacher activities to benefit exceptional children.

Exercises and Discussion Topics

1. Plan an informational meeting for a large group of parents (thirty to thirty-five people) on the etiology, course, treatment, and prognosis of a form of exceptionality with which you are familiar. Present your program to your study group. Invite the group members to critique your program and performance from the perspective of a parent of a child with an exceptionality.

2. Plan a series of at least four informational meetings for a small group of parents (six to eight people). Select a different topic from the one you discussed in the first exercise. Present one meeting from this series to your study group. Invite group members to critique your program and performance from the perspective of a parent.

3. Instruct your study group in the use of Parent Effectiveness Training (PET), Systematic Training for Effective Parenting (STEP), or another commercially available parent education program.

4. Research the literature and write a brief paper on "discussion group atmosphere."

5. Plan a series of behavior management training lessons for a small group of parents (ten to twelve people) using a theoretical model of your choice. Present one lesson to your study group. Invite the members of the group to critique your performance from the perspective of a parent of a child with an exceptionality.

6. Write a lesson or series of lessons for training parents to increase their effectiveness in the IEP meeting.

References

Baker, B. L., and M. C. McCurry. 1984. School-based parent training: An alternative for parents predicted to demonstrate low teaching proficiency following group training. *Education and Training of the Mentally Retarded* 19: 261–67.

Dinkmeyer, D., and G. D. McKay. 1976. *Systematic training for effective parenting: Leader's manual.* Circle Pines, Minn.: American Guidance Services.

Gilliam, G. 1975. Parent training. *Health Education* 6 (5): 11–12

Gordon, T. 1970. *Parent effectiveness training.* New York: Peter Wyden.

Hallenback, M., and M. Beernink. 1989. A support program for parents of students with mild handicaps. *Teaching Exceptional Children* 21 (3): 44–47.

Hanline, M. F., and A. Halvorsen. 1989 Parent perceptions of the integration transition process: Overcoming artificial barriers. *Exceptional Children* 55 (6): 487–92.

Hietsch, D. G. 1986. Father involvement: No moms allowed. *Teaching Exceptional Children* 18 (4): 258–59.

James, R., and G. Etheridge. 1978. Training for inner city parents in child rearing: Why fried chicken franchises for parenting don't work. ERIC Document ED197004.

Johnston, J. C., and A. Zemitzsch. 1988. Family power: An intervention beyond the classroom. *Behavioral Disorders* 14: 69–79.

Katz, S., J. Borten, D. Brasile, M. Meisner, and C. Parker. 1980. Helping parents become effective partners: The IEP process. *The Pointer* 25 (1): 35–45.

Kelly, E. J. 1974. *Parent-teacher interaction: A special educational perspective.* Seattle: Special Child Publications.

Meyer, D., P. Vadasy, R. Fewell, and G. Schell. 1985. *A handbook for The Father's Program: How to organize a program for fathers and their handicapped children.* Seattle: University of Washington Press.

Mitchell, L. S. 1989. Turn that open house into a full house. *Exceptional Times* 1 (1): 2.

Phillips, K. M. 1985. Parents as partners: Developing parent support groups. *Teaching: Behaviorally Disordered Youth* 1: 29–36.

Rutherford, R. B., and E. Edgar. 1979. *Teachers and parents: A guide to interaction and cooperation.* Boston: Allyn and Bacon.

Shea, T. M. 1977. *Camping for special children.* St. Louis: Mosby.

Shea, T. M. 1978. *Teaching children and youth with behavioral disorders.* St. Louis: Mosby.

Singler, G. H., L. Irvin, and N. Hawkins. 1988. Stress management training for parents of children with severe handicaps. *Mental Retardation* 26: 269–77.

Walker, J. E., and T. M. Shea. 1988. *Behavior management: A practical approach for educators.* 4th ed. Columbus, Ohio: Charles E. Merrill.

CHAPTER NINE

School, Home, and Community Programs

> Ms. P., parent of a thirteen-year-old son with mental retardation:
>
> *"My girlfriend's little boy, he's in a special ed classroom, too. She talked to me, she talked to me a lot before my boy went into that room. She really let me know how it was, how the kids picked up, when they didn't pick up. And then her son and my boy would talk. It's like Tony would tell Jason what it's like. My girlfriend's son Tony was already in special ed when Jason went in so it wasn't really spooky for him, because Tony give him ideas of what it was like."*

Chapter Topics and Objectives

Throughout the nation, thousands of parents are volunteering services in the classrooms and schools. Others, unable to go to school, demonstrate interest in their children's formal education by contributing time and effort to committee work and special projects. Some parents act as advocates for children with exceptionalities in the community. Others participate in their children's education through home-teaching programs.

This chapter discusses several ways to involve parents and help them be effective in classroom, school, home, and community services for children with exceptionalities. To act as paraprofessionals, instructors, volunteers, and home teachers, parents need special skills. This chapter discusses techniques for preparing them for these roles, such as observation, demonstration, role playing, instructional coaching, and modeling. Resource centers are also important aids that supplement parents' efforts to educate their children.

The effectiveness of parent collaboration in the classroom, school, home, and community depends in large part on teachers' and parents' attitudes and expectations for the activities. Brown (1978) and Croft (1979) suggested several premises for positive, productive parent-teacher collaboration:

1. Both parents and teachers are concerned about the education and general welfare of the child. Each must understand their importance, as well as the importance of the other, as active members of the child's educational team. Parents and teachers will participate in cooperative programming as their living and working conditions and personal abilities and skills allow. The first step toward effective collaboration is to recognize, understand, and accept the concerns and expectations that each person brings to the efforts.

2. Both parents and teachers are effective treatment providers. Each party must recognize the other's areas of expertise in fostering the child's education. Each must recognize that the other has much to offer, yet much to learn about, children with exceptionalities.

3. Parents and teachers must recognize and change as necessary the social-emotional and physical environment in which they work with the child. Neither can function effectively in an environment lacking needed facilities, furnishings, equipment, and materials.

4. Parents and teachers must recognize the importance of each other's goals for the child and themselves and consider both sets of goals in planning. Consensus on common goals is essential for effective collaboration.

5. Parents and teachers must have training in the processes of collaboration and in the skills and knowledge needed to participate in activities. Through training sessions carefully organized to present the needed skills and knowledge, parents and teachers grow in confidence and are better able to help the child.

6. Parents and teachers function more comfortably and effectively when they have well-defined rules of operation. Each must know the when, where, how, who, what, and why of their collaborative activities.

7. Both parties need encouragement and positive reinforcement. They need supervision to increase their effectiveness.

8. Finally, parents and teachers must be persistent and patient in their efforts to become effective in helping the child with exceptionalities.

Chapter Nine • School, Home, and Community Programs **215**

In this chapter, we will:

- Describe ways to prepare parents to work with children with exceptionalities.
- Discuss the various roles parents may assume in collaborative efforts to educate their children.

Parent Training Techniques

Adults do not naturally possess the knowledge and skills to be effective teachers. Most parents need training to be effective in teaching their children.

Learning instructional skills involves several stages (Blackard 1976; Haring 1976): Parents must acquire the skills and become proficient in using them for instruction and behavior management. They must maintain the skills in conditions similar to those in which they learned them, and they must learn to generalize and adapt the skills to new or different conditions.

This section reviews several techniques for training parents to teach their children, including observation, instructional coaching, modeling, and role playing. These techniques are useful for classroom and school paraprofessionals, tutors, volunteers, teacher assistants, and home teachers. Because research on the effectiveness of these techniques in parent training is scant (Clements and Alexander 1975), teachers should carefully monitor and evaluate their effectiveness in specific settings.

Observation

Practitioners in parent education recommend that parents receive training in objective observation of classroom procedures and behavioral incidents (Croft 1979; Miller 1975; Shea and Bauer 1987). Croft emphasized that such training should be a prerequisite for active involvement in the classroom, and Miller thought it especially important for parents learning to be behavior modifiers.

Training in observation helps parents overcome personal biases when observing interpersonal interaction, increasing their awareness of their own interaction in the process. Parents' observations can also help teachers responsible for explaining to parents their child's therapeutic and instructional objectives and programs. Careful observation during periodic visits may better equip parents to evaluate their children's progress and to adapt specific techniques for use at home.

Croft (1979) developed two checklists to help parents develop their powers of observation (Figures 9.1 and 9.2). One focuses on student motivation, language development, emotional conditions, academic learning program, and opportunities for creative expression. The second guides parents in evaluating their children's physical environment, materials and equipment, personnel, and instructional program. Parents benefit most from these and similar observation schedules when they can discuss their observations with a teacher either during or immediately after the observation period. The teacher can then clarify parents' perceptions and misperceptions of what they observed.

Shea and Bauer (1987) suggested the following guidelines for training parents to observe specific behaviors:

1. Parents' first observations should not be in their children's classrooms, unless an observation booth or one-way viewing mirror is available. They should observe another child, teacher, or classroom group. This restriction prevents parents' emotional responses to their children from interfering with objectivity.

2. Parents' first observations should be brief (ten to fifteen minutes) and focus on a specific behavior or behaviors (attending, out-of-seat, hand raising, and so on). Parents should count the frequency or duration of the selected behavior. As their observational skills increase, parents can broaden their focus and increase the length of their observations.

3. Parents should first observe with a teacher or paraprofessional. The staff person can explain the activities under way in the classroom and discuss children's and teachers' behaviors. As parents' skills develop, they can observe independently, but a staff person should remain available to discuss observations and respond to questions and concerns.

Instructional Coaching

Clements and Alexander (1975) found that parent training programs often use instructional coaching. This procedure precisely specifies how parents are to instruct their children, either through consultation, written lesson plans, videotapes, programmed materials and texts, or a combination of these (Baker and McCurry 1984).

Whatever aids augment instructional coaching procedures,

FIGURE 9.1 • *Observation Check Sheet*

Name of Observer: _____ Date: _____

Instructions: Please sit down in an unobtrusive place where you can see most of the classroom. In order to observe objectively it is best to limit your interactions with the children. If they should approach you and talk with you, answer them, but do not encourage a lengthy conversation. If they want you to do something with them, refer them to the teacher.

Give yourself time to take in the total environment. Absorb the general atmosphere, look all around the room, listen to the sounds, and generally acquaint yourself with the surroundings and the people. When you are comfortable, begin to focus on more specific aspects of the curriculum.

In this classroom we want to:

1. Increase the Child's Awareness and Knowledge about the Physical World

	Check
Does the program encourage the development of curiosity through materials and displays that lead a child to explore?	___
Do you hear children asking questions?	___
Do the teachers encourage children to ask questions?	___
Are the children free to touch and explore and actively experiment with materials in the classroom?	___
Do the teachers foster a child's interest in new things?	___
Are there opportunities for freedom of choice in a variety of learning activities?	___

2. Develop Language Abilities

Are the children encouraged to express themselves verbally?	___
Are there a variety of language-motivating materials available to the child? (Records, books, puppets, dramatic play materials?)	___
Do you hear children expressing ideas and feelings?	___
Do the activities encourage verbal interaction between and among the children?	___
Do the teachers introduce new concepts and terminology?	___
Do the teachers name objects and verbalize clearly about procedures to the children?	___

3. Foster Mental and Emotional Health

Do the children appear comfortable in the classroom?	___
Do the children seem self-confident?	___
Are the teachers respectful of the child who is different?	___
Do the children seem secure in the routines and methods used by the teachers?	___
Are disciplinary methods fair and reasonable?	___
Are the teachers sufficiently firm and flexible?	___
Do you see examples of building a child's strong self-concept?	___
Do teachers value individual children?	___
Are children learning responsibility for their actions and choices?	___
Are children learning to care for others?	___

(cont.)

FIGURE 9.1 *Continued*

4. Teach Cognitive Skills

Are there materials designed to teach children concepts like large and small, geometric shapes, numbers, colors, letters? _____

Are there small group and individual instruction times set aside during the day? _____

Is plenty of time allotted for working with learning materials? _____

Do the children get immediate feedback about the correctness of the concepts they are learning? _____

Are children allowed to learn at their own pace? _____

Do teachers use praise to encourage children? _____

5. Encourage Creative Expression

Are there many art materials and opportunities for creative expression available? _____

Are there opportunities for dramatic play and imaginative involvement? _____

Are there music and creative movement activities? _____

Are children encouraged to use their imaginations? _____

Is the individual child given space and time to daydream or simply to be alone? _____

This observation form is intended to provide a framework for looking more closely at various aspects of the curriculum. You can expand on these as you work with us in our program. We value your comments and invite your suggestions.

Comments and Suggestions:

Source: From *Parents and Teachers: A Resource Book for Home, School, and Community Resources* (pp. 176–78) by Doreen J. Croft, © 1979 by Wadsworth Publishing Company, Inc., Belmont, Calif. 94002. Reprinted by permission of the publisher.

Clements and Alexander suggested the following general guidelines for parent trainers:

- Provide the parents with clear, concise, and specific directions.
- Begin by working with highly specific behaviors and actions.
- Reinforce parents' efforts as well as their successes.
- Offer the parents immediate or near-immediate feedback on their performance.
- Ask parents to discuss their perceptions of the training pro-

Chapter Nine • School, Home, and Community Programs **219**

gram and their performance to enhance their understanding and motivation.

Modeling

Modeling, a process of observation and imitation, is one of the most common forms of human learning. Theorists have described modeling variously as observational learning, identification, copying, vicarious learning, social facilitation, and contagion (Walker and Shea 1988).

> *This method of parent training may be employed in vivo (where the teacher engages in the task or demonstrates the activity in the actual situation and environment in which the parent[s] is to perform, while the parent observes) or in individual or group training sessions with only the teacher and parents present. (Clements and Alexander 1975, 7)*

To teach a skill using modeling, parents and teacher repeat the following three steps until the parent has mastered the skill:

FIGURE 9.2 • *What to Look for in a School Visit*

Name of Observer: _____ Date: _____

1. Physical Aspects

	Check
Ample indoor and outdoor space? (A minimum of thirty-five square feet indoors and fifty square feet outdoors per child.)	_____
Space for running and plenty of large-muscle activities?	_____
Variety of physical activities encouraged through good design?	_____
Isolation quarters?	_____
Place for quiet contemplation?	_____
Supervision taken into account in overall design? Can children be easily seen and supervised, or are there many areas not easily covered at all times?	_____
Hygienic conditions? (Clean sinks, toilets, safe conditions, heating facilities, drafts, fire extinguishers well located, well lighted, children appear healthy?)	_____

2. Equipment

Sterile equipment leads to limited and sterile responses. Are children able to get many different ideas in use of materials, and are they free to explore and question and work out their curiosity? Can most equipment be used in many ways? _____

(cont.)

FIGURE 9.2 *Continued*

Are there enough equipment and materials to go around? _____

Is all equipment in good condition? (Painted, sanded, no sharp or broken edges?) Do puzzles have all pieces? Are books in good repair? Is most equipment readily available for children? _____

3. People

Do you get the feeling the school is friendly? _____

Is it too quiet or too hectic? _____

Do you hear lots of "No, No"? _____

Do the teachers seem interested, relaxed, but busy? _____

Are the needs of children cared for, or are there some who seem left out and ignored? _____

What is the ratio of adults to children? (Recommended minimum of one adult to ten children. A better ratio is one to five or six depending on age of children.) _____

Are visitors apparently welcome at any time, or is it necessary to make an appointment? _____

Are children free to express themselves verbally and explore physically without constant direction from adults? _____

Does there appear to be a mutual trust and respect among staff and children? _____

Do the teachers have plenty of physical contact (hugging, holding) with children? Or do they seem to be too busy setting up and cleaning up? _____

4. Program

Does the daily routine offer a comfortable balance between free play and organized activities? Does it allow for flexibility within an organized routine? _____

Do the various areas show adequate preplanning? _____

Are the areas inviting and appealing to children? _____

May children move freely within well-supervised areas? Or do they have to all do the same things at the same time? _____

Are there "escape hatches" for those who do not want to participate with the group? _____

Do art work and creative play areas seem stereotyped? That is, are materials precut; are children required to all make the same thing to take home; are some activities special and not always available whenever children want them? _____

Is there a good variety of small- and large-muscle activities available—music, stories, nature studies? Do tools and materials (such as carpentry) provide for successful experiences rather than frustration and failure? _____

Are there well-planned, cognitively oriented activities with appropriate teaching guidance by an adult? _____

Are there many self-help, self-correcting tasks to engage the children so they can learn at their own pace? _____

Source: From *Parents and Teachers: A Resource Book for Home, School, and Community Resources* (pp. 178–80) by Doreen J. Croft, © 1979 by Wadsworth Publishing Company, Inc., Belmont, Calif. 94002. Reprinted by permission of the publisher.

1. The teacher, a paraprofessional, or a trained parent demonstrates the target skill or activity with the child as the parent trainee observes. The demonstrator offers verbal or written instructions before the demonstration and follows it with a discussion.
2. The parent practices the activity with the child while the trainer observes.
3. The parent and trainer critique the parent's performance.

Because of the complexity of modeling, Clements and Alexander (1975) suggested that it be carefully evaluated. Among the variables the teacher using modeling should monitor are the persons involved (child, parent, and teacher), the specific skill or activity being learned, the instructional setting, and the instructional method.

Role Playing and Behavioral Rehearsal

Role playing is an activity in which participants assume a specific role in a demonstration or simulation. It is a technique that takes into account both the cognitive and the emotional components of the incident being acted out.

For role playing to be effective, the teacher and parents, together, must agree on its purpose, whether in a group setting or family conference, and agree on the situation to be enacted. Role playing is most effective when used to teach new behaviors and skills, select the most effective behavior or skill for a given situation, determine the behavior or skill the parent will be most comfortable using in a given situation, and explore the emotional components of a situation. Webster (1977) divided role playing into three phases: selecting and clarifying the situations and roles to act out, acting out the roles, and discussing the thoughts and feelings evoked by the process.

Behavioral rehearsal is a variation on role playing in which

> *parent(s) actually engage in the activity or task in other environments or situations than those in which they will be expected to perform. Role-playing may be utilized, in which the teacher or another parent assumes the role of the child if appropriate to the activity the parent is to engage in. This is not a prerequisite to behavioral rehearsal, however, and in numerous activities, it may be more expedient to have the parent "walk through" the activity both physically and verbally under the direction and guidance of the teacher. Behavioral rehearsal may also be covert, in which case the parent imagines the situation, task, or activity and cognitively rehearses his behavior in a sequential or systematic way.* (Clements and Alexander 1975, 7)

Another variation is simulation training, which allows parents to learn in an arranged environment approximating as closely as possible the realities of their lives with their children and others. Through simulation techniques, parents not only learn the details of specific techniques but also learn to interact productively.

In simulation training, parents act both as players and observers. Members of the training group suggest simulation topics that are significant to them. Audiovisual and videotaping methods can provide useful feedback during the training.

Because simulation training can respond to parents' individual needs and interests. Wagonseller and Mori (1977) recommended its use in small groups of parents of exceptional children. It enhances parents' motivation, encourages both cognitive and affective self-evaluation, and adapts to parents' speeds, levels, and styles of learning. Perhaps most important, simulation allows parents to try out interactions in a safe environment, where they need not fear harming or embarrassing their children or themselves.

Parent Roles

Parents as Paraprofessionals

Parents can improve their behavior management and instructional skills in a variety of classroom and school functions. While improving their personal competencies, parents can also be instrumental in improving classroom and school services for their children (Shea and Bauer 1987).

Paraprofessionals in the classroom relieve the teacher of many routine but necessary tasks, freeing the teacher to plan, coordinate, and supervise instruction. With the extra time, teachers can personalize and individualize the child's educational program.

Wood (1975) recommended that parents be trained as *support teachers* for severely emotionally disturbed children. In this role, parents are responsible for a broad spectrum of helping activities, including the instruction of children under supervision. Serving as instructors, parents not only support the teacher's efforts to individualize the children's programs but also acquire teaching skills they can use at home.

Soar and Kaplan (1976) developed a taxonomy of the activities teachers and paraprofessionals can share in the classroom (Figure 9.3). A comprehensive list of classroom activities, the taxonomy offers a common basis for teachers' and paraprofessionals' discussions. They can then assign or take on responsibilities according to

Chapter Nine • School, Home, and Community Programs **223**

their training, experience, competency, and legal and ethical responsibilities. Parents and teachers may want to add or delete activities in the taxonomy to fit the children and setting in which they are functioning. When completing the taxonomy, parents and teachers should perform the following tasks independently:

1. Study the activities in the taxonomy and decide which should be modified, added, or eliminated.
2. Place a check mark (√) by those activities for which they take personal responsibility.
3. Write S next to those activities for which they share responsibility.
4. Leave unmarked those activities whose assignment is unclear.

After marking the form individually, the teacher and paraprofessional meet for the following purposes:

1. Discuss each activity to ensure mutual understanding of the parameters of the activity and each person's responsibility.
2. Reach consensus on each shared (S) and unmarked activity.
3. Complete the form and post it in the classroom or office for reference and review.

FIGURE 9.3 • *Classroom Activities*

Teacher	Paraprofessional (Parent)		Both
		Housekeeping Activities	
_____	_____	Dusting, cleaning, and so on	_____
_____	_____	Helping children with clothing	_____
_____	_____	Arranging furniture	_____
_____	_____	Keeping order	_____
_____	_____	Posting items on the bulletin board	_____
_____	_____	Monitoring children on the bus, during lunch and snacks, in the lavatory, and during recess	_____
_____	_____	Other: _____	_____
		Clerical Activities	
_____	_____	Collecting money	_____
_____	_____	Collecting papers	_____

(cont.)

FIGURE 9.3 *Continued*

____ ____	Taking attendance	____
____ ____	Duplicating and distributing materials	____
____ ____	Filling out routine reports	____
____ ____	Administering tests	____
____ ____	Taking inventory	____
____ ____	Maintaining an instructional materials file	____
____ ____	Keeping records	____
____ ____	Other: _____	____

Materials Activities

____ ____	Locating materials	____
____ ____	Making bibliographies	____
____ ____	Setting up displays and demonstrations (preparing materials)	____
____ ____	Other: _____	____

Instructional Activities

Teaching

____ ____	Tutoring	____
____ ____	Organizing play activities	____
____ ____	Selecting and developing materials	____
____ ____	Large or small group teaching	____
____ ____	Disciplining	____
____ ____	Organizing groups for instruction	____
____ ____	Making judgments	____
____ ____	Other: _____	____

Planning

____ ____	Planning and organizing meetings	____
____ ____	Planning bulletin boards	____
____ ____	Planning small or large group lessons	____
____ ____	Other: _____	____

Evaluation Activities

____ ____	Grading papers	____
____ ____	Keeping anecdotal records	____
____ ____	Making systematic observations	____
____ ____	Organizing case studies	____
____ ____	Evaluating materials	____
____ ____	Making tests	____
____ ____	Interpreting test results	____
____ ____	Other: _____	____

Source: Adapted from Soar and Kaplan 1976, 77.

Soar and Kaplan suggested that parents and teachers review the taxonomy three or four times annually to assure that they are meeting their responsibilities. This review allows changes in responsibilities that may be necessary to respond to changes in the student population, personnel training and experience, instructional materials, student objectives, and work setting. Teachers should not assign all routine, unstimulating activities to parents. Both parties should share desirable and undesirable classroom activities.

Parents who function as paraprofessionals need training. Croft (1979) suggested the following sequence of activities for training parents in their duties.

1. *School orientation.* This training session offers general background information about the school program, its practices and procedures, and provides an informal welcome and get-acquainted time, a tour of the school and facilities, refreshments, and a question-and-answer period.
2. *Small-group meetings.* In these sessions, parents discuss their feelings and expectations and learn their roles and duties. An experienced parent paraprofessional currently teaching in the school can lead the discussion.
3. *Practice observations and visits.* Trainees, as individuals or in a small group, observe classroom procedures and discuss their observations with a teacher or qualified professional or paraprofessional.
4. *Classroom assistance.* After training with a supervisor, who may be a trained parent paraprofessional, parents follow the daily routine in their assigned classrooms. At the end of the session, supervisor and trainee evaluate and discuss the trainee's performance.
5. *Group meeting.* After all parents have had at least one opportunity to assist in the classroom and discuss their experiences, they meet together to reassess and clarify their duties as paraprofessionals.
6. *Revision of work schedule.* Periodically, professionals and paraprofessionals meet as a group to evaluate and revise as necessary the parent-teacher relationship in the classroom.

Informal discussions and individual conferences may supplement these formal training sessions if they will benefit the trainees.

In addition to serving as teacher assistants, parents of children with exceptionalities can serve as assistants for field trips, parties, and special events; and as library, clerical, lunchroom or cafeteria, and playground and physical education assistants. They can help various specialized personnel also, such as music and art teachers, physical and occupational therapists, psychologists and counselors, social workers, and others.

Parents as Instructors

Frequently, educators in both regular and special education settings overlook parents' skills and talents in children's formal educational process. Often, parents' vocations or avocations prepare them to contribute significantly to instructional programs. Much depends on the students' instructional objectives and the teacher's ability to integrate the lesson content into the curriculum.

With minimal guidance, parents can become effective instructors. They can prepare and conduct brief lessons or more extended minicourses related to their occupations, hobbies, and other interests.

Bauer and associates (1987) provide two examples of activities in which parents serve as instructors. In the first, parents serve as teachers of minicourses or leisure activities. In this activity, parents bring some area of personal or professional expertise into the classroom or school to share with students. Bauer and associates suggest that to initiate the activity, teachers send the parents an interest survey or letter to ascertain their willingness to share their interests, hobbies, or talents. In an individual meeting with the parents who agree to participate, the details of the course (number of days, dates, information students need prior to the presentation, materials, costs, etc.) are discussed. It is prudent to review the proposed activity prior to the presentation; parents may have too much or too little information for the time allotted. After the course is completed, evaluations can be made by using parents' and students' responses to the activity. The teacher should follow up the activity with a letter of appreciation to the parent.

The second activity suggested by Bauer and associates is the "Parent Career Day." In this activity, parents discuss their occupation with the students. To organize a parent career day, teachers should send an interest survey or letter to the parents to determine their interest and willingness to participate and present a lecture to the class. Again, preplanning the presentation with the parents is recommended.

Parents as Volunteers

Parent volunteers can contribute significantly to the quality of the services offered to their children. Along with teachers and paraprofessionals, they can become an integral part of the child's educational team.

The National School Volunteer Program cited four reasons for using volunteers in the classroom and school (Greer 1978):

1. Relieving the professional staff of nonteaching duties
2. Providing needed services to individual children to supplement the work of the classroom teacher
3. Enriching the experiences of children beyond that normally available in school
4. Building better understanding of school problems among citizens and stimulating widespread citizen support for public education.

Though parents are the most frequent volunteers, siblings, elementary and secondary school students, college students, senior citizens, business and professional people, members of church and civic groups, and other members of the community also volunteer in the schools. The major prerequisite is a willingness to help children with exceptionalities. Volunteers should be personable in their relationships with others, dependable in discharging assigned duties, and willing and able to follow instructions.

The special education parent volunteer works under the direct supervision of a professional teacher, therapist, administrator, or other qualified staff person—and occasionally under a teacher assistant. Volunteers generally work on task-specific activities, either individually or in small groups. For example, volunteers may check a child's home or class assignments, assist during field trips and special events, serve as a companion or guide for a child, reinforce acceptable behavior and work, or prepare instructional materials and equipment (Greer 1978).

Volunteers should participate in a brief preservice training program, as well as in on-the-job training. Preservice training workshops introduce volunteers to special education, school, and classroom processes and procedures and spell out their roles and functions. The training emphasizes the importance of confidentiality and attendance and offers an opportunity to discuss the program with experienced volunteers and to visit the classroom to observe and discuss the program with the teacher. On-the-job training is a continuous process in which volunteers learn the specific activities for which they will be responsible.

The prudent teacher matches tasks with the volunteers' abilities, interests, and special skills. A questionnaire completed by potential volunteers during recruitment or preservice training can help teachers assign tasks and develop schedules (Figure 9.4). Individual interviews can supplement questionnaire data if necessary.

Bauer and associates (1987) suggested several ways that parent volunteers can help: as room parents, as classroom and school volunteers while children are present, as classroom and school volunteers after school hours, and as assistants to perform tasks related to the classroom and school in the home. Table 9.1 lists activities in each of these categories suggested by several authors (Stahl 1977; Bauer et al. 1987; Shea and Bauer 1987).

Parent partner programs offer other volunteer opportunities.

FIGURE 9.4 • *Parent-Volunteer Questionnaire*

Date _____
Parents' Names _____
Child's Name _____ Telephone Number _____
Teacher's Name _____

Parents! We need your help. Please consider helping with the activities and projects listed on this questionnaire. Check all those activities for which you can volunteer service. Your participation will help us provide an interesting, stimulating, individualized educational program for your children.

Mother   Father

_____   _____   I would like to assist in the classroom on a regular basis. The times I have available are:

                  Days   Hours
                  _____   _____
                  _____   _____

_____   _____   I would like to assist *occasionally* in the classroom.
                  (check one)
                  a.   Contact me _____
                  b.   I will contact the school _____

_____   _____   I would like to assist from my home.

(cont.)

In-Classroom Activities

_____ _____ Read a story to the children.
_____ _____ Assist children in a learning center.
_____ _____ Assist individual children with learning and remedial tasks.
_____ _____ Assist with the music program.
_____ _____ Assist with the art program.
_____ _____ Assist with the movement activities program.
_____ _____ Work puzzles and play table games with the children.
_____ _____ Help with cooking projects.
_____ _____ Assist with writing activities.
_____ _____ Assist with carpentry projects.
_____ _____ Assist with homemaking projects.
_____ _____ Assist with the care of classroom pets.
_____ _____ Assist with gardening and horticultural projects.
_____ _____ Assist children during recess, snack time, lunch, and free time.
_____ _____ Take a child for a walk.
_____ _____ Assist with field trips.

Home-Based Activities

_____ _____ Make instructional materials: games, flash cards, puppets, costumes, charts.
_____ _____ Type.
_____ _____ Help with costumes for dress-up events.
_____ _____ Cut out and catalog pictures from magazines, catalogs, and newspapers for instructional use.
_____ _____ Help repair classroom furnishings and instructional materials and equipment.
_____ _____ Help construct new furnishings and equipment for the classroom.
_____ _____ Organize parties for birthdays and holidays.
_____ _____ Babysit for parents who are volunteering their service to the classroom.
_____ _____ Care for classroom pets during vacations.
_____ _____ Make props and sets for plays, parties, and special events.
_____ _____ Make room and bulletin board decorations.

(cont.)

FIGURE 9.4 *Continued*

_____ _____ Make posters.

_____ _____ Assemble and staple materials.

_____ _____ Research and organize field trips.

_____ _____ Help plan and conduct parent activities, such as meetings, educational training programs, and conferences.

_____ _____ Research and contact sources for free instructional supplies (computer cards and paper, wood scraps, boxes, carpet, print shop discards, spools, pencils, paper).

_____ _____ Make items to sell for fund raising.

_____ _____ Assist with fund-raising activities.

_____ _____ Plan and organize social events.

What other activities could you help with?

A. In the classroom:

B. At home:

What other family members or friends are interested in volunteering services to the children?

A. _____

B. _____

Your comments, concerns, and questions are welcome.

Teachers may be able to pair parents to help each other with their children. For example, parents may go shopping together, share the names of physicians and dentists who treat children with exceptionalities, attend meetings together for mutual support, or just simply talk about their progress and problems in raising their children.

Teachers should take care to train the partners and supervise their relationship in a partner program. Partner training should remind parents to share but not attempt to solve the other parent's problems, to use active listening skills, to maintain objectivity, and to guard confidentiality. Teachers should meet with parent partners at least once a month to ensure they are exchanging accurate information and building a healthy relationship.

TABLE 9.1 • *Parent-Volunteer Activities*

Room Parents
- Foster working relationships among classroom, school, home, and community workers
- Coordinate parent-volunteer program
    — Recruit volunteers
    — Help in preservice and on-the-job training programs
    — Schedule volunteers
- Oversee classroom, school, and community committees
- Coordinate parties, field trips, special events, student performances, and parent meetings

Classroom Volunteers during School Hours
- Serve as managers of learning centers
    — Schedule, supervise, and assist children
    — Prepare materials and equipment
- Assist with arts and crafts, music, carpentry, sewing, gardening, cooking, science, and so on
- Assist with recreational activities, large-group activities
- Assist individual children in reading, writing, spelling, and arithmetic
- Organize and supervise snack time, free time, and so on
- Supervise personal hygiene activities (handwashing, toileting)
- Prepare and operate audiovisual equipment
- Assist with routine evaluation of home and class assignments

Parent Volunteers
- Parent-volunteer activities in the school *during* school hours may include the following:
    — Serve as bulletin board and display designers and constructors
    — Assist in researching, organizing, and supervising field trips
    — Supervise cafeteria, lunchroom, playground, hallways
    — Locate reference materials and other resources needed by the professional staff
    — Assist in the library, audiovisual center, physical education equipment center, and office
    — Accompany teachers on home visits
    — Serve as interpreter for non-English-speaking parents
    — Serve as manager of all-school learning center
    — Coordinate all-school special event, festival, and holiday activities
    — Assist in the evaluation of materials, curriculum, and equipment
    — Serve as clerical assistant (typing, filing, duplicating, counting and depositing money, taking attendance, taking lunch count, answering the phone, sorting mail, scheduling appointments)
- Parent-volunteer activities in the classroom and school *after* school hours may include the following:
    — Create and construct learning materials (games, flashcards, individual project charts, study carrels, filmstrips, movies, slide presentations)
    — Conduct and supervise tutoring programs
    — Care for equipment, materials, furnishings, physical facilities
    — Clean, paint, and repair materials, equipment

(Continued)

TABLE 9.1 *Continued*

—Confer with other parents and community persons related to school and classroom programs
—Serve on various education-related committees
- Parent-volunteer activities *in the home and community* may include the following:
  —Organize and operate tutoring centers
  —Construct and repair instructional materials
  —Coordinate and supervise Saturday and evening field trips and special events
  —Locate community resources for utilization in school and classroom programs
  —Organize and conduct fund-raising activities
  —Serve as members and officers in various community organizations, agencies, boards, and committees bearing on the welfare of exceptional children
  —Participate in groups that lobby at the local, regional, state, and federal levels for the benefit of exceptional children

Sources: Adapted from Stahl 1977; Bauer et al., 1987; Shea and Bauer 1987.

Parents can help train other parents in more direct ways as well. Hall, Grinstead, Collier, and Hall (1980) used parents to implement their "Responsive Parenting" program. In this program, parents who had successfully completed at least one behavior change project, had demonstrated a grasp of the principles and practices of behavior modification, and had shown enthusiasm became apprentice group leaders. As apprentices, they took on increasing responsibilities for a small instructional group. If they attended meetings regularly, gave appropriate instructions and feedback to the members, and helped each member produce workable behavior change programs, they became group leaders. After directing three successful groups, parents could apprentice as program directors.

Hall and associates suggested several advantages of this approach. Parents can relate to parent trainers as people who have "been there." In addition, parents are less likely to be in awe of a parent trainer than of a professional and are less likely to reject a program as impractical if another parent has used it successfully. Using parents as trainers also helps ease the personnel shortage and reduce the cost of the training program.

However, Hall and associates cautioned against the indiscriminate use of parents as trainers. Their program was geared to middle-class parents with strong academic and social skills, who already possessed many skills for leading groups. Another study of a program using parent trainers yielded inconsistent results (Edgar et al.

1981). In this study, some group participants rated parent communication skills low, though they accepted information they received from parent trainers as correct.

Parents on Committees

Parent participation as chairpersons or members of classroom and school committees can contribute significantly to the exceptional child's education. Through committee work, parents not only contribute to the classroom and school but also receive indirect training in serving exceptional children's needs through program development, operation, staffing, and evaluation. They develop appreciation for staffing concerns, curriculum development, fiscal exigencies, materials and equipment needs, and other demands of instructional programming.

An advisory committee can serve as a liaison between school or classroom and home and community, functioning as a permanent parent-to-parent communications committee to announce meetings, special events, legislative happenings, personnel changes, and so on. The school or classroom advisory committee can assume responsibility, in cooperation with the professional staff, for organizing and directing several ad hoc or temporary committees.

Ad hoc committees, like advisory committees, should be broadly representative of the parents in the classroom or school. They form to accomplish specific tasks and disband once they have attained their objectives and have reported to the advisory committee. Ad hoc committees are essentially "working" (Shea and Bauer 1987) or "action" (Pasanella and Volkmor 1977) groups with limited functions and short lives. Service on ad hoc committees is ideal for busy parents with limited time to devote to committee work.

Berger (1981) conducted an informal survey of 350 parents that duplicated a 1977 Gallup poll of public attitudes toward public schools. Of the respondents, 82 percent indicated a willingness to serve on one or more of the following committees:

Discipline and related problems	Curriculum
Student-teacher relations	Teacher evaluation
Home study and work habits	Career education
Extracurricular activities	Athletic programs
Student assessment and test results	Handicapped students
Educational innovations	Public relations of schools

Community use of school buildings	Work-study programs
Educational costs and school finance	Student dropouts
Education for citizenship	School facilities
Progress of recent graduates	School transportation

Parent committees may undertake a wide range of activities. Committees may be involved in fund raising or planning special projects (parties, field trips, open houses, dramatic presentations). They may collaborate on curriculum and program evaluation and may review textbooks and instructional materials. Committees may be responsible for developing newsletters and performing public relations activities.

Whether serving on a classroom, school advisory, or ad hoc committee, committee members can benefit from the following guidelines (Pasanella and Volkmor 1977):

- Remember the committee's purpose and objectives. Stick with the task at hand.
- Remember that people's attitudes toward exceptionality change slowly. Be patient.
- Be confident in the committee's ability to accomplish the assigned task. Approach the task positively.
- Start small. Take one step at a time.
- Function within the system. Become an integral part of the classroom or school.
- Seek financial, administrative, informational, and other assistance when necessary.
- Use committee expertise at home first. Once the task is accomplished, the committee can help other schools, classrooms, and communities.
- Do not impede progress by becoming unnecessarily aggressive or antagonistic. However, do not be too passive.

Parents as Home-Based Teachers

In recent years, teachers have increasingly advocated home programs for children with exceptionalities. Programs to train parents as home-based teachers vary greatly in structure, content, and personnel requirements. Programs may simply teach parents how to monitor their children's work on teacher-assigned projects, or they may train parents to teach highly specific readiness skills and academic knowledge to supplement or reinforce school instruction. Content may emphasize parent-child interpersonal interaction or may focus on instruction in specific skills.

One of the more traditional ways parents work with their children in the home is parent-supervised home study or homework. Horner (1987) suggests that there are several reasons parents become discouraged when supervising their children's homework. The children may experience failure at home similar to the failure they experience at school, frustrating both the parents and the child. Parents may not have consistent teaching skills; thus, the potential for tension between parent and child exists. Parents may have personal time contraints, and the child may be deprived of time needed for leisure and relaxation. Finally, parents may feel guilty if they are unable to help the child.

Parents may also serve as tutors for their children. Mehan and White (1988) used parents as home instructors in a Chapter I compensatory education program. Parents worked with their children for fifteen minutes at least three days a week, and they submitted a tutoring log to document participation. The parents were trained and received ongoing support in meetings with the staff. Mehan and White found that children exhibited long-lasting improvement in reading ability, as measured by a group-standardized reading test. They concluded that parent tutoring can be an effective supplement to a compensatory education program. However, a substantial number of the eligible parents did not participate in the tutoring program.

Thurston (1989) suggests four steps for working with parents to make home-tutoring experiences successful. The first step involves parents in the selection of materials. Parents, according to Thurston, are more comfortable practicing previously learned skills with their children than teaching them new skills. The parents may collaborate in selecting both the subject and the materials. Materials should not be too difficult nor present so much new information that the child is overwhelmed.

Once the materials are selected, Thurston suggests that parents be provided with basic instruction in tutoring. Parents should engage in tutoring with their child at a regular time and in a specific place. Sessions should be ten or fifteen minutes in duration and without interruptions. The tutoring time should be a pleasant experience for both parent and child, with the child receiving praise for effort and correct responses.

The third step involves instructing the parents in error correction procedures. The parents are taught strategies to help children learn when they are doing a good job and when they are making errors. Simple guidelines for giving praise are taught, as well as a correction procedure that provides the student with the appropriate response. When the child is not concentrating, the parent is instructed to remain supportive and positive, slow down the pace of the lesson, review the directions, and give praise.

The final step suggested by Thurston involves record keeping. The parents are urged to keep tutoring periods brief and to document progress. Children may keep a listing of new words, a chart of spelling scores, or a similar system to represent their efforts and progress.

Since parents traditionally help their children with homework or tutor them, several professionals have developed innovative procedures for helping children at home. Three such procedures are the "Writer's Suitcase" (Bushman, Costanzo, and Engle 1989), the "Transactional Family Systems Model" (Hedlund 1989), and "Coincidental Teaching" (Schulze, Rule, and Innocenti 1989).

The Writer's Suitcase involves parents in their children's early literacy experiences. The suitcase is a box, case, or any other type of container packed with materials for writing, which is taken home by each student in the class in turn. It contains a variety of supplies needed to write books, letters, poems, picture stories, sentences, paragraphs, and words. There are different types of paper, pencils, crayons, stapler, paper clips, and bookbinding supplies; folders for the student's finished work; and a parent's evaluation form. The purpose of the suitcase is to facilitate communication between parents and school personnel. Parents are encouraged to share the suitcase experience with their child, so that they will be able to see firsthand the child's capabilities and progress. Because the suitcase contains a variety of materials at various developmental levels, parents can learn what materials are appropriate for their child. Active participation is encouraged between parent and child and between parent and teacher. In addition, both parent and child experience that writing can be fun. A sample evaluation form for the Writer's Suitcase project is presented in Figure 9.5.

The Transactional Family System Model (Hedlund 1989) offers a home-based intervention system for severely handicapped, medically fragile infants and their families. The goal of this program is to foster positive interaction between parents and their babies by helping parents become sensitive to their infants' behavioral cues. In the project, four steps are used to involve the parents in working with their child. First, the parents are educated about the significance of

FIGURE 9.5 • *Writer's Suitcase Evaluation Form*

Dear Parents:

Thanks for working on Writer's Suitcase with your child. Could you please answer a few questions to help us keep Writer's Suitcase working for our children?

How long did you work together?

What materials did your child like the best?

Were there any other materials you seemed to need that were not included?

Do you have anything you'd like to share about working with your child? Thanks much!

Ms. C.

---

their baby's unique body language. They are then helped to become attuned to their personal interactional style and learn how that style affects the child. In the third step, professionals in the program provide parents with guided practice and encouragement to help them adapt their interactional styles as the infant develops. Finally, through the project, parents develop a sense of competence, which helps them to see their child as a competent, developing individual.

In Coincidental Teaching (Schulze, Rule, and Innocenti 1989), teachers help parents identify opportunities to teach particular social skills to their children in a variety of natural settings with a variety of people. The program is based on the assumption that when social skills are taught "coincidentally" in many situations, they generalize more readily to other situations and settings. In this project, small groups of parents are instructed in the use of the naturally occurring opportunities during the course of a day to encourage their children to practice social skills. The teacher helps parents select appropriate social skills to teach, instructs them on how to recognize opportunities to teach the selected skills, and shows them how to prompt (graduated from verbal, to modeling, to physical guidance) and praise. In a study of seventeen families, it was found that, on average, the families conducted between nine and twenty coincidental teaching episodes a week.

Vantour and Stewart-Kurker (1980) developed a lending library to motivate parents and children in home study programs. They rewrote the instructions in commercially available instructional materials to make them easy to use by parents and children at home.

Teachers wrote *prescriptions* to specify the book, cards, games, and other materials the child should take home from the library. The system allowed teachers to coordinate library materials with classroom lessons.

Parent Resources

The Parent Resource Center

Establishing a parent resource center is an effective way to meet the informational and social-emotional needs of the parents (Edmister 1977; Karnes and Franke 1978). The center staff should select materials and equipment carefully to respond to the parent users' needs.

Borrowers can use materials, such as the following, at the center or borrow them for home or classroom.

- *For parents.* Books, pamphlets, periodicals, filmstrips and audiotapes, cassettes, films, and teaching packages on a broad range of topics related to raising children with exceptionalities.
- *For teachers.* Textbooks and journals on exceptionality, parent education, and training materials and kits.
- *For children.* Toys, books, periodicals, records, and educational games.

The center can also provide important services to parents, children, and teachers, serving as a facility for individual study, small-group meetings, conferences, informal discussions, and social activities. If located in a standard classroom, staff can furnish it with library facilities such as bookcases, storage cabinets, audiovisual equipment, and tables and chairs. One area of the room can serve as an audiovisual viewing area, another as a small-group discussion center, and another as a private place for individual conferences or study activities. The center can also include a play or discovery area for children.

Edmister (1977) recommended that the center contain the following equipment: film projector and screen, filmstrip and slide projector, videotape monitor, cassette recorder and tapes, typewriter, record player, a desk and chair for the staff person and storage, file cabinet, library tables and chairs, and display stands.

The center may share this equipment with school personnel. Regularly scheduled hours, including some late afternoon and evening hours for parents and teachers unable to visit the center during traditional working hours, are important, as is a standard lending policy. The center might lend books and pamphlets for two weeks, for example, toys and games for one week, and films, videotapes, and filmstrips for two days. Ideally, a parent-professional committee supervises the center, with day-to-day operation the responsibility of parent volunteers.

Parents as Resources

As parents become empowered, collaborating as full partners in the education of their children, they gain specific expertise. Parents may be resources for other parents and may contribute in both training and providing support to other parents.

Ball, Coyne, Jarvis, and Pease (1984) recruited the graduates of a community-based training course for parents of developmentally disabled children as training assistants for additional courses. The training program consisted of parents applying behavioral principles and developing intervention programs for teaching self-help skills and modifying behavior problems. Ball and associates used these parents in troubleshooting and developing intervention strategies collaboratively with other parents. In their study, Ball and associates found that no decrement in teaching effectiveness occurred as the result of substituting a parent volunteer for a professional. In addition, using parents was cost-effective. Parents were also perceived as best able in lending credibility to the project and motivating other parents to participate. The parent trainers furnished insights from the parent's point of view, gave practical suggestions, and provided real-life examples. Ball and associates cautioned, however, that parents must be able to generalize novel problems to be good trainers.

Parents can provide support for other parents both in group settings and individually. Kratochvil and Devereux (1988) suggest that parents of handicapped children provide unique and highly valued support for each other. Parent associations are a source of support, especially in urban centers. It helps parents to see other parents who are coping and to share frustrations that arise from caring for a handicapped child. Parents of older handicapped children may find the benefits of parent associations diminish over time, however. Although long-term members see value in helping and encouraging new parents, their own needs with older handicapped children may remain unmet. Kratochvil and Devereux suggest that when long-term members experience renewed grief, they tend to view the grief as a breakdown in their adjustment, something difficult to admit or share, thereby acting in accordance with the theory that grief has closure and adjustment should be continuous.

Bauer and associates (1987) suggest that parents may serve as partners for parents new to special education. They recommend that teachers approach a small number of positive parents who are willing to function as partners to parents whose children have just recently begun receiving services. Guidelines should be set regarding the parent-partner contact; for example, new parents with concerns or questions may be given the telephone number of a preselected parent partner. Parents who are serving as partners should be alerted to possible uncomfortable questions. In addition, teachers should be aware of the need to terminate relationships if they become unhealthy. Parent partners should be aware that they are enlisted in the program not to counsel but to provide support and information to parents.

Summary

This chapter discusses ways for parents to participate in classroom, school, home, and community programs. Parents should receive training before they work in the school or teach their children at home. The chapter discusses several training techniques, including observation, instructional coaching, modeling, and role playing. Parents can play many roles at school and at home. They can work as paraprofessionals, instructors, and volunteers in the classroom; serve on classroom and school committees; and participate as home-based instructors and home study supervisors. The chapter describes appropriate activities for each role and identifies programs and techniques available to help parents be effective in each setting. The final pages of the chapter discuss resources for parent training, including parent resource centers and parents as resources.

Exercises and Discussion Topics

1. Observe a teacher and paraprofessional working in a classroom or resource room. Note each person's role and function; then interview both about their views of their roles. Using the information from the observations and interviews, develop a taxonomy of classroom or resource room functions. Compare your taxonomy with the Soar and Kaplan taxonomy in Figure 9.3.

2. Develop an agenda for a parent-paraprofessional training program for your classroom or a hypothetical classroom. Present the agenda to your study group for discussion and evaluation.

3. Develop and administer a questionnaire to several parents on their instructional and volunteer contributions to a classroom program. Develop a plan for incorporating the results into a training program.

4. Using data on a specific child and parent, develop a series of five lessons for parents to teach their children at home.

5. Develop a plan for using parent committees in your classroom and school. Determine each committee's purpose, role, function, composition, and operation. Critique your plan with your study group.

6. Research and write a brief paper on "parents in classroom, school, home, and community education programs."

References

Baker, B. L., and M. C. McCurry. 1984. School-based parent training: An alternative for parents predicted to demonstrate low teaching proficiency following group training. *Education and Training of the Mentally Retarded* 19: 261–67.

Ball, T. S., A. Coyne, R. M. Jarvis, and S. S. F. Pease. 1984. Parents of retarded children as teaching assistants for other parents. *Education and Training of the Mentally Retarded* 19: 64–69.

Bauer, A. M., M. Barger, C. Dunn, B. Farrell, K. Goehl, C. Harvey, and T. Whitlow. 1987. *Parent involvement training modules.* Indianapolis: Division of Special Education, Indiana Department of Education.

Berger, E. H. 1981. *Parents as partners in education: The school and home working together.* St. Louis: Mosby.

Blackard, K. 1976. Introduction to the family training program: Working paper, 1–15. Seattle: Experimental Education Unit, Child Development and Mental Retardation Center, University of Washington.

Brown, S. L. 1978. A structure for early parent involvement. In *Parents on the team*, eds. S. L. Brown and M. S. Moersch, 113–122. Ann Arbor: University of Michigan.

Bushman, S., T. Costanzo, and S. Engle. 1989 Writer's suitcase. Unpublished manuscript, University of Cincinnati.

Clements, J. E., and R. N. Alexander. 1975. Parent training: Bringing it all back home. *Focus on Exceptional Children* 7 (1): 1–12.

Croft, D. J. 1979. *Parent and teachers: A resource book for home, school, and community relations.* Belmont, Calif.: Wadsworth.

Edgar, E., T. Singer, C. Ritchie, and M. Heggelund. 1981. Parents as facilitators in developing an individual approach to parent involvement. *Behavioral Disorders* 6: 122–27.
Edmister, P. 1977. Establishing a parent education resource center. *Childhood Education* 54:62–66.
Greer, J. V. 1978. Using paraprofessionals and volunteers in special education. *Focus on Exceptional Children* 10 (6): 1–15.
Hall, M. C., J. Grinstead, H. Collier, and R. Hall. 1980. Responsive parenting: A preventive program which incorporates parents training parents. *Education and Treatment of Children* 3: 239–59.
Haring, N. G. 1976. *Systematic instructional procedures: An instructional hierarchy.* Final report of a program for the National Institute of Education, Washington, D.C.
Hedlund, R. 1989. Fostering positive social interactions between parents and infants. *Teaching Exceptional Children* 21 (4): 45–48.
Horner, C. M. 1987. Homework: A way to teach problem solving. *Academic Therapy* 22: 239–44.
Karnes, M. B., and B. Branke. 1978. *Family involvement.* Urbana: Institute for Child Behavior and Development, University of Illinois.
Kratochvil, M. S., and S. A. Devereux. 1988. Counseling needs of parents of handicapped children. *Social Casework* 69 (7): 420–26.
Mehran, M., and K. R. White. 1988. Parent tutoring as a supplement to compensatory education for first-grade children. *Remedial and Special Education* 9 (3): 35–41.
Miller, W. H. 1975. *Systematic parent training: Procedures, cases, and issues.* Champaign, Ill.: Research Press.
Pasanella, A. L., and C. B. Volkmor. 1977. *To parents of children with special needs: A manual on parent involvement in educational programming.* Los Angeles: California Regional Resource Center, University of Southern California.
Shea, T. M., and A. M. Bauer. 1987. *Teaching children and youth with behavioral disorders.* 2d ed. Englewood Cliffs, N.J.: Prentice-Hall.
Shulze, K. A., S. Rule, and M. S. Innocenti. 1989. Coincidental teaching: Parents promoting social skills at home. *Teaching Exceptional Children* 21 (2): 24–27.
Soar, R. S., and L. Kaplan. 1976. Taxonomy of classroom activities. In *Building effective home-school relationships,* eds. I. J. Gordon and Breivogel, W. F. Boston: Allyn and Bacon.
Stahl, N. A. 1977. Twenty-five ways to harness parent power. *Early Years* 8 (2): 56.
Thurston, L. P. 1989. Helping parents tutor their children: A success story. *Academic Therapy* 24 (5): 579–87.
Vantour, J. A., and E. A. Stewart-Kurker. 1980. A library for exceptional children promotes home-school cooperation. *Teaching Exceptional Children* 13 (1): 4–7.
Wagonseller, B., and A. Mori. 1977. Applications of the simulation tech-

nique as a training instrument for teachers and students. *Focus on Exceptional Children* 9 (5): 10–12.

Walker, J. E., and T. M. Shea. 1988. *Behavior management: A practical approach for educators.* 4th ed. Columbus, Ohio: Charles E. Merrill.

Webster, E. J. 1977. *Counseling with parents of handicapped children: Guidelines for improving communications.* New York: Grune and Stratton.

Wood, M. M. 1975. *Developmental therapy: A textbook for teachers as therapists for emotionally disturbed young children.* Baltimore: University Park Press.

SECTION THREE

Special Issues in Collaboration

Throughout this text, we have discussed the recurrent theme of the family as a complex social system. Rather than being seen individuals, parents and children are seen as members of social systems, which must be understood if effective parent-teacher collaboration programs are to be developed.

As discussed in Chapter 1, the family as a social system is changing. Family conditions are quite different today than they were when Public Law 94-142 came into effect in 1975. Today, most children live in single-parent or blended families. These families confront limited resources, and often, maintaining the family must take precedence over parents' concerns for their children's educational program. Many children spend more time in substitute care and in school than with their parents.

Society is becoming more ethnically diverse. Hodgkinson (1985) suggests that by the year 2000, one in three Americans will be nonwhite. Moreover, projections suggest that by the year 2020, the Hispanic population will equal or surpass the African-American population of the United States.

An issue that affects all families, regardless of their type, conditions, or ethnicity, is life transitions. As families develop over time, they go through changes or transitions. Some transitions are predictable; others are not. During these transitions, stress often occurs in the family. Specific plans and activities can be developed to mitigate this stress.

In this section, we address societal issues that impact on collaboration. In Chapter 10, we discuss issues related to families from diverse cultures and the collaboration with siblings and extended family members. The issues of children in substitute care and family involvement in child maltreatment are also discussed. In Chapter 11, we discuss the role of transitions and collaborative activities that mitigate the stress unique to families at these times. Chapter 12 applies the materials presented throughout the text in an extended illustration of a parent-teacher collaboration program in a special education setting.

CHAPTER TEN

Special Issues in Family Collaboration

Mr. L., parent of an eleven-year-old boy with behavioral disorders, who had recently gained custody of his son (the child had been removed from his mother's home and placed in a foster home):

> *"I offer this advice to parents trying to put their families back together. Don't feel sorry for yourself. Do not throw away all those dreams that you had for the little baby in your arms in the hospital. Don't sell this child short. You're all not going to die from this. So why should we despair and throw away our hope? Aspire to hope. You'll make it."*

Chapter Topics and Objectives

Several issues complicate collaboration with some families of children with exceptionalities. Nonmajority culture families have special values aand interaction patterns that must be addressed for effective collaboration to occur. In addition, due to changes in family structure that have occurred in recent years, siblings and extended family members may be the effective agents in the lives of some children.

Family systems may include interaction patterns that are abusive to children. In some family systems, the child must be removed for his or her safety, and the family members must learn appropriate parenting skills. In these situations, children may not be living with their biological family. Unique issues related to separation and loss exist for children in substitute care and in families involved in child maltreatment.

In this chapter, we will:

- Describe issues related to families from diverse cultures.
- Discuss collaboration with siblings and extended family members of children with exceptionalities.

- Explore issues related to children in substitute care.
- Explore issues related to children in families in which they are maltreated.
- Discuss counseling for families with children with exceptionalities.

Families from Diverse Cultures

In a discussion of the current state of collaboration between home and school, Lightfoot (1981) discussed boundary setting or territoriality between parents and teachers. Territoriality exists, she suggests, because of stereotypes about minority parents and teachers. Schools, she contends, organize public ritualistic occasions such as PTA meetings, open houses, or newsletters that permit little or no true collaboration, negotiation, or criticism between parents and teachers. Interactions between parents and teachers tend to be little more than institutionalized means for establishing boundaries under the guise of polite conversation and collaboration. In work with minority families, territoriality must be diminished before true collaboration can take place.

Teachers must be competent to address the specific needs of their culturally different students. Cross (1988) offers a framework for understanding the knowledge and skills needed by educators serving minority children. There are five keys to the provision of culturally competent services:

1. An awareness and acceptance of ethnic difference. The special educator must acknowledge cultural differences and become aware of how they affect the helping process. Teachers should accept that each culture finds some behaviors, interactions, or values more important and desirable than others, and that there may be a mismatch between the teacher's and the family's perceptions.

2. Self-awareness of one's personal culture. Teachers should examine how they define family, identify desirable life goals, and view students and behavioral problems from their personal cultural perspective.

3. Recognition of the dynamics of differences. Special educators and families bring to any interaction a unique history of interactions with each other's cultural group and the influences of current political relationships between those groups. Collaborators must recognize culturally prescribed patterns of communication, etiquette, and problem solving. Teachers should recognize that some families exhibit behaviors that are adjustment reactions to living in a culturally foreign environment.

4. *Knowledge of the family's culture.* Teachers should explore the significance of the child's behavior as it relates to his or her cultural group.

5. *Adaptation of skills.* Teachers should adjust the helping process to compensate for cultural differences. Work with families can incorporate culturally enriching experiences that teach the origins of stereotypes and prejudices. Various activities that are culturally specific should be legitimized and incorporated into collaboration plans.

There are four major cultural groups in U.S. schools: African-American, Hispanic-American, Asian-American, and Native American (Olion and Gillis-Olion 1984). These cultural groups are increasing dramatically, with Hispanics representing the fastest-growing population in the nation. By the year 2000, one-third of the population of the United States will be African-American, Hispanic-American, and Asian-American (Yates 1987).

According to Chavkin (1989), research demonstrates that the notion that minority parents don't care about their children's education is a myth. In a survey of African-American and Hispanic-American parents, results clearly demonstrated that parents, regardless of ethnicity or minority status, were concerned about their children's education. For example, 95 percent of the parents responded "I want to spend time helping my children get the best education" and expressed a strong interest in a variety of roles and activities related to their children's education. Minority parents were interested in being involved in school decisions and evaluation (Williams and Chavkin 1987).

African-Americans

Lightfoot (1978) reported that the educational values of African-American families and white middle-class teachers were not seriously mismatched. Both groups valued education, but both reported misperceptions of the other group's values. When African-American parents did not participate in school events, teachers assumed that the parents were apathetic rather than that the parents were simply unable to attend or had been excluded from participation in the past. African-American parents reported that the teachers did not believe that their children could achieve in school. Developing involvement, Lightfoot reports, is a slow and tentative process.

Comer (1980) found that collaboration develops slowly among both parents and teachers. However, parents did collaborate on three levels: as members of curriculum, personnel, and decision-making committees; as tutors and assistants on field trips; and as participants in activities such as fund raisers, social events, and conferences.

Hispanic-Americans

Lynch and Stein (1987) reported that Hispanic families were satisfied with their children's special education program. They were less knowledgeable and less involved in their children's education than the parents of Anglo and Black students receiving similar services.

Language is a serious barrier to the involvement of Hispanic-American parents in their children's education. Lynch and Stein (1987) suggest several ways to involve families from diverse linguistic and cultural backgrounds as collaborators in their children's education:

- Analyze existing parent involvement and determine the difference between the current program and the needs of the cultural community to be served.
- Develop a position paper and invite leaders of the various cultural groups and organizations to support the parent-teacher collaboration effort.
- Develop grant applications that support the employment and training of parents from various cultural groups as liaisons between school and parents.
- Work with other community groups and organizations to disseminate information and training about special education.
- Develop training packages with nontechnical print materials in the appropriate language. Make these materials available in local churches, community centers, markets, and other businesses.
- Provide in-service programs to school personnel that describe and sensitize them to cultural and linguistic differences.
- Recruit and employ school personnel who represent a wide range of cultural and linguistic backgrounds.

Asian-Americans

Chan (1986) suggests that family pride and shame have an impact on the functioning of Asian-American families. Individual academic achievements promote family pride; negatively valued behaviors, such as handicapping conditions, result in collective shame. Asian-Americans' great respect for and confidence in teachers may inhibit communication. Yao (1988) suggests that communicating with teachers may be viewed as disrespectful, as checking up on them. Asian-American parents, sensitive to nonverbal communication, may, as Yao suggests, construe a teacher's causal gestures as an attitude of indifference.

Morrow (1987) has three suggestions for teachers working with Asian-American parents. First, teachers should develop an understanding of the culture's values, because many American values—such as openness, independence, and directness—are not valued by Asian-Americans. Also, teachers should recognize the need for the family to save face, to initiate interactions by "talking around" a subject, and to spend time establishing personal rapport. Morrow's third suggestion is to develop a sense of trust, since Asian-Americans revere education and rarely question an educator's decisions.

Native Americans

Native Americans demonstrate cultural values that may challenge the collaborative efforts of majority culture teachers. Native American families tend to be strongly grounded in tradition. The culture maintains that time is infinite; consequently, students' time may be perceived by others as being used inefficiently and work completed as satisfying present needs rather than future needs. Native American families are typically noncompetitive and often share property and child-raising responsibilities. Specific traditions held by Native American families vary with tribal origins. Uthe-Reyno and MacKinnon (1989) suggest that by visiting students' homes, attending cultural events, and studying native legends, history, and language, teachers can demonstrate respect for the culture of the Native American family.

Low-Income Families

Minority families are frequently residents of low-income areas and live in the inner city. In a study of low-income families,

Brantlinger (1987) found that parents are concerned about the quality of the education their children received, and that they had generally positive attitudes about special education. Negative evaluations of special education classes were situation-specific and not concerned with the child's program in general. Low-income parents, however, were generally unaware of the cascade of services available in special education and were not familiar with concepts such as due process, least restrictive environment, and mainstreaming.

Bermudez and Padron (1988) offer several suggestions for increasing minority parent collaboration in their children's education:

- Encourage parents to view the program as an opportunity.
- Treat parents as interested partners in their children's education.
- Provide specific strategies and skills for social and economic survival.
- Praise and recognize parents' participation.
- Schedule activities when it is most convenient for parents to participate.
- Provide instruction in English as a second language when needed.
- Select topics that increase parents' understanding of the school-home partnership, including bilingual education, parents' rights, health and nutrition, substance abuse, and child development.

Chavkin (1989) reports that though minority parents want to be involved, appropriate structures and strategies do not currently exist for their collaboration. She contends that teachers alone cannot get minority parents involved; rather, attention at the policy-making and school district level is needed. A commitment by individual teachers, however, is a beginning in efforts to challenge current programming that limits the collaboration of parents from diverse cultures.

Collaboration with Siblings and Extended Family Members

Siblings spend a great deal of time with their brother or sister with disabilities and often assume a significant child care role (Weinrott 1974). In some instances, Weinrott suggests, siblings may be more committed, more enthusiastic, and more successful when offering assistance to their brother or sister than other caregivers. Schreibman, O'Neill, and Koegel (1983) suggested that not only can siblings act as effective instructional agents in the home, but they benefit, personally, through increased knowledge and social skills.

Swenson-Pierce, Kohl, and Egel (1987) describe a program in which siblings were taught to work with their brother and sister with severe handicaps. The siblings were successful, using prompts proficiently and consistently. The disabled children increased in independent performance of the taught skills. Swenson-Pierce and associates caution, however, that teachers working with siblings need to be flexible and sensitive to both family and individual needs. Some siblings will not make effective instructional agents, regardless of training. Also, older siblings are more desirable as home teachers; if the siblings are very close in age, problems may arise as a consequence of competition and rivalry.

Milstead (1988) cautioned that the feelings of siblings should be considered in collaboration with families. Siblings may react to the stress resulting from having a disabled family member through changes in behavior or feelings of loneliness, insecurity, or incompetence. Menke (1987), however, in a study of siblings of chronically ill children, found that the school-age child worried about the sibling with the chronic illness. Almost half of the siblings expressed protective concerns about their ill brother or sister. Support group participation may help some siblings live more effectively with their chronically ill brother or sister (Kramer and Moore 1983).

Though grandparents may provide considerable support for the family with an exceptional member, little attention has been given to working with grandparents. George (1988) describes a program for grandparents that emphasized maintaining a positive relationship with the child's parents and their potential helpfulness to the family. In group meetings, therapeutic methods for working with grandparents so that they might provide support for the family were discussed.

Child Maltreatment and Substitute Care

Child Maltreatment

Child abuse is a generic term that includes nonaccidental physical injury, neglect, sexual molestation, and mental injury (Zirpoli 1986). According to Public Law 93-247, child neglect is the physical or mental injury, sexual abuse, negligent treatment, or maltreatment of a child under the age of eighteen by a person who is responsible for the child's welfare under circumstances that indicate that the child's health or welfare is harmed or threatened thereby (in Rose 1980).

Nearly 2 million official reports of child maltreatment were made in the United States in 1985 (American Humane Association 1987). However, the actual incidence of child maltreatment is unknown. Though each state has a reporting procedure as required by Public Law 93-247, statute definitions and reporting procedures vary greatly from state to state (Rose 1980). The incidence of child abuse is difficult to determine because the child may not be taken for medical care, the child may be taken to a different doctor or hospital for each injury, the injury may not be detected, private physicians may not report the abuse, and public health personnel vary in their interpretation of state and local abuse laws (Parke and Collmer 1975).

Child maltreatment is not a single fixed incident but an ongoing interaction between parents and children (Cicchetti, Toth, and Hennessy 1989). In a thorough review of the literature, Youngblade and Belsky (1989) concluded that maltreatment is associated with dysfunctional parent-child relations. The effects of child maltreatment, however, are not limited to family relationships; there are repeated indications that maltreatment is associated with problems in peer relations.

Youngblade and Belsky suggested that children who are abused tend, as adults, to abuse their children. Abused children, however, do not grow up to be abusive when they experience some compensatory relationship with a spouse, schoolmates, or a nonparental adult. These experiences presumably enhance the individual's feelings of worthiness while at the same time provide appropriate behavioral models for child care. Abused children need therapeutic experiences that instill a sense of trust and self-worth and provide them with the behavioral skills needed to deal with others, particularly in affectively charged situations. If these experiences occur, there is every reason to expect that the effects of child maltreatment can be ameliorated.

Crittenden (1989) suggests that children who have been maltreated demonstrate a hierarchy of needs. First, they need to be able to predict events in their environment; otherwise, they cannot organize their personal behavior. After they have a sense of predictability, they need to learn socially appropriate means to achieve desired ends. In their families, the means they have learned for achieving desired ends have been abusive and violent. Next, they need to learn to communicate openly and trustingly and to master developmentally appropriate cognitive and language skills. They need carefully regulated, umambiguous, and consistent affective experiences in order to develop trust. Finally, they need to develop the self-confidence, motivation, and self-control necessary to enjoy and benefit from the intellectual stimulation of educational programs.

In a family systems model, such as applied in this text, the special educator may be a source of support for families who maltreat their children. Within the systems model, the actions of any individual family member, even the maltreating member, are not seen as the expression of the problem of the individual member but of the overall functioning of the family system (Asen et al. 1989). The systems approach focuses on the interactions of the family within the ecological context. The special educator and the special education program may be a part of the family's ecological context.

Though special educators need information in order to interact effectively with families who maltreat their children, it is not their function to treat the maltreatment or to counsel the family. Family counseling for maltreatment is the function of trained, specialized professionals.

Asen, George, Piper, and Stevens (1989) describe several patterns of child abuse. The first pattern is helplessness and help-recruiting abuse. These families appear to have a limited range of skills for dealing with everyday family issues. In the extended context of the family, school personnel, extended family members, and therapists attempt to help the inexperienced family. Repeated offers of help and its acceptance by the family lead to a situation in which the helper, knowingly or unknowingly, becomes involved to a point that he or she assumes parental tasks. Outside help then becomes a problem in its own right. Interactions with families involved in this pattern should emphasize the family's strengths while diminishing staff expertise. These families may need help in interactions within their extended ecological context to make members within that extended context reduce their codependent relationships with the family.

The second pattern described by Asen and associates is professional abuse. In this pattern, professionals become overinvolved in the family to the extent that they assume parenting duties. The overinvolved professional, however, will remain involved with the family only as long as the problem continues. Consequently, the family may pace the professional helper by showing just enough improvement to keep the helper motivated, engaged, and interested in the family's problem. When working with these families, the professionals must separate themselves from the family system and objectively evaluate it and their relationship with it.

Transgenerational abuse occurs when grandparents are involved in raising their son's or daughter's children, either because they have accepted the caretaking role or because they share the same residence. In many situations, this repeats the cycle of poor parenting and frequently results in abuse. In other cases, keeping the child's birth parents dependent may give the grandparents a second chance at parenting. In such situations, unresolved problems relating to the birth parent's own childhood may be reactivated. In these families, the goal of assistance is to decrease the activity of the grandparents and increase the differentiation of functions between the parents and the grandparents. Authority within the family may then be shifted to the parents, and a potentially more appropriate child-raising context may emerge.

The fourth pattern Asen and associates describe is stand-in abuse. In these families, one parent is closely engaged with the child, and the relationship between the parents is distant. Consequently, an attack on the child may represent a means of punishing the partner without undermining the marriage. The family may adopt a pattern of behavior in which, at a time of crisis, one child is singled out and punished, or the child learns to behave in such a way as to elicit abuse. The primary issue for the professional working with these families is to find a way to help the parents resolve their marital conflict without abusing the child.

In some families, a pattern of distance-regulating abuse occurs. The child may learn that the only way to achieve close physical contact with mother or father is to evoke punishment. Closeness is experienced through the act of punishment and the subsequent hugs and comforting that result from the parent's feelings of guilt. In families who regulate personal distance with abuse, there are predictable sequences of outbursts of violence. The purpose of violence is to stabilize the family at a point where there is neither too much closeness nor too much distance. Work with these families necessitates involving them in positive experiences characterized by closeness.

In other families, transferred abuse occurs. In these families, it is difficult to understand the patterns underlying the abuse, because intense experiences from the past can be transferred to the present. These families need help in differentiating between their present and past experiences.

Cultural abuse may also occur in families. If these parents are challenged regarding their disciplinary practices, they state that their behavior is appropriate within their culture, even though the behavior may not be acceptable to child care authorities and teachers. The parents may state that their particular way of dealing with their children's behavior is an inherited practice. In work with these families, it may be necessary to involve other families from the same culture who do not abuse their children. The message to be communicated is: We recognize that your culture may have different disciplinary practices, but in this community, the law and children's service authorities take a firm stand opposing abuse. The parents should be urged to rethink their interactions with their children and to be made aware of the risk they are taking of losing their child if they continue to be abusive.

The final pattern of abuse described by Asen and associates is denied abuse. In these families, the child is injured but the cause of the injury is denied by the abusive family. In order to work effectively with such families, the professional must shift the focus of intervention from questioning "Who did this?" to pointing out positive patterns of interaction within the family. The professional should emphasize interactions demonstrating that the family's parenting is "good enough" to keep the child rather than focus on behavior demonstrating that their parenting is "bad enough" to remove the child.

These patterns of family interactions emphasize the function of abuse within the family and the extended ecological context in which the family functions. Again, though each of these patterns suggests activities on the part of the professional, the teacher's role is not to treat abusive families but to refer any evidence or suspicion of abuse to the appropriate authorities. However, it is essential that teachers understand the dynamics of child maltreatment within the family system.

Substitute Care

Children enter substitute care (care by individuals other than the child's birth parents) either voluntarily or through the intervention of a social agency. Children may live in either formally or informally constituted foster homes or families or with adoptive parents.

In a study of foster parents' self-reported needs for training, Noble and Euster (1981) found that over half of the parents they surveyed were interested in learning more about managing child behavior and communicating with their foster children. In a study of the foster parents of handicapped children, Arkava and Mueller (1976) found that though all foster parents incurred additional expenses in caring for their foster children, foster parents of handicapped children spent twice as much as other foster parents, particularly for equipment.

Families who are providing substitute care for children confront a wide range of issues. Elbow (1986) suggests that these families must master the developmental tasks of a biologically formed family and develop guidelines for the process of becoming a family whenever a new child enters the family system. She contends that these tasks are challenged by a distortion of the family cycle; whereas biological families begin with dependent relationships and move toward individualization and independence, substitute families begin far apart and must move toward closeness. Unlike biological families, substitute families share no history or experiences with the foster children. In addition, family boundaries are strained with the intrusion of the adoption or social agency. These boundaries are further challenged by the child's ties or sense of loyalty to previous caregivers. Finally, the child and parents may have unresolved individual issues. Parents may have expectations of parenthood that are not fulfilled by the foster or adopted child and may experience a lack of family or cultural support for their nonbiological parenthood.

When an older child enters a family for adoption, several predictable sources of stress emerge (Gill 1978). Initially, there is an adjustment process between the child and the family, which begins as a "honeymoon" of appropriate behavior, followed by a long period of testing, and finally, an incorporation into the family system. The child experiences conflicting loyalties to current and previous foster and biological parents. A shift eventually occurs in the system, and relationships within the family change. Parents may doubt their ability to cope with the child's behavior and with their feelings of being rejected by the child. In addition, new demands for support and communication are placed on the marital relationship.

The issues of foster care and adoption are confusing to children. Proch (1982) found that only 28 percent of the children in his sample could differentiate between foster care and adoption. The children either did not know what they were or considered them the same. Brodzinsky, Schechter, and Brodzinsky (1986) found that children's understanding of adoption undergoes clear, systematic changes with age, and that they are more limited in their understanding of adoption than most mental health professionals and parents previously realized.

Brodzinsky and associates summarize the behavior of older children who have been adopted; their summary may be applicable to all foster and biological families. They suggest that attempts by school-age children to understand the basis of their parent's relinquishment—that is, displays of sadness and anger—are actually normal, age-appropriate, inevitable components of the experience. Much like reactions to a parent's death or divorce, they represent children's grief and mourning in response to parental loss. Unlike children of divorce, however, these children are struggling with the loss of parents for whom they may have only vague and distorted memories. Their loss is even more pervasive and potentially problematic as they enter adolescence and begin to deal with issues of identity.

When working with these families, teachers should recognize that becoming a family is a developmental process. As Elbow (1986) suggests, the usual bonding and attachment patterns are not present. Rather, substitute families are faced with the challenge of preserving the child's individual identity while providing strong parental roles and family security. Teachers should also recognize that families providing foster and adoptive homes for children may have limited access to developmental and behavioral information on the children.

Counseling Families

As we suggested in our discussion of child maltreatment, teachers are not therapists and therefore not qualified to counsel parents and families. Kratochvil and Devereux (1988), however, suggest that many parents need counseling because they continue to experience periods of grief. Perhaps these parents did not receive the help they needed to deal with their feelings in the past because they appeared to be well-adjusted. Some families may need periodic counseling for the purpose of normalizing their uncomfortable "down" periods. The teacher's role at this time is to provide support and recognize the strengths of the family. Coleman (1986) suggests that in the following situations, families' needs are beyond the scope of teacher's abilities, and the family should be referred to an appropriate professional or agency for assistance.

- Parents experience a period of unusual financial difficulty, marital discord, or emotional upheaval.
- Parents routinely express feelings of helplessness or depression.
- Parents feel unable to control their child.
- Parents report that the child is habitually in trouble with juvenile authorities.
- Parents chronically appear to be under a high level of stress.

- Parents impose on the teacher's time at home or school with their personal problems.

Boyer (1986) suggests some special considerations for counselors working with parents of children with disabilities. The parents may appear to be defensive and resistant clients due to past experiences with professionals. In addition, family therapy may be ongoing and continue throughout the child's lifetime. In order to work successfully with these families, therapists must know about resources and services in the community. Extended family members may need to be involved in counseling. As a final caution, Boyer suggests that counselors be aware of the personal emotional impact the family may have on the counselor.

Boyer offers several objectives for counselors of families with children who are disabled. Counselors can help family members develop and express realistic expectations for themselves and one another, maximize resources and find adequate time and opportunity for personal renewal, learn to share feelings and receive support from each other on a continuing basis, and develop more positive self-concepts.

Summary

This chapter discusses a variety of special issues in collaborations with parents of children with exceptionalities. These special issues concern families from diverse cultures, work with siblings and extended family members, children who are in substitute care or who are maltreated, and families whose needs exceed collaboration with teachers.

Keys to the provision of culturally competent services are described, followed by a description of the four major cultural groups in American schools. Ways of working with siblings and extended family members are also presented. Child maltreatment is presented through a family systems perspective, and the special needs of children in substitute care and their caregivers are discussed. The chapter concludes with a discussion of families in need of counseling and of the indicators that a family should be referred for special help.

Exercises and Discussion Topics

1. Lightfoot (1981) contends that traditional parent collaboration activities, such as PTA meetings and open house, are means for

establishing boundaries between parents and teachers. Discuss in which ways this is true for work with families from diverse cultures. Describe ways in which you agree or disagree with the statement.

2. One of the five keys to providing culturally competent services is developing knowledge of the family's culture. In what ways can a teacher discover the significance of a child's behavior as it relates to his or her cultural group?

3. Describe ways in which you would involve your students' siblings in the education of their brother or sister with an exceptionality. How would you involve grandparents and other extended family members?

4. Discuss the implications of viewing child maltreatment through the family systems perspective.

5. Describe several issues confronting families providing substitute care for children.

6. Discuss indicators that a family's needs exceed those that may be addressed through parent-teacher collaboration.

References

American Humane Association. 1987. *Highlights of official child neglect and abuse reporting.* Denver: The American Humane Association.

Arkava, M. L., and D. N. Mueller. 1976. Components of foster care for handicapped children. *Child Welfare* 58: 339–45.

Asen, K., E. George, R. Piper, and A. Stevens. 1989. A systems approach to child abuse: Management and treatment issues. *Child Abuse and Neglect* 13: 45–48.

Bermudez, A. B., and Y. N. Padron. 1988. University-school collaboration that increases minority parent involvement. *Educational Horizons* 66 (2): 83–84.

Boyer, P. A. 1986. The role of the family therapist in supportive services to families with handicapped children. *Clinical Social Work Journal* 14 (3): 250–61.

Brantlinger, E. A. 1987. Making decisions about special education placement: Do low-income parents have the information they need? *Journal of Learning Disabilities* 20 (2): 94–101.

Brodzinsky, D. M., D. Schechter, and A. B. Brodzinsky. 1986. Children's knowledge of adoption: Developmental changes and implications for adjustment. In *Thinking about the family: Views of parents and children,* eds. R. D. Ashmore and D. M. Brodzinsky, 205–32; Hillsdale, N.J.: Lawrence Erlbaum.

Chan, S. 1986. Parents of exceptional Asian children. In *Exceptional Asian children and youth*, eds. M. K. Kitano and P. C. Chinn, 36–53. Washington, D.C.: Eric Exceptional Child Education Report.

Chavkin, N. F. 1989. Debunking the myth about minority parents. *Educational Horizons* 67 (4): 119–23.

Cicchetti, D., S. Toth, and K. Hennessy. 1989. Research on the consequences of child maltreatment and its application to educational settings. *Topics in Early Childhood and Special Education* 9 (2): 33–55.

Coleman, M. C. 1986. *Behavior disorders: Theory and practice.* Englewood Cliffs, N.J.: Prentice-Hall.

Comer, J. 1980. *School power: Implications of an intervention project.* New York: The Free Press.

Crittenden, P. M. 1989. Teaching maltreated children in the preschool. *Topics in Early Childhood Special Education* 9 (2): 16–32.

Cross, T. 1988. Services to minority populations: What does it mean to be a culturally competent professional? *Focal Point* 2 (4): 1–3.

Elbow, M. 1986. From caregiving to parenting: Family formation with adopted older children. *Social Work* 31: 366–70.

George, J. D. 1988. Therapeutic intervention for grandparents and extended families of children with developmental delays. *Mental Retardation* 26: 369–75.

Gill, M. M. 1978. Adoption of older children: The problem faced. *Social Casework* 59: 272–78.

Hodgkinson, H. 1985. *All one system.* Washington, D.C.: Institute for Educational Leadership.

Kramer, R. F., and I. M. Moore. 1983. Childhood cancer: Meeting the special needs of health siblings. *Cancer Nursing* 2: 213–17.

Kratochvil, M. S., and S. A. Devereux. 1988. Counseling needs of parents of handicapped children. *Social Casework* 69 (7): 420–26.

Lightfoot, S. L. 1981. Toward conflict resolution: Relationships between families and schools. *Theory into Practice* 20 (2): 97–104.

Lightfoot, S. L. 1978. *Worlds apart: Relationships between families and schools.* New York: Basic Books.

Lynch, E. W., and R. C. Stein. 1987. Parent participation by ethnicity: A comparison of Hispanic, black, and Anglo families. *Exceptional Children* 54: 105–111.

Menke, E. M. 1987. The impact of a child's chronic illness on school-aged siblings. *Children's Health Care* 15: 132–40.

Milstead, S. 1988. Siblings are people, too! *Academic Therapy* 23 95: 537–40.

Morrow, R. D. 1987. Cultural differences—Be aware. *Academic Therapy* 23 (2): 143–49.

Noble, L. S., and S. D. Euster. 1981. Foster parent input: A crucial element in training. *Child Welfare* 60: 35–42.

Olion, L., and M. Gillis-Olion, 1984. Assessing culturally diverse exceptional children. *Early Child Development and Care* 15: 203–31.

Parke, R. D., and C. W. Collmer. 1975. Child abuse: An interdisciplinary analysis. In *Review of child development research, Vol. 5*, ed. E. M. Hetherington. Chicago: University of Chicago Press.

Proch, K. 1982. Differences between foster care and adoption: Perceptions of adopted foster children and adoptive foster parents. *Child Welfare* 61: 259–69.

Rose, T. C. 1980. Child abuse and the educator. *Focus on Exceptional Children* 12 (9): 1–13.

Schreibman, L., R. E. O'Neill, and R. L. Koegel. 1983. Behavioral training for siblings of autistic children. *Journal of Applied Behavior Analysis* 16: 129–38.

Swenson-Pierce, A., F. L. Kohl, and A. L. Egel. 1987. Siblings as home trainers: A strategy for teaching domestic skills to children. *Journal of the Association for Persons with Severe Handicaps* 12: 53–60.

Uthe-Reyno, M. G., and D. L. MacKinnon. 1989. Teacher's modeling encourages learning in Indian students. *Educational Horizons* 67 (4): 163–65.

Weinrott, M. R. 1974. A training program in behavior modification for siblings of the retarded. *American Journal of Orthopsychiatry* 44: 362–75.

Williams, D. L., and N. F. Chavkin. 1987. *Final report of the parent involvement in education project.* Washington, D.C.: National Institute of Education, Contract No. 400-83-0007, Project P-2.

Yao, E. 1988. Working effectively with Asian immigrant parents. *Phi Delta Kappan* 42: 223–25.

Yates, J. R. 1987. Current and emerging forces. *Counterpoint* 7 (4): 4–5.

Youngblade, L. M., and J. Belsky. 1989. Child maltreatment, infant-parent attachment security, and dysfunctional peer relationships in toddlerhood. *Topics in Early Childhood Special Education* 9 (2): 1–15.

Zirpoli, T. J. 1986. Child abuse and children with handicaps. *Remedial and Special Education* 7 (2): 29–48.

CHAPTER ELEVEN

Family Transitions

Ms. J., parent of a sixteen-year-old son with mental retardation:

"Just when we seem to get settled, something comes up. Like this year, my son says, 'When am I going to a new school?' I asked him, 'Why do you think you're going to a new school?' And he said, 'Cause I don't stay anyplace, and I've had Ms. M. last year and this year. I always go to a new school.' And that's the truth, it seems like he's always going some place new. And its hard on the girls, because they feel that I pay more attention to him than to them. I lose time at work until we have the bus straightened out. He's got to figure out how this teacher and school do things different. It's hard, but I guess that's how they do things in special ed."

Chapter Topics and Objectives

Transitions are the changes that occur in families as they move from one stage or state of functioning to another. As a consequence of the changes in the family system in contemporary society, discussed in Chapters 2 and 10, transitions cause stress in families with members with exceptionalities (McDonald et al. 1989). The sources of stress within the family include changes in the status of the child with the disability, changes in the socioeconomic status of the family, changes in marital status, or changes in the child's education and training program.

Various factors, which either protect the family or make the family vulnerable, determine the adaptations that individuals within the family make to transitions at various times in the family's history. Hetherington (1989) found that the effects of family transitions depend on the characteristics of the child with the exceptionality, the child's age and gender, the availability of needed resources, subsequent life experiences, and interpersonal relationships. In addition, the adaptations that individuals make to a specific transition are shaped by experiences that preceded that transition.

In this chapter, we will:

- Describe the nature of transitions in families with exceptional members.
- Discuss various perspectives on collaboration that may facilitate transitions.
- Present strategies to assist families in transitions.

Transitions in Families with Members with Exceptionalities

Transitions are not one-time propositions but represent a passage or evolution (Lazari and Kilgo 1989). They are recurrent, lifelong processes that all individuals experience. Lazarri and Kilgo suggest that for families with exceptional members, the transition process includes three phases: preparation, implementation, and follow-up. It is important that professionals working with families in transition remember that both the exceptional child and the family are making the transition and that both are experiencing the stress of the change. When the special education student leaves the familiar environment of either the home or the school, both the students and the parents confront the possibility that the transition will be a failure (Kovanc and Warren 1984).

Two transition periods that have received particular attention in the literature are the transitions from preschool to public school and from school to work. These transitions are especially complex and difficult because parents must interact with various private and public agencies; these agencies determine their child's eligibility and vary in the quality of services they provide to child and family (Smith and Strain 1988). In addition, the focus of the interventions offered may vary from agency to agency (Harbin 1988).

Transition from Preschool to Public School

Diamond, Spiegel-McGill, and Hanrehan (1988) suggest that a child's transition from preschool or child care service to public school may be the most abrupt and permanent break with the past he or she will experience until leaving home as a young adult. This is complicated by specific differences that exist among various early childhood programs regarding behavioral expectations for students (Hains, Fowler, and Chandler 1988). Jones (1989) suggests that preschool programs usually have fewer children, individualized instruction, and immediate, personalized reinforcement. In public schools, however, children are encouraged to work in large groups and function independently.

Jones contends that Public Law 99-457 has increased the number of potential transitions in students' early childhood. Transitions may occur during any of the following program changes: from home to an infant intervention program, from home to a preschool program, from home to preschool, from early intervention program to preschool, from preschool to kindergarten, and from kindergarten to first grade. The potential for stress exists at each of these transitions due to changes in personnel, program goals, and policies and to differences in the effectiveness of the program.

Transition from School to Work

Wehman, Kregel, and Barcus (1985) perceive the transition from school to work as a carefully planned process that establishes and implements a plan for either employment or further training for students who leave school. These students generally have attended school for a period of three to five years. Wehman and associates state that, in practice, systematically planned transitions are usually not available.

Kovanc and Warren (1984) suggest that in the transition from school to work, parents become aware that, unlike the special educational system, community and work environments may not provide the support needed by the individual to ensure success. In addition, when the community provides the student with opportunities to function independently, this independence may become threatening to both the parents and the student. Parents' unresolved grief is often reactivated when the child leaves school. The parents tend to have recurring thoughts of "what may have been" if their child had not been exceptional.

Perspectives on Collaboration to Facilitate Transitions

McDonald and associates (1989) endeavored to ascertain parents' perspectives on the transition from a program for handicapped infants to a preschool. In structured interviews, they explored the parents' perceptions of appropriate time frames, preparation activities, and level of involvement needed to facilitate effective transitions. The majority of parents answered that six months to one year was needed to decide on a change in placement. This time was necessary to adequately explore potential program options. All the parents in the survey expressed a desire to be involved in planning the transition, particularly by being provided with program descriptions and tours of potential placement facilities. The parents desired staff assistance during the transition in the form of information and support on an individual-family basis. Ninety-six percent of the parents wanted staff follow-up from the originating program to the new program.

McDonnell, Wilcox, and Boles (1986) offer a different perspective in a national study designed to identify the scope of the postschool services needed by individuals exiting public school programs. They suggested that if significant progress is to be made in the transition of students with severe disabilities from school to work and community life, changes at both the local and state levels are needed. They urge the implementation of individual transition training for students with disabilities. Such training must begin early in the student's high school career. Transition activities should be an integral part of the student's individualized education program and should culminate in a formal transition plan. Throughout the process, parents must be informed of available service options and how to gain access to them.

Ferguson, Ferguson, and Jones (1988) emphasize that transitions must be understood within a systems framework. In a qualitative study, they found that transition is not a single-component process; parents reported bureaucratic, family life, and status components in transitions. Among the families studied, transitions were better understood when perceived as separate processes or components.

The bureaucratic transition is the process whereby the agencies and professionals involved with the family change from representatives of the special education system to representatives of the adult service system. Families reported that several patterns occur within bureaucratic transition. In one pattern, some families felt professional abandonment—a realization that special education services are ending but with little certainty that community services will begin and provide needed assistance. Implicit in abandonment are feelings of helplessness and that professionals have given up hope with regard to their child.

A second pattern of bureaucratic transition is a surrender to professional expertise. In this situation, the parents give up their responsibilities to the professional agency. The third pattern is assimilation, in which the parents feel the need to become professionals themselves by starting programs and providing services with other parents for their children. The final bureaucratic pattern is an engagement with professionals. In this pattern, parents worked enthusiastically with professionals to design and implement programs of active involvement or collaboration.

Ferguson and associates described three patterns of family life transitions, which involve disruptions in established family routines and changes in family responsibilities that previously had made life manageable. Some parents reacted with resignation and fatigue when coping with the adult service system, which did not follow the mandated procedures and programs they had become accustomed to in the public school system. Other parents reported being forced to be self-reliant, which they resented. In this transition pattern, passive resignation is replaced with a sense of anger and injustice. In the final family life transition pattern, parents reported a natural and collective self-reliance. In this pattern, parents used social supports to cope with transitions.

The third and final transition pattern described by Ferguson and associates is a status transition. In this pattern, parents confront the issue of treating their children with disabilities as adults. The parents were concerned about losing their proactive control over the children's lives to professional care providers because their children were functioning as adults with adults.

The perspective offered by Ferguson and associates has several implications for services to families. It suggests that professionals using a single-pattern approach to transition may find that they miscommunicate with parents. The three-component approach to transitions implies that parents may be successful in one or two patterns of transition while needing assistance in other patterns. Ferguson and associates suggest that normalization necessitates a reduction of parental restrictions and control over their children and an increase in parental advocacy. Acceptance of transitions as a multiple process enhances professional understanding of parents' concerns and actions.

Strategies to Assist Families in Transition

The goals of transition planning appear to be simple and straightforward. They include selecting a placement that is appropriate for the student's needs and acceptable to the parents, ensuring a smooth transfer from the old to the new placement, and initiating service in a timely fashion (Fiechtl, Rule, and Innocenti 1989). However, specific strategies may be needed to help parents successfully accomplish these apparently simple goals. Making the transition from home or a service program to school, or from school to work and community, requires that parents devote considerable time and energy to learning about various potential new programs, the individualized education program or other planning procedures used in the new program, their legal rights and responsibilities as well as those of their child, and the special education or related services offered by the new program (Hanline, Suchman, and Demmerlie 1989).

The optimum role that parents may assume during transition planning is that of a participant who is encouraged and nurtured by professionals who are sensitive to each family's needs and desires. Everson and Moon (1987) suggested several participant responsibilities, derived from the literature, that can be assumed by parents and families; these responsibilities are summarized in Table 11.1. Professionals should not assume that all parents are readily prepared to take on these responsibilities. Each responsibility may require that the parents be given training, education, and information.

As a result of their study of parents' perceptions of transitions, McDonald and associates (1989) recommended the following strategies to assist parents in transition. First, the transition should be initiated six months to a year prior to the projected change. Parents should be consulted with regard to how they wish to be involved in the planning and implementation of the transition. During planning, the family should be helped in projecting future changes and environments, beyond the specific transition under consideration. Finally, follow-up support should be provided

TABLE 11.1 • *Participant Responsibilities of Parents and Family Members in Transition*

Attend individualized education program meetings

Provide information to the team on family and student needs as well as the specific responsibilities the family is able and willing to assume

Advocate for a plan that integrates the student into the community and decreases dependence on the family and social service agencies

Focus the team on the individual student's and family's needs

Request information on residential, recreational, guardianship, financial, medical, social, behavioral, sexual, and other areas of service and concerns

Support programming that complements skills needed in the transition

---

Source: Adapted from Everson and Moon 1987.

to the family. McDonald and associates suggest a four-step process to facilitate transitions:

1. Determine the time frame of the transition in collaboration with the parents.
2. Add the transition goals to the individual family plan.
3. Establish a time line, including specific activities for both parents and staff, such as tours, program descriptions, and observations (an example time line is presenteded in Table 11.2).
4. Provide follow-up services.

Lazzari and Kilgo (1989) suggest that goals for transition plans may be very broad, such as to learn what a transition is and why it is important to the family; to identify the information and skills needed by the family for the transition into a new program; or to identify the transitions that may occur within the next five years. They describe several skills that parents can be taught to help them collaborate in transitions, such as record keeping (how to maintain

TABLE 11.2 • *Transition Plan Time Line*

Transition Plan: Joey Ling Family

June 1991	Conference to discuss the need to change the program in one year
August 1991	Conference to discuss the parents' involvement in the transition process
September 1991	Conference to review the individual family plan (IFP), to initiate plans for tours and visitations, and to provide program descriptions
November 1991	Visitations and observations; transition goals added to IEP and IFP
December 1991	Visitations and observations continue; develop program goals to facilitate change
March 1992	Conference to discuss progress and evaluate visits and tours
	Continue program goals to facilitate change
June 1992	IEP forwarded to new program
August 1992	Follow-up telephone communication
October 1992	Follow-up telephone communication
January 1993	Check with family
February 1993	Final telephone communication to check on all arrangements

a telephone log, record conference notes, and keep a notebook to document contacts), communicating effectively, and conducting classroom observations.

Planning for the transition from school to work must begin three to five years before it is anticipated that the student will leave school. A program that is responsive to the needs of students and their families and that will enable them to effectively cope with this transition should include the following goals (D'Alonzo, Owen, and Hartwell 1985; Halpern 1985):

- Develop appropriate life skills, educational goals, and objectives for all secondary students.
- Emphasize job-seeking and maintenance skills as well as community survival skills training.
- Provide supervised on-site job training.
- Support special and regular educators, providing students with appropriate programming.
- Increase collaboration between community agencies and special education and between special education and vocational education.

Wehman, Kregel, and Barcus (1985) describe three stages in the transition preparation process. The first is appropriate instruction, which is provided by the school. The second stage is the planning process itself. There must be a formal, individualized student transition plan, developed collaboratively by parents, student, school, community, and employment agency personnel. Interagency cooperation should be emphasized, and vocational alternatives and opportunities available to the student should be discussed. The final stage is placement into meaningful employment, which is the desired outcome of the transition.

Summary

In this chapter, the various transitions that confront a family with an exceptional member are discussed. Transition is presented as a lifelong issue and a process rather than an event. Various models to facilitate transition are presented. Specific strategies including planning, projecting time frames, and providing follow-up are suggested. Through these strategies, the individual needs of each child and family are addressed.

Exercises and Discussion Topics

1. Interview the parent of a child with an exceptionality. What are some issues regarding transition that emerge during the interview?

2. Discuss the various transitions that may occur in the educational career of a child, from home-based, early intervention infant programming through leaving the educational system at age eighteen or twenty-one.

3. Give an example of each of the three components of transition reported by Ferguson, Ferguson, and Jones (1988): bureaucratic, family life, and status.

4. What steps can be undertaken to facilitate transitions?

References

D'Alonzo, B. J., S. D. Owen, and L. K. Hartwell. 1985. Transition models: An overview of the current state of the art. *Techniques* 1 (6): 429–36.

Diamond, K. E., P. Spiegel-McGill, and P. Hanrehan. 1988. Planning for school transition: An ecological developmental approach. *Journal of the Division for Early Childhood* 12 (3): 245–52.

Everson, J. M., and M. S. Moon. 1987. Transition services for young adults with severe disabilities: Defining professional and parental roles and responsibilities. *The Journal of the Association for Persons with Severe Handicaps* 12: 87–95.

Ferguson, P. M., D. L. Ferguson, and D. Jones. 1988. Generations of hope: Parental perspectives on the transitions of their children with severe retardation from school to adult life. *The Journal of the Association for Persons with Severe Handicaps* 13 (3): 177–88.

Fiechtl, B., S. Rule, and M. S. Innocenti. 1989. It's time to get ready for school. *Teaching Exceptional Children* 22 (1): 63–65.

Hains, A. H., S. A. Fowler and L. K. Chandler. 1988. Planning school transition: Family and professional collaboration. *Journal of the Division for Early Childhood* 12 (2): 108–15.

Halpern, A. S. 1985. Transition: A look at the foundations. *Exceptional Children* 51 (6): 479–86.

Hanlin, M. F., S. Suchman, and C. Demmerlie. 1989. Beginning public preschool. *Teaching Exceptional Children* 55 (6): 487–92.

Harbin, G. L. 1988. Implementation of PL 99-457: State technical assistance needs. *Topics in Early Childhood Special Education* 8 (1): 24–36.

Hetherington, E. M. 1989. Coping with family transitions: Winners, losers, and survivors. *Child Development* 60: 1–14.

Jones, S. D. 1989. The transition facilitator model: A project to enhance preschool transitions. Cincinnati, Ohio: University of Cincinnati, unpublished manuscript.

Kovanc, J. T., and N. J. Warren. 1984. Graduation: Transitional crisis for mildly developmentally disabled adolescents and their families. *Family Relations* 33:135–42.

Lazzari, A. M., and J. L. Kilgo. 1989. Practical methods for supporting parents in early transitions. *Teaching Exceptional Children* 22 (1): 40–43.

McDonald, L., T. Z. Kysela, P. Siebert, S. McDonald, and J. Chambers. 1989. Parent perspective: Transition to preschool. *Teaching Exceptional Children* 22 (1):4–8.

McDonnell, J., B. Wilcox, and S. M. Boles. 1986. Do we know enough to plan for transition? A national survey of state agencies responsible for services to persons with severe handicaps. *The Journal of the Association for Persons with Severe Handicaps,* 11: 53–60.

Smith, B. J., and P. Strain. 1988. Early childhood special education in the next decade. Implementing and expanding PL 99-457. *Topics in Early Childhood Special Education* 8 (1): 37–47.

Wehman, P. H., J. Kregel, and J. M. Barcus. 1985. School to work: Vocational transition for handicapped youth. In *Competitive employment for persons with mental retardation: From research to practice,* eds. P. Wehman and J. H. Hewitt. Richmond, Va.: Commonwealth.

CHAPTER TWELVE

Programming for Parent Collaboration: An Illustration

Mr. B., parent of an eight-year-old boy with learning disabilities:

"After all the conferences when B. J. repeated kindergarten, then failed first grade, before they called him 'learning disabled' and gave him extra help, everybody was telling us what he wasn't doing. They never told us what they were doing, just that he wasn't measuring up. Then, before school even starts, the first year he was going to be in special ed, we get a letter from Ms. M. It tells us what her goals are for the kids who get extra help from her, who to call if we have any questions, and an invitation to come in the day before for a brown-bag lunch. She even made the coffee, punch for the kids, and cookies. She kept saying 'we'll be working on this' and 'we'll be working on that' instead of 'your kid is not working and why aren't you doing something about it?' "

Chapter Topics and Objectives

Meeting the needs of several parents and their children with exceptionalities collaboratively requires careful planning and organization. This chapter offers a detailed, step-by-step illustration of the parent-teacher collaboration program model. This illustration, which brings together the material presented in Chapters 4 through 9, is not a model or ideal program, because each program must focus on participants' special needs. However, it does show how teachers can go about planning and carrying out a program using the ideas in this text.

The illustration assumes a hypothetical group of children in a self-contained special education class; however, the procedures and activities are readily applicable, with limited modifications, to other special educational service programs, such as resource rooms or special day schools. The planning and scheduling framework is an August-to-May school calendar.

In this chapter, we will:

- Present a detailed hypothetical illustration of the application of the parent-teacher collaboration model.
- Plan a comprehensive parent-teacher collaboration program applicable in your present or future work setting.

The Class

The hypothetical classroom serves eight children with mild disabilities in a non-categorical program for children identified as behavior-disordered, learning-disabled, and educable mentally handicapped and for children with combinations of these exceptionalities. Two children are from one-parent families; one child is in foster care; the others live with their natural parents or stepparents. Parents in three families work full-time outside the home. The families represent a range of socioeconomic levels and ethnic backgrounds.

One teacher (Mrs. Paul) and one full-time paraprofessional (Mr. Kevin) work in the classroom. The teacher assistant, Mr. Kevin, has legal certification to substitute in the teacher's absence. Mrs. Paul is competent in several skills that are important to collaboration, such as interviewing and leading groups. Both Mrs. Paul and Mr. Kevin are committed to encouraging parent involvement. Although not active in the program, the school principal (Mr. Hanes) supports the teacher's and assistant's efforts.

The parents of two children (Mrs. Daniels and Mr. and Mrs. Ming) serve as examples throughout the chapter. They are generally representative of the class's parents.

Program Introduction

Mrs. Paul and Mr. Kevin meet in late August to begin planning the parent-teacher program. They decide that, at a minimum, they will offer the following services to the parents of the children in the class:

- A welcome letter and follow-up telephone call (Chapter 5)
- A parent orientation meeting (Chapter 8)

- An intake and assessment interview (Chapter 4)
- An optional home visit, with an opportunity for the child to participate (Chapter 9)
- Periodic report cards, including task analysis forms (Chapter 5)
- An individualized education program conference (Chapter 6).

In addition, they decide to recruit parents for a class advisory committee to help organize and schedule individual and group activities for parents. And they decide to determine parents' interest in serving as instructors and volunteer aides. Mrs. Paul and Mr. Kevin except other parent-teacher activities to develop from the individual intake and assessment interviews.

Two weeks before the first day of school, Mrs. Paul mails a personalized letter to each family welcoming parents to the class and inviting them to the orientation meeting (Figures 12.1 and 12.2).

After about a week, Mrs. Paul calls each home to follow up on the written invitation and to determine approximate attendance. This attendance estimate helps Mrs. Paul and Mr. Kevin to prepare sufficient materials and refreshments for the group. Mrs. Paul is careful not to pressure the parents to attend the orientation meeting. If parents say they cannot attend the orientation meeting, she makes an appointment for an intake and assessment interview.

Before the orientation meeting, Mrs. Paul and Mr. Kevin prepare a file folder for each family. They will record each family's contacts and activities during the year on the Parent Collaboration Log in the file (Figure 12.3). The file will also store all letters, notes, and messages the parents receive from and send to the school during the year, as well as pre- and postconference notes.

Parent Orientation Meeting

At the orientation meeting, Mrs. Paul's main goal is to communicate information to parents. However, she also plans a discussion and question-and-answer period to allow parents to address immediate problems and to dispell new parents' concerns about their child's placement in special education.

The meeting agenda includes the following items:

- A description of the special education program and class, its purpose and objectives, and the integration of children into regular classes
- A description of the parent-teacher program

FIGURE 12.1 • *Welcome Letter for Parents of a Returning Student*

August 20, 19__

Dear Mrs. Daniels:

I was very happy to learn that Mary is in our class again this year. The gains we saw in Mary's skills and behaviors last year promise another successful year together.

This year we plan to continue Mary's individualized program, emphasizing behavior management and socialization. We will continue work on self-help skills, language and communication, reading, and arithmetic. The children will again attend physical education each day with Mr. Lansing.

To begin the school year, we are planning a parent orientation meeting on August 31, 19__, at 7:00 PM I would really enjoy visiting with you and sharing some information you may find useful this school year. During the meeting, I will introduce the school staff, and we will tour the building.

In the near future, I would like to meet with parents individually to discuss their child's individualized educational program and to review the goals and objectives we established last May. During the conference, we will discuss expectations for Mary this year.

Parent-teacher involvement programs will continue this year. I think you will agree that this cooperative programming contributes a great deal to Mary's success. I will telephone you about these matters in a week or two.

Both Mr. Kevin, our teacher's assistant, and I are looking forward to another rewarding and productive school year. With your support and assistance, we are sure Mary will make significant progress. Please feel free to contact us at Springvalley School (555-8477).

Sincerely,

Sarah Paul
Teacher

- A formal introduction of the special education program and the school staff, including the special education teacher and teacher's assistant, appropriate regular class teachers, principal, psychologist, social worker, nurse, school secretary, and others
- Presentation and handouts on "who to call for what": information on transportation, food service, lunch program, absences,

FIGURE 12.2 • *Welcome Letter for Parents of a New Student*

August 20, 19__

Dear Mr. and Mrs. Ming:

I am very happy to welcome you and John to Springvalley School for the 19__ – __ school year. Your child is a member of the special education program here at Springvalley and has been assigned to our special class. He will attend regular class part-time as soon as we determine the best type and amount of participation for him.

Let me introduce myself. I have taught exceptional children at Springvalley for four years. Mr. Kevin, our teacher's assistant, has been at Springvalley School for two years. In our class, we provide individualized programming for each child. The program stresses behavior management and socialization. In addition, the children work on self-help skills, language and communication, reading, and arithmetic. John will also participate in physical education each day with Mr. Lansing, the school physical education teacher.

To begin the school year, we are planning an orientation meeting for parents on August 31, 19__, at 7:00 PM. We would enjoy visiting with you and sharing information you may find useful this school year. During this meeting, you will meet the school staff, and we will tour the building.

In the near future, I'll be meeting with parents to discuss their child's individualized educational program and to review the year's goals and objectives. During this conference, we will discuss the expectations for John this school year.

As parents new to our class, you may be particularly interested in our parent-teacher involvement program. This program helps us get to know each other and conduct activities to help John. It is also a good way for you to learn more about John's educational program. I will telephone you about these matters in a week or two.

Both Mr. Kevin and I are looking forward to a rewarding and productive school year. With your support and assistance, we are sure John will make significant progress. Please feel free to contact us at Springvalley School (555-8477).

I look forward to seeing you on August 31.

Sincerely,

Sarah Paul
Teacher

FIGURE 12.3 · *Parent Collaboration Log*

Parent Name(s) _____

Child's Name _____ Birthdate _____

Home Phone Number _____ Work Phone Number _____

Date File Opened _____ _____

Activities   Date

I. INTAKE AND ASSESSMENT
   A. Intake and Assessment Conference(s)   _____

   B. Intake and Assessment Completed   _____

II. SELECTION OF GOALS AND OBJECTIVES
   A. Parents' Needs Form Returned   _____
   B. Parents' Activities Form Returned   _____
   C. Goals and Objectives Conferences   _____

   D. Parent-Teacher Involvement Plan Completed   _____

III. ACTIVITY ATTENDANCE
   A. Individual Conferences
      1. Home Visit   _____
      2. Child Evaluation Conference   _____
      3. IEP Conference   _____
      4. _____   _____
      5. _____   _____

   A. Group Meetings
      1. Orientation Meeting   _____
      2. _____   _____
      3. _____   _____
      4. _____   _____
      5. _____   _____

IV. EVALUATION
   A. Evaluation Form Returned   _____
   B. Evaluation Conference   _____

Phone Contacts

Date   Reason/Results
_____   _____
_____   _____

(cont.)

FIGURE 12.3 *Continued*

Other Contacts (Letters, notes, and so on)
Date	Description	Reason/Results
_____	_____	_____
_____	_____	_____
_____	_____	_____
_____	_____	_____

Parent-Teacher Association, health services, occupational and physical therapy, testing, and so on
- A tour of the classroom and school, including visits with staff people at their work stations
- A discussion and question-and-answer period
- Refreshments and informal discussion in the classroom.

The day after the orientation meeting, Mrs. Paul mails a "nice to have seen you again" or "sorry you couldn't make it" note to each family, enclosing meeting handouts in the latter. In the notes, Mrs. Paul lets parents know she will contact them within a week to make an appointment for an intake and assessment conference.

Intake and Assessment

The welcome letter and orientation meeting have introduced parents to the parent-teacher collaboration program. Now it is time to enter phase I of the model, the intake and assessment.

During this phase, Mrs. Paul meets individually with parents in one or more conferences. Through interviewing techniques, she determines parents' perceptions of their needs and interests in their child's program.

Mrs. Paul plans carefully for this phase. She lists the fourteen parents of her students, establishing priorities for intake and assessment. She decides to interview the two families new to the program first, for she anticipates that these parents will need at least two conferences for intake and assessment. She expects one conference to be adequate for parents of returning children.

Chapter Twelve • *Programming for Parent Collaboration* **281**

Mrs. Paul plans to confer with all parents before mid-September; and she establishes a calendar schedule for these conferences and other activities she and Mr. Kevin have planned for the month. For example, they plan to send home a newsletter toward the end of the month, have each parent complete a Parents Needs Form and a Parents' Activities Form, and hold an informational group meeting on "Rights and Confidentiality."

Mrs. Paul develops the following agenda for intake and assessment conferences:

1. Review the child's diagnostic findings and the reason for special education placement.
2. Review the roles of classroom and support staff in the child's education.
3. Review the parents' role and functions in the child's education.
4. Interview parents (Chapter 4).
5. Explain the Parents' Needs Form and Parents' Activities Form and ask parents to complete and return the forms within one week (Appendices C and D).
6. Respond to parents' questions and concerns.

Parents of children returning to the program will be familiar with some of the information, so Mrs. Paul will not need to discuss items 1, 2, and 3 in great depth. Parents of children new to the program will require more detailed discussions of most items.

Selection of Goals and Objectives

After completing the intake and assessment conferences, Mrs. Paul schedules conferences to select goals and objectives for the parents' involvement. By this time, Mrs. Paul has received the needs and activities forms from seven of the eight families. The needs and activities forms completed by Mrs. Daniels and Mr. and Mrs. Ming, our representative parents, are presented in the Supplementary Material section at the end of this chapter. In a telephone conversation, she learns that one parent cannot participate in parent-teacher activities because of family, work, and community commitments. She accepts the parent's reasons and lets her know that she is welcome to join the program at a later date and that she will receive periodic report cards, newsletters, an invitation to the IEP conferences, and occasional notes and telephone calls during the year.

Before each goals and objectives conference, Mrs. Paul and Mr.

Kevin review all available information on each family, including the forms they completed. To help organize this large quantity of information, Mrs. Paul summarizes and enters the information on Program Development Forms (Figures 12.4 and 12.5). She and Mr. Kevin discuss each parent's needs and prepare a tentative list of goals and objectives.

At the beginning of the conference, Mrs. Paul reviews the information she has on parents' needs and interests and asks the parents if they have any additions, corrections, questions, or comments. She asks parents which items are most important to them and then states the items most important to her as the child's teacher. Mrs. Paul and the parents then compare and discuss their ideas until they reach a consensus on their common goals for collaboration. Thus, she and the parents work as equal partners for the child's benefit. Mrs. Paul writes her goals and the parents' goals on the Program Development Form.

Once they agree on goals, Mrs. Paul and the parents write specific objectives designed to accomplish each goal, again discussing both parties' ideas and reaching a consensus. Mrs. Paul records the agreed-upon objectives on the Program Development Form.

During this process, both parents and teacher are aware that they cannot accommodate all their personal needs and interests in a single school year. Thus, they defer work on some low-priority goals and objectives.

Activity Selection and Implementation

Next, Mrs. Paul works with parents to select or design activities to meet the objectives (phase 3 of the model). She may accomplish this task during the goals and objectives conference or during a special conference focusing specifically on activities. Mrs. Paul schedules remaining conferences so that phase 3 activities will be complete by mid-October.

To prepare for the conference, Mrs. Paul develops a list of activities that will meet the target objectives, be consistent with the information on the Parents' Activities Forms, and fit with parents' personalities, life-styles, and desired level of participation. At the beginning of the conference, Mrs. Paul and the parents review their objectives and the information on the Parents' Activities Form. They then devote the remainder of the conference to selecting the activities, negotiating, and compromising if necessary. Mrs. Paul then enters the activities on the Program Development Form.

FIGURE 12.4 • *Program Development Form for a Returning Student*

Parent's Name Luane Daniels   Teacher's Name Sarah Paul

Child's Name Mary Daniels   Date 9-13-

I	II	III	IV
Assessment	Goals and Objectives	Activities	Evaluation
Sloman and Webster Vineland Needs Assessment Form	Goals: I To apply behavioral techniques and instructional methods at home as in school II To develop my own skills for dealing with Mary's behaviors III To continue communication between school and home	Objective IA: —Appropriate reading directed by teacher —Classroom observation by babysitter Objective IIA: —Directed reading Objective IIIA: —Passport —Monthly phone calls	Process: IA, IIA Were readings available to Mrs. Daniels and the sitter? IIA Did Mrs. Burden observe in the classroom? IIIA Was the passport used between home and school? IIIA Did the teacher make monthly phone calls?
—Gives up too easily —Is independent and reliable once she knows she can do something —Uses instructional methods at home —Works with babysitter for consistency	Objectives: IIA To use a problem-solving technique independently IIIA To continue using the passport to maintain communication and consistency between home and school IA Mrs. Burden (Mary's sitter) to demonstrate one new behavioral technique in dealing with Mary's behavior		Content: IA Did the readings help in developing one new behavior management technique? IIA Can Mrs. Daniels now use a problem-solving technique? IIIA Was communication between home and school adequate?

FIGURE 12.5 • Program Development Form for a New Student

Parents' Names James & Lynn Ming   Teacher's Name Sarah Paul
Child's Name John Ming   Date 9-6-84

I Assessment	II Goals & Objectives	III Activities	IV Evaluation
Sloman and Webster Vineland Needs Assessment Form	Goals: I To increase general information about John's exceptionality II To increase knowledge about John's rights, confidentiality, and reasons for placement III To increase skills in disciplining John and in behavior management IV To increase John's participation in the family	Objectives: IA Individual conferences with teacher, parent, and special education supervisor Observation of teacher in classroom IIA Group meeting Objective IIIA Individual conference Observation of teacher in classroom IIIB Work with the teacher in classroom Behavior management parent groups IVA Parent partner	Process: IA Did conferences take place? Did Mr. and Mrs. Ming observe in the classroom? IIA Did Mr. and Mrs. Ming attend the group meeting? IIIA Did Mrs. Ming work with the teacher in the classroom? IIIB Did Mr. and Mrs. Ming participate in behavior management groups? IVA Were parent partners available to the Mings?
—Perceive John as demanding —Concerned John doesn't express affection —John's poor self-help skills cause stress to family —Both parents express the need to discuss feelings —Want information on exceptionality and placement	Objectives: IA To define behavior disorders and describe reasons for placement IIA To understand the rights of handicapped children IIIA To decrease John's hitting behavior at home IIIB To demonstrate two techniques useful in dealing with John's behaviors IVA To perform one social-community activity with John per month		Content: IA Verbal reporting to teacher IIA Verbal reporting to teacher IIIA Behavior counts: has John's hitting decreased? IIIB Teacher observation IVA Report of parent partner

When the activities are selected, Mrs. Paul prepares a parent-teacher activities plan for the remainder of the school year. She and Mr. Kevin enter all group and individual activities on monthly calendars, which they will modify during the school year as necessary.

From program development forms and her notes, Mrs. Paul writes a summary of the individual and group activities all parents will participate in during the year. She records the following activities:

- Newsletter (all parents)
- Periodic report cards with task analysis forms (all parents)
- Informational meetings (all parents)
- Monthly telephone calls (Mrs. Daniels, Mr. and Mrs. Lang, Mr. and Mrs. Pulley)
- Biweekly telephone calls (Mrs. and Mrs. Martinez)
- Passport (Mrs. Daniels, Mr. and Mrs. Ryan)
- Individual conferences (Mr. and Mrs. Ming)
- Behavior management training group (Mr. and Mrs. Ming, Mr. and Mrs. Lang, Mr. Webster)
- Directed readings (Mrs. Daniels and Mary's babysitter)
- Parent partners (Mrs. and Mrs. Ming with Mr. and Mrs. Ryan)
- Observations in classroom (Mary Daniels's sitter, Mr. and Mrs. Ming)
- Daily report cards (Mr. and Mrs. Martinez)
- Classroom assistance (Mr. and Mrs. Ming)
- Parent Advisory Committee.

While completing the calendar, Mrs. Paul attempts to balance parents' individual needs with those of the group. Consequently, she plans as many activities as possible that respond simultaneously to several parents' objectives. To facilitate scheduling, the teacher completes a calendar for each month of the year. Examples are shown in the Supplementary Material section at the end of this chapter.

Evaluation

With scheduling completed, Mrs. Paul turns her attention to evaluation, phase 4 of the parent-teacher collaboration model. She evaluates both the process (availability of activities and participation) and the content (knowledge, practices, and skills learned) of the parent program. The evaluative criteria should be objective. To evaluate process, she considers the following questions, among others:

- Are the activities available?
- Are the activities taking place or scheduled as planned?
- Do the parents (teacher) attend the activities?
- Do the parents (teacher) participate in the activities?

Mrs. Paul's content evaluation responds to the following questions:

- Did the desired behavior change occur?
- Are the partipants demonstrating the designated level of skill or knowledge?
- Is the activity content responding to participants' needs?

Mrs. Paul writes her process and content evaluation techniques—determined with parents during the activities conference—on the Program Development Form.

Mrs. Paul will evaluate individual parent-teacher activities in a conference in which she and parents will discuss their progress toward their objectives and ways to improve their progress if they are dissatisfied. She may use the annual IEP conference for this evaluation. To evaluate workshops and group meetings, Mrs. Paul designs and distributes evaluation forms for participants to complete and return.

Mrs. Paul periodically evaluates the overall impact of the parent-teacher collaboration program, asking herself and parents two key questions:

- Is the program meeting parents' (teacher's) goals and objectives?
- Do parents (teacher) feel positive about the program?

To answer the first question, Mrs. Paul develops a summary sheet of goals and objectives and invites parents' help in judging the program's effectiveness in meeting them. To assess parents' perceptions of the program, she decides to use an anonymous questionnaire (Figure 12.6). Parents indicate which activities they liked or disliked and which they viewed as meaningful or irrelevant. The questionnaire also requests program ideas for the next school year.

Chapter Twelve • Programming for Parent Collaboration **287**

Summary

This text presents a broad spectrum of parent-teacher activities, each activity selected for its potential value to parents and teachers sharing a commitment and responsibility for educating children with exceptionalities. These suggested activities are but printed symbols on paper unless they motivate others to action.

Parent and teacher collaboration begins with the following:

- *You, the reader.* You are responsible for helping the exceptional child grow and learn. Collaboration begins with a good heart and a sincere wish to provide the best possible education for children. It begins with openness and acceptance of parents' and children's special needs and preferences.
- *Study.* Collaboration begins with a critical study of this text and other literature on parents and teachers working together. It requires a commitment to continuously seek new or more effective activities and techniques.

FIGURE 12.6 • *Parent Collaboration Program Evaluation Form*

May 24, 19__

Dear _____:

    The Parent-Teacher Involvement Program is your program, designed with you and for you. We want it to meet your needs and the needs of your child. Thus, it is important to know what you like and dislike about the program and what activities you would and would not participate in next year.

    To help in the planning of next year's program and to make it more responsive to your needs, we invite you to complete and return the attached questionnaire. Please be frank. If you wish to remain anonymous, do not sign the form. Anonymous or signed, your responses will be held in the strictest of confidence.

    Thank you for your help.

Sincerely,

Sarah Paul
Teacher

FIGURE 12.6 Continued

Please make an X in the appropriate columns to the right of each activity listed in the left column. Indicate whether you participated in the activity and how you felt about it. For meetings and workshops, please indicate if you wanted to attend but were unable to. Comments and suggestions are welcome.

ACTIVITY	I was involved in this activity.	I wanted to participate but could not.	I would participate again next year.	My rating of this activity is:			
				Excellent	Good	Fair	Poor
Intake/Assessment Conferences							
Parent Orientation Meeting							
Open House							
Rights and Confidentiality Meeting							
Newsletter							
Passport							
Telephone Calls							
Individual Conferences							
Parent Partners							
Behavior Management Group							
Other:							
Other:							

Use the space below to comment on this year's program and make suggestions for next year.

- *Analysis.* Collaboration begins with objective analysis of your personal needs, the child's needs, and parents' needs.
- *Planning.* Planning a parent-teacher collaboration program requires full consideration of the goals and objectives of collaboration, the resources available, the most desirable activities, and the potential barriers. The teacher's professional judgment is the most powerful planning tool.
- *Knowledge of exceptional children and parents.* Collaboration means recognizing and working with professional strengths and weaknesses when selecting and carrying out activities.
- *Action.* Collaboration begins with one activity, then another, and another, until a comprehensive program of services for parents of children with exceptionalities is realized.

Exercises and Discussion Topics

1. Plan a comprehensive parent-teacher collaboration program for the parents of the children assigned to your program (or to a hypothetical program). The program may be at the preschool, elementary, or secondary level, categorical or noncategorical, self-contained or resources-based.

2. Apply the parent-teacher collaboration model in your plan.

Chapter Supplement

Confidential   Date: __Sept. 4__

Parent's Name __LUANE DANIELS__

Child's Name __MARY DANIELS__

Introduction:
   Listed below are several statements describing concerns common to the parents of exceptional children. The items may or may not concern you at this time. Please complete only those items that currently concern you.
   The information on this form is used *only* to help plan and implement a parent-teacher involvement program. All information is held in strict confidence.

Directions:
1. Read each statement carefully.
2. Circle the number on the 1–5 scale that most closely approximates your current need in each area. Circle *1* to indicate a low priority need and *5* to indicate a high priority need.
3. Below the 1–5 scale are several statements suggesting ways you may prefer to meet your stated needs. Please check only *two* of the four statements listed below each item.
4. You may write additional comments in the space provided.

I. I need the opportunity to discuss my feelings about my exceptional child and myself with someone who understands the problem.

              (Circle the appropriate number.)

         ①   2   3   4   5
        Low   High
       Priority   Priority

              (Check *only* two statements.)
   _____ I prefer to talk to a professional.
   _____ I prefer to talk to the parent of an exceptional child.
   _____ I prefer to be referred to another agency for counseling.
   _____ I prefer to read articles and books discussing the reactions of parents of exceptional children.
   ✓ I prefer __JUST TALKING TO YOU EVERY NOW AND THEN.__
   __I FEEL FINE ABOUT MARY AND WHAT SHE'S DOING.__

II. I would like to talk with other parents and families who have exceptional children.

              (Circle the appropriate number.)

         ①   2   3   4   5
        Low   High
       Priority   Priority

              (Check *only* two statements.)
   _____ I prefer to be in a discussion group.
   _____ I prefer to participate in social gatherings (picnics, parties, potluck dinners).
   ✓ I prefer to meet informally.
   _____ I prefer to participate in general meetings, workshops, lectures, demonstrations, and other informational gatherings.
   _____ I prefer _____

III. I would like to learn more about my child's exceptionality.

(Circle the appropriate number.)

1   ②   3   4   5
Low   High
Priority   Priority

(Check *only* two statements.)
- ✓ I prefer to obtain information through reading.
- ___ I prefer to observe teachers and other professionals working with my child and then discuss my observations.
- ✓ I prefer individual parent-teacher conferences.
- ___ I prefer a parent-teacher discussion group.
- ___ I prefer _____

IV. I would like to learn more about how children develop and learn, especially exceptional children.

(Circle the appropriate number.)

1   ②   3   4   5
Low   High
Priority   Priority

(Check *only* two statements.)
- ✓ I prefer to obtain information through reading.
- ___ I prefer to participate in a formal behavior management training course.
- ___ I prefer a parent-teacher discussion group.
- ___ I prefer individual training in my home by a teacher or other professional.
- ___ I prefer to attend meetings at which specialists present information on behavior management.
- ✓ I prefer **TO MEET WITH YOU ABOUT MY SPECIFIC QUESTIONS.**

VI. I would like to work with a teacher or other professional so that I can use the same instructional methods at home that the school uses.

(Circle the appropriate number.)

1   2   ③   4   5
Low   High
Priority   Priority

(Check *only* two statements.)
- ___ I prefer to observe my child in school.
- ___ I prefer to attend a training program in observation.
- ___ I prefer to attend a course in instructional methods.
- ___ I prefer to work with the teacher in my child's classroom.
- ✓ I prefer in-home training by a teacher or other professional.
- ✓ I prefer to learn through readings, newsletters, telephone communication, and similar resources.
- ___ I prefer _____

VII. I would like _____

(Circle the appropriate number.)

1   2   3   4   5
Low   High
Priority   Priority

(Write the appropriate statements.)
- ___ I prefer _____
- ___ I prefer _____

Comments: I'M AFRAID WITH MY JOB AND ALL, I CAN'T GET TO SCHOOL THAT OFTEN. I'D REALLY LIKE TO KEEP UP OUR WRITTEN LOG AND PHONE CALLS. MAYBE THIS YEAR WE CAN GET MARY'S SITTER INVOLVED.

Thank you.

Confidential Date: Sept. 4
Parent's Name: LUANE DANIELS
Child's Name: MARY DANIELS

Introduction:
Listed below are thirty-five topics and activities generally believed of interest to the parents of exceptional children. Not all parents are interested in any single item, nor is any parent interested in all the items.

Your response to this questionnaire is used *only* to assist in planning and implementing a parent-teacher involvement program for you. All information is held in strict confidence.

Directions:
1. Read the entire form carefully.
2. In Column A check 15 items of interest to you.
3. In Column B rank 5 of the 15 items you checked in Column A. Number the item of highest priority to you 5, the next highest 4, and so on.
4. You may write additional comments in the space provided.

A	B	
✓		1. Help my child learn.
✓		2. Build my child's self-confidence.
		3. Select activities to help my child learn (books, games, toys, projects, experiences).
✓	3	4. Teach my child to follow directions.
✓		5. Help my child enjoy learning.
		6. Assist my child in language development.
✓		7. Teach my child problem-solving skills.
		8. Fulfill my role as (father) (mother) to my child.
✓		9. Avoid emotional involvement in my child's emotional outbursts.
✓		10. Protect my child from getting hurt.
		11. Care for my child when he or she is sick or injured.
✓	4	12. Discipline my child.
✓		13. Deal with my child's misbehavior.
✓		14. Teach my child respect for people and property.
✓	5	15. Teach my child to express feelings in a socially acceptable manner.
		16. Teach my child to show love, affection, and consideration for other family members.
		17. Teacn my child to live in harmony with the family (television, bedtime, meals, sharing, responsibilities).

___ ___		18. Develop a positive and productive relationship with my child.
✓ 2		19. Develop my problem-solving skills.

How can I obtain information on the following topics affecting my child:

___ ___	20.	Art activities
___ ___	21.	Creative dramatics
___ ___	22.	Educational games and activities
___ ___	23.	Exercise
___ ___	24.	Health and hygiene
___ ___	25.	Music
___ ___	26.	Nutrition and diet
___ ___	27.	Puppetry
✓ ___	28.	Recreation
✓ ___	29.	Sleep
___ ___	30.	Toys

Other topics and activities of interest to me are:

✓ 1	31.	HELPING MARY'S BABYSITTER DEAL WITH HER.
___ ___	32.	_____
___ ___	33.	_____
___ ___	34.	_____
___ ___	35.	_____

Thank you!

Confidential   Date: Sept 6

Parent's Name __James and Lynn Ming__

Child's Name __John Ming__

Introduction:
Listed below are several statements describing concerns common to the parents of exceptional children. The items may or may not concern you at this time. Please complete only those items that currently concern you.

The information on this form is used *only* to help plan and implement a parent-teacher involvement program. All information is held in strict confidence.

Directions:
1. Read each statement carefully.
2. Circle the number on the 1–5 scale that most closely approximates your current need in each area. Circle *1* to indicate a low priority need and *5* to indicate a high priority need.
3. Below the 1–5 scale are several statements suggesting ways you may prefer to meet your stated needs. Please check only *two* of the four statements listed below each item.
4. You may write additional comments in the space provided.

I. I need the opportunity to discuss my feelings about my exceptional child and myself with someone who understands the problem.

(Circle the appropriate number.)

1   2   3   4   **(5)**
Low   High
Priority   Priority

(Check *only* two statements.)

- **X** I prefer to talk to a professional.
- **X** I prefer to talk to the parent of an exceptional child.
- ___ I prefer to be referred to another agency for counseling.
- ___ I prefer to read articles and books discussing the reactions of parents of exceptional children.
- ___ I prefer _____

II. I would like to talk with other parents and families who have exceptional children.

(Circle the appropriate number.)

1   2   3   4   **(5)**
Low   High
Priority   Priority

(Check *only* two statements.)

- ___ I prefer to be in a discussion group.
- ___ I prefer to participate in social gatherings (picnics, parties, potluck dinners).
- ___ I prefer to meet informally.
- ___ I prefer to participate in general meetings, workshops, lectures, demonstrations, and other informational gatherings.
- **X** I prefer _to talk to people in very small groups._

III. I would like to learn more about my child's exceptionality.

(Circle the appropriate number.)

1   2   3   **(4)**   5
Low   High
Priority   Priority

(Check *only* two statements.)

- ___ I prefer to obtain information through reading.
- **X** I prefer to observe teachers and other professionals working with my child and then discuss my observations.
- **X** I prefer individual parent-teacher conferences.
- ___ I prefer a parent-teacher discussion group.
- ___ I prefer _____

IV. I would like to learn more about how children develop and learn, especially exceptional children.

(Circle the appropriate number.)

1   **(2)**   3   4   5
Low   High
Priority   Priority

(Check *only* two statements.)

- **X** I prefer to obtain information through reading.
- ___ I prefer to participate in a formal behavior management training course.
- ___ I prefer a parent-teacher discussion group.
- **X** I prefer individual training in my home by a teacher or other professional.
- ___ I prefer to attend meetings at which specialists present information on behavior management.
- ___ I prefer _____

VI. I would like to work with a teacher or other professional so that I can use the same instructional methods at home that the school uses.

(Circle the appropriate number.)

1	2	3	④	5
Low Priority				High Priority

(Check *only* two statements.)

__X__ I prefer to observe my child in school.
_____ I prefer to attend a training program in observation.
_____ I prefer to attend a course in instructional methods.
__X__ I prefer to work with the teacher in my child's classroom.
_____ I prefer in-home training by a teacher or other professional.
_____ I prefer to learn through readings, newsletters, telephone communication, and similar resources.
_____ I prefer _____

VII. I would like _more information about why John is in this class._

(Circle the appropriate number.)

1	2	3	4	⑤
Low Priority				High Priority

(Write the appropriate statements.)

__X__ I prefer _to talk to you and someone in charge._
_____ I prefer _____

Comments: _We need more information about why John changed rooms. At the I.E.P. they said it would help him. We'll do anything that will help, but would like to know what we can do to make it possible for him to go back to his old school and not be in a special room._
Thank you.

Confidential   Date: _Sept 6_
Parent's Name _James and Lynn Ming_
Child's Name _John Ming_

Introduction:
  Listed below are thirty-five topics and activities generally believed of interest to the parents of exceptional children. Not all parents are interested in any single item, nor is any parent interested in all the items.
  Your response to this questionnaire is used *only* to assist in planning and implementing a parent-teacher involvement program for you. All information is held in strict confidence.

Directions:
  1. Read the entire form carefully.
  2. In Column A check 15 items of interest to you.
  3. In Column B rank 5 of the 15 items you checked in Column A. Number the item of highest priority to you 5, the next highest 4, and so on.
  4. You may write additional comments in the space provided.

A	B	
X		1. Help my child learn.
		2. Build my child's self-confidence.
		3. Select activities to help my child learn (books, games, toys, projects, experiences).
X		4. Teach my child to follow directions.
X		5. Help my child enjoy learning.
		6. Assist my child in language development.
		7. Teach my child problem-solving skills.
		8. Fulfill my role as (father) (mother) to my child.
X		9. Avoid emotional involvement in my child's emotional outbursts.
X		10. Protect my child from getting hurt.
		11. Care for my child when he or she is sick or injured.
X	2	12. Discipline my child.
X	3	13. Deal with my child's misbehavior.
X	4	14. Teach my child respect for people and property.
		15. Teach my child to express feelings in a socially acceptable manner
		16. Teach my child to show love, affection, and consideration for other family members.
X	5	17. Teach my child to live in harmony with the family (television, bedtime, meals, sharing, responsibilities).
		18. Develop a positive and productive relationship with my child.
X		19. Develop my problem-solving skills.

How can I obtain information on the following topics affecting my child:

A	B	
		20. Art activities
		21. Creative dramatics
		22. Educational games and activities
X		23. Exercise
		24. Health and hygiene
		25. Music
		26. Nutrition and diet
		27. Puppetry
X		28. Recreation
X		29. Sleep
		30. Toys

Other topics and activities of interest to me are:

A	B	
X	1	31. *What makes kids' behavior disordered?*
		32.
		33.
		34.
		35.

An Example of a Teacher's Monthly Schedule for September

SEPTEMBER

Monday	Tuesday	Wednesday	Thursday	Friday
			1 Meet with principal, nurse, social worker about newsletter "welcome"	2
5	6 Conference: 10:30 AM Mr. & Mrs. Smith	7	8 Conference 6:30 PM Mr. Webster	9
12 Conference: 9:00 AM Mrs. Daniels	13 Conference: 10:30 AM Mr. & Mrs. Smith	14	15 Conference: 4:30 PM Mr. & Mrs. Long	16 Conference: 8:15 AM Mrs. Ming
19 Conference: 8:00 AM Mr. & Mrs. Pulley 3:30 PM Mr. & Mrs. Ryan	20	21 Conference: 9:30 AM Mr. & Mrs. Holmes 3:30 PM Mr. Webster	22	23 Send Newsletter: a) Welcomes b) Who to call for what c) Children's accomplishments
26 Additional conferences as needed	27 Follow up calls on needs and activities forms	28 Parent Meeting: Rights and confidentiality 7:00 PM	29	30

An Example of a Teacher's Monthly Schedule for February

FEBRUARY

Monday	Tuesday	Wednesday	Thursday	Friday
			2 Observation: Mary's sitter 10:00–10:00 AM	3
6 Fill out periodic report cards this week Call Holmes	7 Call Daniels	8 Behavior Management Group: 10:00 AM	9 Observation: Smith: 10:00–11:00 AM	10 Check on Parent Partners
13 Send periodic report cards to students' homes	14 Call Long	15 Parent Advisory Group Meeting 7:00 PM	16 Call Pulley	17
20 Conference: 4:00 PM Smith	21 Readings for Mrs. Daniels	22 Behavior Management Group: 10:00 AM	23	24
27 Newsletters: Language Accomplishments	28			

299

APPENDIX A

Cases for Study and Role Playing

The case studies in this appendix represent a variety of exceptionalities and parent needs. Students without access to children with exceptionalities or their parents can use these cases to complete the chapter exercises in this book.

Marshall P., Age 8 Years, 4 Months

Diagnosis: Educable mental retardation.
Academic skills: Marshall's reading and mathematics skills are beginning first-grade level. He functions well with concrete facts and has great difficulty with abstractions. He successfully manipulates objects, pictures, and so on to perform tasks. He is very interested in books and "reads" pictures well.
Language: Marshall is very verbal. His social language is a strength. Marshall does not use conceptual language and cannot demonstrate basic concepts such as "in/out" or "up/down."
Behavior: Marshall tries to do all tasks presented to him. His teachers speak of him as a "good kid." He rarely requests help but sits with a task and continues to work at it (right or wrong) until he completes it or the study period ends. He is passive but cooperates with his peers in play and work tasks.
Parent concerns: Mr. and Mrs. P. are upset about Marshall's recent diagnosis of mental retardation. They are angry that the diagnosis came after Marshall repeated kindergarten and first grade and do not understand how their son can suddenly "become retarded." They have hired a tutor to work with Marshall during the summer. They have requested reevaluation of Marshall at a private diagnostic center. Marshall is the only surviving child in this family; a four-year-old sister died in a boating accident

when Marshall was an infant. Both parents are still grieving for their daughter and have stated, "First we lost Jessie, and now this."

Louise S., Age 4 Years, 5 Months

Diagnosis: Moderate mental retardation (Down's syndrome).

Self-help: Louise can dress and undress herself, except that she lacks sufficient fine-motor strength and coordination to manipulate small buttons or snaps and to tie shoes. She frequently states "me do" when her parents or older brother or sister try to help her. Louise attempts all tasks without prompting.

Preacademic skill: Louise can complete wooden puzzles of five or fewer pieces. She sings simple songs, finger plays, and works independently. She will busy herself with toys for extended periods. She rote counts to five and understands the concept of "one."

Language: Louise uses two-word statements to express her needs. She frequently sings and babbles to herself while playing. Her articulation is poor. She receives two twenty-minute speech therapy sessions each week.

Social skills: Louise plays well with both exceptional and nonexceptional peers at preschool. She initiates social interaction with adults. She has begun to "tease" adults around her and to display a sense of humor.

Parent concerns: Louise is the youngest of three children. Her older brother is a college freshman, and her sister is a high school junior. Mr. and Mrs. S. are concerned that Louise's siblings will become responsible for her care as the parents age. Mr. S. is in poor health and is worried about "keeping up" with Louise's needs. Both parents enjoy Louise a great deal. Their only specific concern at this time is Louise's "stubbornness."

Henry L., Age 11 Years, 3 Months

Diagnosis: Behavioral disorders.

Behavior: Henry has great difficulty controlling his behavior in the classroom. He is upset easily and is aggressive verbally and physically. When assigned a task to complete in a specific period, Henry will begin the task, then become distracted. When reminded to return to work, Henry becomes angry and tears up his papers. Henry does not seem aware of the consequences of his actions. Since the beginning of counseling, Henry has gained better control over his impulsiveness.

Academic: Henry is an avid reader of science fiction. His mathematical skills are slightly below grade level. His true ability is difficult to measure because he does not complete tests, worksheets, and other work. His cursive handwriting is barely legible, and his spelling is poor.

Parent concerns: Mr. and Mrs. L. were divorced several years ago, and Mr. L. has custody of Henry. Henry rarely sees his mother, and his grandmother assumes his primary care. Mr. L. is considering remarriage, but Henry has announced that he "hates" his father's fiancée, Ms. J. During a family dinner, Henry threw a plate of food at Ms. J. Mr. L. is considering asking his former wife to assume custody or seeking foster home placement. Three-way counseling with Henry, Ms. J., and Mr. L. has not resulted in much behavior change.

Lisa B., Age 14 Years, 3 Months

Diagnosis: Profound hearing impairment.

Academic skills: Lisa is currently functioning at approximately the 4.5 grade level in reading and written expression and the 6.3 grade level in mathematics.

Language: Lisa uses total communication, signing and speaking simultaneously. Her speech is difficult to understand. She receives three twenty-minute sessions of individual speech therapy weekly. She wears biaural hearing aids but claims these aids do not help her and make her look "ugly." She "forgets" the aids whenever possible.

Social skills: Lisa would like to transfer to the local high school with an interpreter in order to attend school with her neighborhood friends. According to her parents, however, Lisa has little contact with the children in her neighborhood; all her friends attend the special day school for the deaf. Lisa attends Sunday school with nonexceptional peers, but they ignore her. The teacher asked her parents to withdraw her from Sunday school because she was interfering with other students' progress. Several boys in the class called her "doorknob," imitated her signing, talked behind their hands, and otherwise ridiculed her.

Parent concerns: Mr. and Mrs. B. want Lisa to develop her speech and language skills to the maximum. They fear Lisa's Sunday school experience represents hearing people's typical reaction to the deaf. They want their daughter to remain in the protected environment of the school for the deaf as long as possible. They are concerned that Lisa is becoming part of the deaf subculture at her school.

Eileen S., Age 13 Years, 9 Months

Diagnosis: Nonexceptional.
Academic skills: Eileen currently functions at grade level in all subject areas; she reports that her favorite subject is English, and she enjoys writing and illustrating story books for her younger sister.
Extracurricular activities: Though Eileen has taken music lessons (piano) for several years, she is not interested in joining band or choir at her school. She played softball at her elementary school but does not participate in any sports in junior high school.
Parent concerns: Eileen, who was an A student throughout elementary school, is earning Bs and Cs in junior high school. She has only one close friend, a girl who went to elementary school with her. A boisterous leader in elementary school, she has remained outside of extracurricular activities in junior high. Mr. and Mrs. S. are concerned that she isn't a "star" any more and that the large junior high may be too competitive for her. Eileen has expressed no concerns, saying only that even though "a lot more kids are around," the larger school does not bother her. Mr. and Mrs. S. have decided to begin punishing Eileen for any grade lower than a B. They have requested a psychological evaluation.
Teacher concerns: Ms. M., Eileen's homeroom and social study teacher, feels that Eileen is adjusting from a small elementary school to junior high school satisfactorily. The teacher believes that Eileen is working to the best of her ability. Ms. M. is concerned about Eileen's parents' decision to punish her for grades lower than a B. She is very hesitant to refer Eileen for testing.

Rebecca H., Age 9 Years, 5 Months

Diagnosis: Autism.
Self-help: Rebecca cares for her personal hygiene and grooming when reminded. She dresses and undresses herself without help. Though Rebecca's self-feeding skills are good, she eats

only four foods (bananas, graham crackers, peanut butter, and marshmallows). Rebecca has a history of eliminating one "favorite" food from her diet and replacing it with another. She will then eat only those few foods for a month or so before eliminating one and substituting another.

Language: Rebecca uses echolalia (repeating others' words) to communicate her needs. When making a request, she answers her own question ("Do you want a puzzle? Yes.") She receives speech therapy three times a week, and her communication is improving.

Academic skills: Rebecca can word call at the ninth-grade level. She does not demonstrate reading comprehension. She can add and subtract three-digit numbers mentally and is beginning to multiply. She prints carelessly, running words, sentences, and paragraphs together.

Social skills: During free time or recess, Rebecca either walks the perimeter of the room or play area alone or spins an object inappropriately (record player, toy truck wheels). She will use social language if provided a model (please, thank you, hello).

Parent concerns: Mr. and Mrs. H. are very concerned about Rebecca's diet. They want to work with the school to increase the number of foods Rebecca will eat. Both parents have completed a behavior modification course and have successfully used behavioral interventions to control Rebecca's behavior. Rebecca's only sibling, an older brother of fifteen, is embarrassed by his sister's behavior and robotic voice. He spends a great deal of time away from home. The parents are worried about his inability to accept Rebecca.

Michael R., Age 8 Years, 1 Month

Diagnosis: Learning disabilities.

Academic skills: Michael is reading at the first-grade level; his mathematics skills are at the mid-first-grade level. Michael is very verbal and enjoys making up stories. Michael's poor fine motor skills make his printing very labored and difficult to read.

Language: Michael is very verbal and has a large oral vocabulary. He is quite imaginative and performs well above average in sentence completion tasks.

Social skills: Michael is self-conscious about his poor academic functioning. As a result, he exaggerates his abilities in other areas to his classmates. Michael tells involved stories of imagined experiences. This behavior causes his classmates to label him a liar. He is alone most of the time during recess and free play.

Parent concerns: Michael is the younger of two children. His eleven-year-old brother does well in school, plays saxophone, and is the captain of his soccer team. Mr. and Mrs. R. believe that Michael is either lazy, stubborn, or both. Mrs. R. states that she has a cousin who had trouble reading and is now an aeronautical engineer. She suggests that if the teachers could get Michael to work, he would achieve. Mr. and Mrs. R. are very concerned about Michael's progress. They have tried eye exercises, perceptual motor training, a psychologist, and a counselor for short periods of time, with little success. The counselor advised them that special education held the most promise for Michael, so Mr. and Mrs. R. are willing to cooperate with the school in any way.

Raphael G., Age 6 Years, 1 Month

Diagnosis: Moderate mental retardation.

Self-help Raphael is beginning to dress himself. Until he began school in September, his mother or older sister, who share responsibility for his care, dressed and fed him. Raphael appears able to perform these skills but has not had the opportunity to learn and practice them.

Language: Raphael follows simple commands in both Spanish and English. Though his home is bilingual, Mr. and Mrs. G. try to use English with their children. Raphael uses one- or two-word utterances to express his needs. He uses appropriate social language spontaneously (greeting people, please, thank you, and so on). Raphael sings children's songs and makes requests to his mother in Spanish. He uses English in school.

Preacademic skills: Raphael traces his first and last name, names his body parts, and names four colors. He can match letters and order the letters of his first name. He demonstrates one-to-one correspondence and counts to five in English and Spanish.

Parent concerns: Raphael is one of five children. He is the only boy; his sisters are three, nine, fifteen, and seventeen. His older sister, Rosa, shares the primary care for Raphael with his mother. Mrs. G. works part-time some afternoons and evenings. Mr. G. is uncomfortable with the label "mentally retarded." He will not attend parent meetings that include the parents of exceptional children. Both parents belong to the Parent-Teacher Organization. Mrs. G. is finding it more difficult to deal with Raphael now that he is beginning to perform skills independently. Mr. G. is excited about the new things Raphael has learned. However, he has difficulty adjusting to the demands of Raphael's new level of functioning.

Mark N., Age 8 Years, 3 Months

Diagnosis: Moderate mental retardation.

Academic skills: Mark names eight colors; spells his first name orally; recognizes the first four letters of the alphabet; states his full name, address, and age; and sorts by shape and color. He cannot sort by size, report on the weather, or classify. He has difficulty discriminating letters in sorting, and he reverses letters when printing his first name. In mathematics, Mark rote counts to ten and gives one and two objects when requested. He does not recognize numerals.

Self-help: Mark cannot button small buttons, buckle his belt, or tie his shoes. He needs help toileting because of his inability to fasten clothes.

Language: Mark is very verbal. He uses six-word utterances, has a large vocabulary, and uses "up/down," "out/in," "over/under." Mark has difficulty with directional concepts such as "forward/ backward," "away from/ toward," "left/right," and "front/back." He also has trouble sequencing when relating his experiences.

Gross- and fine-motor skills: Mark uses a stencil to produce shapes but cannot hold a pencil correctly and cannot cut along a line. He frequently bumps into objects. Mark cannot ride a trike, jump on two feet, or balance on one foot.

Behavioral/social skills: Mark becomes frustrated with motor tasks and refuses to attempt them. He interacts well verbally with adults and peers.

Parent concerns: A neurologist has diagnosed Mark as "attention-deficit-disordered," but his mother feels he is learning-disabled and should be placed differently. He is distractible and has difficulty completing tasks. Mark is frequently out of his seat.

Teacher's concerns: The current disagreement between Mark's mother and the school district about his diagnosis is of great concern to Ms. B., Mark's teacher. His difficulties attending to tasks and his out-of-seat behavior are becoming disruptive to her class.

Family description: Mark is the youngest of three children and the only boy. His fifteen- and sixteen-year-old sisters assist him in his self-help skills. Father and mother are both very interested in diagnosis and visited several pediatricians and neurologists before they attained the present diagnosis, which they feel is accurate. Both parents disagree with the school district diagnosis of mental retardation; the mother focuses most on Mark's behaviors and self-help skills, the father on academic progress.

Sally G., Age 10 Years, 7 Months

Diagnosis: Multiple handicaps.

Self-help: Sally can remove her pants and socks herself and can remove her coat with verbal cues. She needs help untying her shoes and needs help with all fasteners. Sally can scoop food independently using a weighted spoon but cannot pierce with a fork. She wipes her mouth with a napkin when reminded. She needs help to carry her tray to her place and to open her milk carton. Sally needs physical assistance to perform basic independent living skills, such as hanging her own coat, using a drinking fountain, and choosing a play activity. She cannot wash her hands without assistance because she cannot turn the water faucets herself. She cannot put toothpaste on her brush but can adequately brush her teeth with a reminder to spit rather than swallow. Sally initiates toileting by using the toilet sign and placing the trainer's hand on the fastener of her pants.

Language: Sally has developed many manipulative skills. When rocked or jostled, she gives the trainer a verbal signal and physical prompt to repeat the activity. "Toilet" remains her only expressive sign. She requests objects by reaching for them or by putting the trainer's hand on the desired object.

Motor skills: Sally can pull herself along a scooter-board obstacle course in ninety seconds. She cannot perform bilateral activities, such as pulling apart popbeads, because she lacks strength on her left side. With her right hand weighted in her lap, she can stack only one of five cones using her left hand.

Preacademic skills: Sally can match three everyday objects. She cannot string beads because of her difficulty using both hands. She responds to her name three out of five times but needs a gesture accompanying the verbal cue to "come here," "pick up," and "give me."

Parent concerns: Sally is the oldest child of a single-parent family. Though Sally is still young, her mother worries about future residential placement. Mrs. G. has begun a trust fund for Sally for the placement she prefers, a group home not far from the family's apartment. Sally's five-year-old brother enjoys playing with Sally's wheelchair and adaptive equipment and has begun to ask questions about Sally's not talking, sleeping in diapers, and so on.

Special considerations: This family needs respite care. Mrs. G. currently has an excellent sitter for both children, but finding full-time care during the summer remains a problem. Mrs. G. is quite supportive of Sally's program and follows through to the best of her ability. Occasionally, however, Mrs. G. simply does not have the time or energy to complete home programs for she works full-time and must often work overtime as well.

APPENDIX B

Support and Informational Organizations

The following organizations and agencies provide information and support to parents and teachers of individuals with disabilities. Many publish pamphlets, periodicals, and books that can be used as resources in working with parents and their exceptional children. In addition, state and local departments of mental health, local regional offices for developmental disabilities, and family and children service agencies frequently provide publications or conduct groups for families with members who have exceptionalities.

Alexander Graham Bell Association for the Deaf
3416 Volta Place, N.W.
Washington, D.C. 20007

Allergy Foundation of America
801 Second Avenue
New York, NY 10017

American Association for Gifted Children
15 Gramercy Park
New York, NY 10003

American Association for Maternal and Child Health
P.O. Box 965
Los Altos, CA 94022

Appendix B • Support and Informational Organizations **311**

American Association on Mental Retardation
5101 Wisconsin Avenue
Washington, D.C. 20016

American Coalition for Citizens with Disabilities
1346 Connecticut Avenue, N.W., Suite 1124
Washington, D.C. 20036

American Council for the Blind
1211 Connecticut Avenue, N.W.
Washington, D.C. 20006

American Diabetes Association
18 East 48th Street
New York, NY 10011

American Foundation for the Blind
15 West 16th Street
New York, NY 10011

American Printing House for the Blind
1839 Frankfort Avenue
P.O. Box 6085
Louisville, KY 40206

American Speech-Language-Hearing Association
10901 Rockville Pike
Rockville, MD 20852

Arthritis Foundation
1212 Avenue of the Americas
New York, NY 10036

Asociacion de Padres Pro-Bienestar de Ninos Impedidos de Puerto Rico
Box Q
Rio Piedras, PR 00928

Association for Children and Adults with Learning Disabilities
4156 Library Road
Pittsburg, PA 15234

Association for the Education of the Visually Handicapped
919 Walnut, Fourth Floor
Philadelphia, PA 19107

Association for Persons with Severe Handicaps
7010 Roosevelt Way, N.E.
Seattle, WA 98115

Canadian Association for the Mentally Retarded
Kinsman NIMR Building
4700 Keele Street
Toronto, Ontario
Canada M5R 2K2

Closer Look Information Center for the Handicapped
P.O. Box 1492
Washington, D.C. 20013

Coordinating Council for Handicapped Children
220 South State Street
Room 412
Chicago, IL 60604

Council for Exceptional Children
1920 Association Drive
Reston, VA 22091

Daycare and Child Development Council of America, Inc.
520 Southern Building
805 Fifteenth Street, N.W.
Washington, D.C. 20005

Down's Syndrome Congress
Room 1562
1640 West Roosevelt Road
Chicago, IL 60608

Epilepsy Foundation of America
1828 L Street, N.W., Suite 405
Washington, D.C. 20036

Federation for Children with Special Needs
312 Stuart Street, 2nd Floor
Boston, MA 02116

International Association of Parents of the Deaf
814 Thayer Avenue
Silver Springs, MD 20910

La Leche League International
9616 Minneapolis Avenue
Franklin Park, IL 60131

Leukemia Society of America, Inc.
211 East 43rd Street
New York, NY 10017

March of Dimes
Birth Defects Foundation
1275 Mamaroneck Avenue
White Plains, NY 10065

Muscular Dystrophy Association of America, Inc.
1828 Banking Street, Room 1
Greensboro, NC 27408

National Association for Children with Learning Disabilities
4156 Library Road
Pittsburgh, PA 15234

National Association for Creative Children and Adults
8080 Springvalley Drive
Cincinnati, OH 45236

National Association for the Deaf-Blind
2703 Forest Oak Circle
Norman, OK 73071

National Association for Down's Syndrome
P.O. Box 63
Oak Park, IL 60303

National Association for Retarded Citizens
2709 Avenue E East
P.O. Box 6109
Arlington, TX 76011

National Association for the Visually Handicapped
3201 Balboa Street
San Francisco, CA 94121

National Association of the Deaf
814 Thayer Avenue
Silver Spring, MD 20910

National Black Child Development Institute
1463 Rhode Island Avenue, N.W.
Washington, D.C. 20005

National Committee for the Prevention of Child Abuse
332 South Michigan Avenue
Chicago, IL 60604

National Down's Syndrome Congress
528 Ashland Avenue
River Forest, IL 60305

National Easter Seal Society for Crippled Children and Adults
2023 W. Ogden Avenue
Chicago, IL 60612

National Federation of the Blind
1346 Connecticut Avenue, N.W.
Dupont Circle Building, Suite 212
Washington, D.C. 20036

National Hemophilia Foundation
19 West 34th Street
New York, NY 10001

National Paraplegia Foundation
333 N. Michigan Avenue
Chicago, IL 60601

Appendix B • Support and Informational Organizations **315**

National Society for Austistic Children and Adults
1234 Massachusetts Avenue, N.W.
Suite 1017
Washington, D.C. 20005

National Society for the Prevention of Blindness
79 Madison Avenue
New York, NY 10016

National Tay-Sachs and Allied Diseases Association, Inc.
122 East 42nd Street
New York, NY 10017

PACER (Parent Advocacy Coalition of Educational Rights)
4701 Chicago Avenue South
Minneapolis, MN 55407

Parent Educational Advocacy Training Center
228 S. Pitt Street, Room 300
Alexandria, VA 22314

Parents Anonymous
6733 South Sepulreda
Suite 270
Los Angeles, CA 90045

Parents as Allies
Portland State University
P.O. Box 751
Portland, OR 97207

PAVE (Parents Advocating Vocational Education)
1010 South I Street
Tacoma, WA 98405

Siblings for Significant Change
105 East 22nd Street
New York, NY 10010

Sibling Information Network
Department of Educational Psychology
Box U64, School of Education
University of Connecticut
Storrs, CT 06268

Spina Bifida Association of America
343 S. Dearborn Street, Room 319
Chicago, IL 60604

United Cerebral Palsy Association
66 East 34th Street
New York, NY 10016

APPENDIX C

Worksheets and Forms

This appendix provides worksheets and forms to help teachers design and implement parent-teacher collaboration activities. Readers can use these forms to complete the chapter exercises or to provide models for developing a parent-teacher collaboration program responsive to special needs.

FIGURE C.1 • *Program Development Form*

Parents' Names _____ Teacher _____ Date _____

I	II	III	IV
Assessment	Goals and Objectives	Activities	Evaluation
A. List the assessment techniques used to obtain the data synthesized in IB.	A. List the goals, by priority, derived from the assessment process and mutually agreed on by parents and teacher.	List the activities designed by parents and teacher to meet the objectives in IIB.	A. Process: List the procedures parents and teacher will use to evaluate the processes for carrying out the activities in III.
B. List the needs mutually agreed upon using the assessment techniques in IA.	B. List the objectives derived from the goals in IIA.		B. Content: List the procedures parents and teachers will use to evaluate the content of the activities in III.

FIGURE C.2 • *Parents' Needs Form*

Confidential   Date: _____

Parent's Name _____

Child's Name _____

Introduction:
    Listed below are several statements describing concerns common to the parents of exceptional children. The items may or may not concern you at this time. Please complete only those items that currently concern you.

    The information on this form is used *only* to help plan and implement a parent-teacher involvement program. All information is held in strict confidence.

Directions:
1. Read each statement carefully.
2. Circle the number on the 1–5 scale that most closely approximates your current need in each area. Circle *1* to indicate a low priority need and *5* to indicate a high priority need.
3. Below the 1–5 scale are several statements suggesting ways you may prefer to meet your stated needs. Please check only *two* of the four statements listed below each item.
4. You may write additional comments in the space provided.

I. I need the opportunity to discuss my feelings about my exceptional child and myself with someone who understands the problem.

(Circle the appropriate number.)

1	2	3	4	5
Low Priority				High Priority

(Check *only* two statements.)

_____ I prefer to talk to a professional.
_____ I prefer to talk to the parent of an exceptional child.
_____ I prefer to be referred to another agency for counseling.
_____ I prefer to read articles and books discussing the reactions of parents of exceptional children.
_____ I prefer _____

II. I would like to talk with other parents and families who have exceptional children.

(Circle the appropriate number.)

1	2	3	4	5
Low Priority				High Priority

(Check *only* two statements.)

_____ I prefer to be in a discussion group.
_____ I prefer to participate in social gatherings (picnics, parties, potluck dinners).
_____ I prefer to meet informally.
_____ I prefer to participate in general meetings, workshops, lectures, demonstrations, and other informational gatherings.
_____ I prefer _____

(cont.)

FIGURE C.2 *Continued*

III. I would like to learn more about my child's exceptionality.

(Circle the appropriate number.)

1	2	3	4	5
Low Priority				High Priority

(Check *only* two statements.)

_____ I prefer to obtain information through reading.
_____ I prefer to observe teachers and other professionals working with my child and then discuss my observations.
_____ I prefer individual parent-teacher conferences.
_____ I prefer a parent-teacher discussion group.
_____ I prefer _____.

IV. I would like to learn more about how children develop and learn, especially exceptional children.

(Circle the appropriate number.)

1	2	3	4	5
Low Priority				High Priority

(Check *only* two statements.)

_____ I prefer to obtain information through reading.
_____ I prefer to participate in a formal behavior management training course.
_____ I prefer a parent-teacher discussion group.
_____ I prefer individual training in my home by a teacher or other professional.
_____ I prefer to attend meetings at which specialists present information on behavior management.
_____ I prefer _____.

VI. I would like to work with a teacher or other professional so that I can use the same instructional methods at home that the school uses.

(Circle the appropriate number.)

1	2	3	4	5
Low Priority				High Priority

(Check *only* two statements.)

_____ I prefer to observe my child in school.
_____ I prefer to attend a training program in observation.
_____ I prefer to attend a course in instructional methods.
_____ I prefer to work with the teacher in my child's classroom.
_____ I prefer in-home training by a teacher or other professional.
_____ I prefer to learn through readings, newsletters, telephone communication, and similar resources.
_____ I prefer _____.

FIGURE C.2 *Continued*

VII. I would like _____
_____.

(Circle the appropriate number.)

1	2	3	4	5
Low Priority				High Priority

(Write the appropriate statements.)

_____ I prefer _____
_____.

_____ I prefer _____
_____.

Comments:

Thank you.

FIGURE C.3 • *Parents' Activities Form*

Confidential   Date: _____

Parent's Name _____

Child's Name _____

Introduction:
    Listed below are thirty-five topics and activities generally believed of interest to the parents of exceptional children. Not all parents are interested in any single item, nor is any parent interested in all the items.
    Your response to this questionnaire is used *only* to assist in planning and implementing a parent-teacher involvement program for you. All information is held in strict confidence.

Directions:
1. Read the entire form carefully.
2. In Column A check 15 items of interest to you.
3. In Column B rank 5 of the 15 items you checked in Column A. Number the item of highest priority to you 5, the next highest 4, and so on.
4. You may write additional comments in the space provided.

A	B	
___	___	1. Help my child learn.
___	___	2. Build my child's self-confidence.
___	___	3. Select activities to help my child learn (books, games, toys, projects, experiences).
___	___	4. Teach my child to follow directions.
___	___	5. Help my child enjoy learning.
___	___	6. Assist my child in language development.
___	___	7. Teach my child problem-solving skills.
___	___	8. Fulfill my role as (father) (mother) to my child.
___	___	9. Avoid emotional involvement in my child's emotional outbursts.
___	___	10. Protect my child from getting hurt.
___	___	11. Care for my child when he or she is sick or injured.
___	___	12. Discipline my child.
___	___	13. Deal with my child's misbehavior.
___	___	14. Teach my child respect for people and property.
___	___	15. Teach my child to express feelings in a socially acceptable manner.

FIGURE C.3 *Continued*

——— ——— 16. Teach my child to show love, affection, and consideration for other family members.

——— ——— 17. Teach my child to live in harmony with the family (television, bedtime, meals, sharing, responsibilities).

——— ——— 18. Develop a positive and productive relationship with my child.

——— ——— 19. Develop my problem-solving skills.

How can I obtain information on the following topics affecting my child:

——— ——— 20. Art activities

——— ——— 21. Creative dramatics

——— ——— 22. Educational games and activities

——— ——— 23. Exercise

——— ——— 24. Health and hygiene

——— ——— 25. Music

——— ——— 26. Nutrition and diet

——— ——— 27. Puppetry

——— ——— 28. Recreation

——— ——— 29. Sleep

——— ——— 30. Toys

Other topics and activities of interest to me are:

——— ——— 31. _____
——— ——— 32. _____
——— ——— 33. _____
——— ——— 34. _____
——— ——— 35. _____

Thank you!

FIGURE C.4 • *Behavior Log Form*

Target behavior _____

Observer's name _____ Child observed _____

Day or Date	Time		Antecedents	Consequences	Applied Interventions	Comments
	Begins	Ends				

FIGURE C.5 • *Meeting Evaluation Form*

Date: _____

Meeting Subject: _____

Please circle the responses that best reflect your feelings about this meeting.

1. The subject was:	Not relevant	Somewhat relevant	Relevant	Very relevant
2. The information was:	Not useful	Somewhat useful	Useful	Very useful
3. The manner of presentation was:	Poor	Fair	Good	Very good
4. Audio visual materials and handouts were.	Poor	Fair	Good	Very good

5. Would you like more information on the subject?   Yes   No

6. Comments:

Thanks! By letting us know how you feel, we can better meet your needs.

Your Advisory Committee

FIGURE C.6 · *Parent-Volunteer Questionnaire*

Date _____
Parents' Names _____
Child's Name _____ Telephone Number _____
Teacher's Name _____

    Parents! We need your help. Please consider helping with the activities and projects listed on this questionnaire. Check all those activities for which you can volunteer service. Your participation will help us provide an interesting, stimulating, individualized educational program for your children.

Mother   Father

_____ _____ I would like to assist in the classroom on a regular basis. The times I have available are:

                    Days   Hours
                    _____ _____
                    _____ _____

_____ _____ I would like to assist *occasionally* in the classroom.

    (check one)
    a. Contact me _____
    b. I will contact the school _____

_____ _____ I would like to assist from my home.

In-Classroom Activities

_____ _____ Read a story to the children.
_____ _____ Assist children in a learning center.
_____ _____ Assist individual children with learning and remedial tasks.
_____ _____ Assist with the music program.
_____ _____ Assist with the art program.
_____ _____ Assist with the movement activities program.
_____ _____ Work puzzles and play table games with the children.
_____ _____ Help with cooking projects.
_____ _____ Assist with writing activities.
_____ _____ Assist with carpentry projects.
_____ _____ Assist with homemaking projects.
_____ _____ Assist with the care of classroom pets.
_____ _____ Assist with gardening and horticultural projects.
_____ _____ Assist children during recess, snack time, lunch, and free time.
_____ _____ Take a child for a walk.
_____ _____ Assist with field trips.

FIGURE C.6 *Continued*

Home-Based Activities

_____ _____ Make instructional materials: games, flash cards, puppets, costumes, charts.

_____ _____ Type.

_____ _____ Help with costumes for dress-up events.

_____ _____ Cut out and catalog pictures from magazines, catalogs, and newspapers for instructional use.

_____ _____ Help repair classroom furnishings and instructional materials and equipment.

_____ _____ Help construct new furnishings and equipment for the classroom.

_____ _____ Organize parties for birthdays and holidays.

_____ _____ Babysit for parents who are volunteering their service to the classroom.

_____ _____ Care for classroom pets during vacations.

_____ _____ Make props and sets for plays, parties, and special events.

_____ _____ Make room and bulletin board decorations.

_____ _____ Make posters.

_____ _____ Assemble and staple materials.

_____ _____ Research and organize field trips.

_____ _____ Help plan and conduct parent activities, such as meetings, educational training programs, and conferences.

_____ _____ Research and contact sources for free instructional supplies (computer cards and paper, wood scraps, boxes, carpet, print shop discards, spools, pencils, paper).

_____ _____ Make items to sell for fund raising.

_____ _____ Assist with fund-raising activities.

_____ _____ Plan and organize social events.

What other activities could you help with?

A. In the classroom:

B. At home:

What other family members or friends are interested in volunteering services to the children?

A. _____

B. _____

Your comments, concerns, and questions are welcome.

FIGURE C.7 · *Parent Collaboration Log*

Parent Name(s) _____

Child's Name _____ Birthdate _____

Home Phone Number _____ Work Phone Number _____

Date File Opened _____

Activities	Date

I. INTAKE AND ASSESSMENT
    A. Intake and Assessment Conference(s) _____

    B. Intake and Assessment Completed _____

II. SELECTION OF GOALS AND OBJECTIVES
    A. Parents' Needs Form Returned _____
    B. Parents' Activities Form Returned _____
    C. Goals and Objectives Conferences _____

    D. Parent-Teacher Involvement Plan Completed _____

III. ACTIVITY ATTENDANCE
    A. Individual Conferences
        1. Home Visit _____
        2. Child Evaluation Conference _____
        3. IEP Conference _____
        4. _____ _____
        5. _____ _____

    A. Group Meetings
        1. Orientation Meeting _____
        2. _____ _____
        3. _____ _____
        4. _____ _____
        5. _____ _____

IV. EVALUATION
    A. Evaluation Form Returned _____
    B. Evaluation Conference _____

(cont.)

FIGURE C.7 *Continued*

Phone Contacts

Date   Reason/Results
_____   _____
_____   _____
_____   _____
_____   _____
_____   _____

Other Contacts (Letters, notes, and so on)
Date   Description   Reason/Results
_____   _____   _____
_____   _____   _____
_____   _____   _____
_____   _____   _____

330 *Appendix C* • *Worksheets and Forms*

FIGURE C.8 • *Parent Collaboration Program Evaluation Form*

May 24, 19__

Dear _____:

The Parent-Teacher Involvement Program is your program, designed with you and for you. We want it to meet your needs and the needs of your child. Thus, it is important to know what you like and dislike about the program and what activities you would and would not participate in next year.

To help in the planning of next year's program and to make it more responsive to your needs, we invite you to complete and return the attached questionnaire. Please be frank. If you wish to remain anonymous, do not sign the form. Anonymous or signed, your responses will be held in the strictest of confidence.

Thank you for your help.

Sincerely,

Sarah Paul
Teacher

FIGURE C.8 *Continued*

Please make an X in the appropriate columns to the right of each activity listed in the left column. Indicate whether you participated in the activity and how you felt about it. For meetings and workshops, please indicate if you wanted to attend but were unable to. Comments and suggestions are welcome.

ACTIVITY	I was involved in this activity.	I wanted to participate but could not.	I would participate again next year.	My rating of this activity is:			
				Excellent	Good	Fair	Poor
Intake/Assessment Conferences							
Parent Orientation Meeting							
Open House							
Rights and Confidentiality Meeting							
Newsletter							
Passport							
Telephone Calls							
Individual Conferences							
Parent Partners							
Behavior Management Group							
Other:							

Use the space below to comment on this year's program and make suggestions for next year.

APPENDIX D

Spanish Worksheets and Forms

Today's teachers serve many Spanish-speaking children with exceptionalities and their families, often in bilingual programs. To help develop appropriate programs for these families, this appendix presents Spanish versions of several worksheets and forms used in this text. Readers who serve bilingual children and their parents, or who expect to in the future, can use these forms to complete the chapter exercises or to develop their own programs for Spanish-speaking children and their families.

FIGURE D.1 • *Program Development Form*

FORMULARIO DEL PROGRAMA DE DESARROLLO

Nombre y apellido de los padres: _____ Maestro/a _____ Fecha: _____

I Evaluación	II Metas y Objetivos	III Actividades	IV Evaluación
A. Enumere las técnicas de evaluación que se usaron para obtener los datos resumidos en IB.	A. Enumere los objetivos, en orden de prioridad, que han resultado del proceso de evaluación y sobre los que se han puesto de acuerdo los padres y los maestros.	Enumere las actividades diseñadas por los padres y el maestro o maestra para lograr los objetivos	A. Haga una lista de los métodos que los padres y maestros van a usar para evaluar los procesos diseñados para implementar las actividades en III.
B. Enumere las necesidades sobre las que se han puesto de acuerdo cuando se han usado las técnicas de evaluación en IA.	B. Enumere los objetivos que se han ido desarrollando a base de las metas u objetivos en IIA.		B. *El Contenido:* Enumere los procedimientos que los padres y los maestros van a usar para evaluar el contenido de las actividades en III.

FIGURE D.2 • *Parents' Needs Form*

FORMULARIOS DE NECESIDADES DE LOS PADRES

<u>Confidencial</u> Fecha: _____

Nombre y apellido de los padres: _____

Nombre del niño/a: _____

Introducción:
  A continuación, van a enumerarse una serie de frases que describen temas comunes a los padres de niños excepcionales. Algunos de estos temas pueden no atañer a sus circumstancias en este momento. Por favor complete solamente los párrafos que se apliquen a su situación.
  La información en este formulario es estrictamente para propósitos de planeación e implementación de un programa de colaboración entre padres y maestros. Toda la información es estrictamente confidencial.

Instrucciones:
  1. Lea cada frase cuidadosamente.
  2. En la escala de 1 a 5—el *1* representa baja prioridad y el *5* indica una necesidad de alta prioridad—señale con un circulo la frase que mejor indique su actitud sobre las necesidades descritas.
  3. A continuación de la escala de 1 a 5 hay varias sugerencias para cómo llenar sus necesidades. Por favor señale solamente *dos* de las cuatro frases debajo de cada tema.
  4. Escriba sus comentarios adicionales en el espacio apropiado.

I. Necesito la oportunidad de discutir mis sentimientos hacia mi niño/a excepcional y hacia mí mismo/a en relación a mi hijo/a con una persona que comprenda el problema.
  (Indique el número apropiado con un círculo)

  1   2   3   4   5
  Baja   Alta
  Prioridad   Prioridad

  Señale solamente *dos* reacciones:
  _____ Prefiero hablar con un profesional al respecto.
  _____ Prefiero hablar con el padre o los padres de niños excepcionales.
  _____ Prefiero que me refieran a otra agencia que ofrezca guianza.
  _____ Prefiero leer artículos y libros que discutan las reacciones de los padres de niños excepcionales.
  _____ Prefiero la siguiente opción _____

II. Quisiera reunirme con otros padres y familias con niños excepcionales.
  (Indique el numero apropiado con un círculo)

  1   2   3   4   5
  Baja   Alta
  Prioridad   Prioridad

  (Señale solamente *dos* reacciones)
  _____ Prefiero participar en un grupo de discusión.
  _____ Prefiero participar en reuniones sociales (picnics, comidas informales con otros padres, etc.).

FIGURE D.2 *Continued*

_____ Prefiero que nos reunamos informalmente.
_____ Prefiero participar en reuniones generales, talleres, conferencias, demostraciones, etc.
_____ Prefiero lo siguiente _____

III. Quiero informarme más con respecto a las necesidades especiales de mi hijo/a.

(Indique el número apropiado con un círculo)

1	2	3	4	5
Baja Prioridad				Alta Prioridad

(Señale solamente *dos* frases)

_____ Prefiero informarme a través de lectura.
_____ Prefiero observar a los maestros y otros profesionales trabajar con mi hijo/a y después discutir mis observaciones.
_____ Prefiero conferencias individuales con el maestro/a.
_____ Prefiero un grupo de discusión que incluya a padres y maestros.
_____ Prefiero lo siguiente _____

IV. Quisiera aprender sobre el desarrollo y el proceso de aprendizaje de los niños, especialmente de los niños excepcionales.

(Indique el número apropiado con un círculo)

1	2	3	4	5
Baja Prioridad				Alta Prioridad

(Señale solamente *dos* frases)

_____ Prefiero informarme a través de lectura.
_____ Prefiero participar en un curso formal sobre el manejo de comportamiento.
_____ Prefiero un grupo de discusión entre padres y maestros.
_____ Prefiero recibir entrenamiento individual en mi casa de un maestro/a u otro profesional.
_____ Prefiero atender conferencias en las que varios especialistas presenten información sobre el manejo de comportamiento.
_____ Prefiero lo siguiente _____ _____

VI. Quisiera trabajar con un maestro/a para poder aplicar los mismos métodos de instrucción en mi casa que se aplican en la escuela.

(Indique con un círculo el número apropiado)

1	2	3	4	5
Baja Prioridad				Alta Prioridad

(Señale solamente *dos* reacciones de las siguientes)

_____ Prefiero observar al niño en la escuela.
_____ Prefiero atender un programa de entrenamiento en técnicas de observacion.

FIGURE D.2 *Continued*

_____ Prefiero atender un curso en métodos de instrucción.
_____ Prefiero trabajar con el maestro/a en el salón de clase.
_____ Prefiero recibir entrenamiento de un maestro u otro profesional en mi casa.
_____ Prefiero informarme a través de lecturas, boletines de noticias, por teléfono, etc.
_____ Prefiero lo siguiente _____

VII. Quisiera lo siguiente _____

(Indique el número apropiado con un círculo)

1	2	3	4	5
Baja				Alta
Prioridad				Prioridad

(Anote aquí la frase apropriada)

_____ Prefiero lo siguiente _____

_____ Prefiero lo siguiente _____

Comentarios:

Muchas gracias.

FIGURE D.3 • *Parents' Activities Form*

Confidencial   Fecha: _____

Nombre y apellido de los padres: _____

Nombre del niño/a: _____

Introducción:
   A continuación van a enumerarse treinta y cinco temas y actividades que generalmente resultan de interés para los padres de niños excepcionales. No todos los padres estarán interesados en un solo tema, ni estarán todos interesados en todos los temas.
   Sus respuestas en este formulario se usarán *únicamente* para la planeación e implementación de un programa colaborativo para ustedes. Toda la información es estrictamente confidencial.

Direcciones
   1. Lea todo el formulario cuidadosamente.
   2. En la columna A señale 15 frases que le parezcan interesantes.
   3. En la columna B enumere en orden de prioridad 5 de las 15 frases que indicó en la columna A. El tema de más alta prioridad debe numerarse 5; el próximo de más alta prioridad debe numerarse 4, y así los 5.
   4. Escriba sus comentarios adicionales en el espacio apropiado.

Columna		Tema
A	B	
___	___	1. Ayudar a mi hijo/a a aprender.
___	___	2. Desarrollar la confianza de mi hijo/a en sí mismo.
___	___	3. Seleccionar actividades para ayudar a mi hijo/a a aprender (libros, juegos, juguetes, proyectos, experiencias).
___	___	4. Enseñar a mi hijo/a a seguir instrucciones.
___	___	5. Ayudar a mi hijo/a a gozar del proceso de aprendizaje.
___	___	6. Ayudar a mi hijo/a a desarrollar destrezas de lenguaje.
___	___	7. Enseñarle destrezas para resolver problemas.
___	___	8. Cumplir con mi papel como (padre) (madre).
___	___	9. Evitar involucrarme en las crisis emocionales del niño/a.
___	___	10. Cuidar de que el niño no se haga daño.
___	___	11. Cuidar el niño/a cuando este enfermo o se haya hecho daño.
___	___	12. Disciplinar al niño.
___	___	13. Manejar el comportamiento inapropiado del niño.
___	___	14. Enseñarle a respetar a la gente y a las cosas.
___	___	15. Enseñarle a que exprese sus sentimientos de una manera aceptable a la sociedad.

(cont.)

FIGURE D.3 *Continued*

_____ _____	16. Enseñarle a demostrar amor, afecto y consideración con respecto a otros miembros de la familia.
_____ _____	17. Enseñarle a vivir en armonía con la familia (televisión, hora de acostarse, comidas, generosidad, responsabilidades).
_____ _____	18. Desarrollar una actitud positiva y productiva hacia mi hijo/a.
_____ _____	19. Desarrollar destrezas para resolver problemas.

Como puedo obtener información sobre los siguientes temas con relación a mi hijo/a?

_____ _____ 20. Activadades de arte
_____ _____ 21. Drama creativo
_____ _____ 22. Juegos y activadades educacionales
_____ _____ 23. Ejercicio
_____ _____ 24. Salud e higiene
_____ _____ 25. Música
_____ _____ 26. Nutrición y dieta
_____ _____ 27. Títeres
_____ _____ 28. Recreación
_____ _____ 29. Sueño
_____ _____ 30. Juguetes

Otros temas y actividades de interés:

_____ _____ 31. _____
_____ _____ 32. _____
_____ _____ 33. _____
_____ _____ 34. _____
_____ _____ 35. _____

Muchas Gracias!

FIGURE D.4 • *Behavior Log Form*

Objetivo de comportamiento: _____

Nombre del observador: _____   Nombre del niño/a: _____

Día o Fecha	Hora		Antecedentes	Consecuencias	Intervención	Comentarios
	Empieza	Acaba				

FIGURE D.5 • *Meeting Evaluation Form*

FORMULARIO DE EVALUACION DE LA REUNION

Tema de la reunión: _____   Fecha: _____

Indique con un círculo la respuesta que mejor refleje lo que usted sintió con respecto a esta reunión:

1. El tema fue   no aplicable   algo necesario   importante   muy importante

2. La información que
   se presentó fue: no aplicable   algo práctica   práctica   muy práctica

3. El estilo de
   presentación fue: malo   regular   bueno   muy bueno

4. Los materiales
   audiovisuales
   fueron: malos   regulares   buenos   muy buenos

5. Quiere más información sobre este tema?   sí   no

6. Comentarios

Gracias. Informándonos sobre sus reacciones, podemos servirle mejor.

Comité de Asesoría

Appendix D • Spanish Worksheets and Forms 341

FIGURE D.6 • *Parent-Volunteer Questionnaire*

FORMULARIO DE PADRES VOLUNTARIOS

Nombre y apellido de los padres _____ Teléfono: _____
Nombre del niño/a _____
Nombre del maestro/a _____

¡Padres! Necesitamos su ayuda; por favor considere ayudarnos con las actividades y proyectos que mencionamos en este formulario. Indique en cuales actividades puede ofrecernos sus servicios voluntarios. Para ofrecer un programa educacional interesante, estimulante e individualizado para su hijo/a necesitamos su ayuda.

Padre   Madre

_____ _____ Podría ayudar en el salón de clase con regularidad. Dispongo de las siguientes horas:

              Días   Horas
              _____   _____
              _____   _____

_____ _____ Podría ayudar en el salón de clase ocasionalmente.

(indique a o b)

a. Llámeme _____

b. Yo me pondré en contacto con la escuela _____

_____ _____ Quisiera asistir en mi casa.

En las Actividades del Salón de Clase

_____ _____ Leyendo cuentos a los niños.

_____ _____ Ayudando a los niños en el centro de aprendizaje.

_____ _____ Ayudando a los niños individualmente con tareas de aprendizaje y trabajo remedial.

_____ _____ Asistiendo en el programa de música.

_____ _____ Asistiendo en el programa de arte.

_____ _____ Asistiendo en el programa de actividades de movimiento.

_____ _____ Asistiendo en los juegos y actividades de los niños.

_____ _____ Asistiendo en los proyectos de cocina.

_____ _____ Asistiendo en proyectos de redacción.

_____ _____ Asistendo en proyectos de carpintería.

FIGURE D.6 *Continued*

_____	_____	Ayudar en proyectos caseros.
_____	_____	Asistiendo en el cuidado de los animales.
_____	_____	Ayudando en proyectos de jardinería y horticultura.
_____	_____	Ayudando a los niños a las horas de recreo, almuerzo, etc.
_____	_____	Sacando a los niños a caminar.
_____	_____	Asistiendo en excursiones por fuera de la escuela.

En Mi Casa

_____ _____ Trabajando en el diseño y construcción de materiales de instrucción: juegos, tarjetas de instrucción, titeres, disfraces, listas, etc.

_____ _____ Pasando trabajos a máquina.

_____ _____ Ayudando a hacer disfraces para funciones de la escuela.

_____ _____ Recortando y catalogando materiales de revistas, catalogos y diarios para uso en el salón de clase.

_____ _____ Ayudando a arreglar los muebles del salón de clase y los materiales y equipo de instrucción.

_____ _____ Ayudar en la construcción de muebles y materiales para el salón de clase.

_____ _____ Organizar fiestas de cumpleaños y otras fiestas especiales.

_____ _____ Asistir en el cuidado de otros niños cuando los padres estén dando servicios voluntarios en la escuela.

_____ _____ Asistir en el cuidado de los animales que pertenecen a la clase durante las vacaciones de la escuela.

_____ _____ Hacer diseños para funciones de teatro, fiestas y otras ocasiones especiales.

_____ _____ Hacer decoraciones para el salón.

_____ _____ Hacer ficheros.

_____ _____ Ordenar y coser materiales de instrucción.

_____ _____ Investigar y organizar excursiones por fuera de la escuela.

_____ _____ Asistir en la organización de actividades para los padres—por ejemplo reuniones, programas de entrenamiento educacional, conferencias, etc.

_____ _____ Investigar y hacer contacto con gente y organizaciones que puedan donar gratis materiales para uso en el salón: por ejemplo, tarjetas de computadores, pedazos de madera, cajas, retazos de tapetes, desperdicios de imprentas, carretes, lápices, papel, etc.

FIGURE D.6 *Continued*

———— ———— Hacer cosas para vender en funciones para beneficiar a la escuela.

———— ———— Asistir en actividades para obtener fondos.

———— ———— Planear y organizar eventos sociales.

Si hay otras actividades en las que usted pueda participar como voluntario/a, por favor descríbalas aquí.

A. En el salón de clase:

B. En la casa:

Que otros miembros de la familia o amigos estarán interesados en prestar servicio voluntario para los niños?

A. _____

B. _____

Les agradecemos sus comentarios y preguntas.

FIGURE D.7 · *Parent Collaboration Log*

Nombre y apellido de los padres: _____

Nombre del niño/a: _____ Fecha de nacimiento: _____

Número del teléfono de la casa: _____ Del trabajo: _____

Fecha en que se ha iniciado el archivo: _____

Actividades   Fecha

I. INGRESO Y EVALUACION
   A. Conferencia de Ingreso y Evaluación   _____

   B. Ingreso y Evaluación completados   _____

II. SELECCION DE METAS Y OBJETIVOS
   A. Formulario de Necesidades de los Padres, Devuelto   _____
   B. Formulario de Actividades de los Padres, Devuelto   _____
   C. Conferencias sobre Metas y Objetivos   _____

   D. Plan de Actividades de Padres-Maestros, devuelto   _____

III. ACTIVIDADES ATENDIDAS
   A. Conferencias Individuales (Descripciones):
      1. Visita a la casa   _____
      2. Conferencia de Evaluación del Niño   _____
      3. Conferencia de IEP   _____
      4. _____ _____
      5. _____ _____

   B. Reuniones de Grupo (Descripciones:)
      1. Reunion de Orientacion   _____
      2. _____ _____
      3. _____ _____
      4. _____ _____
      5. _____ _____

IV. EVALUACION
   A. Formulario de Evaluacion devuelto   _____
   B. Conferencia de Evaluacion   _____

FIGURE D.7 *Continued*

Contactos por Telefono

Fecha	Razon/Resultados
_____	_____
_____	_____
_____	_____
_____	_____

Contactos Adicionales (Cartas, notas, etc.)

Fecha	Descripcion	Razon/Resultados
_____	_____	_____
_____	_____	_____
_____	_____	_____
_____	_____	_____

FIGURE D.8 • *Parent Collaboration Program Evaluation Form*

EVALUACION DEL PROGRAMA PARA PADRES Y MAESTROS

24 de mayo de 19__

Estimado _____:

    El Programa para Padres y Maestros es suyo, diseñado para usted y con usted. Este programa se ofrece esencialmente para atender sus necesidades y las de su niño/a. Es importante saber lo que a usted le agrada y le desagrada en el programa y en qué actividades usted podría participar en este proximo año.

    Para ayudarnos a planear el programa para el próximo año y hacerlo más apropiado para sus necesidades, le pedimos que complete y devuelva este formulario. Por favor, denos sus opiniones francamente. Si prefiere permanecer anónimo, no firme este formulario. Firmado o anónimo, sus respuestas se mantendrán confidenciales.

    Muchas gracias por su ayuda.

Atentamente,

Sarah Paul
Maestra

FIGURE D.8 *Continued*

Por favor indique con una X las columnas apropiados a la derecha de cada actividad anotada en la columna izquierda. Señale si usted participó en la actividad y sus reacciones al respecto. En el caso de reuniones y talleres, indique si usted quiso atender pero no pudo. Le agradeceriamos sus comentarios y sugerencias.

ACTIVIDAD	Participé en esta actividad	Quise tomar parte pero no pude	Quisiera participar el año entrante	Mi evaluación de esta actividad fue:			
				Excelente	Bueno	Mediocre	Malo
Conferencia de Ingreso/Evaluación							
Reunión de Orientación para los Padres							
Casa Abierta							
Reunión sobre Derechos y Confidencialidad							
Boletín							
Pasaporte							
Llamadas Telefónicas							
Conferencias Individuales							
Compañero/a a otros padres							
Grupo de Manejo de Comportamiento							
Otra:							

Comentarios sobre el programa de este año y sugerencias para el año entrante:

Index

Abused children, 253–257
Activities
 classroom, 222–225
 effectiveness of, 188
 evaluation of, 76–77, 183, 184, 195, 285–288
 group, 178–191
 implementation of, 75–76, 182–184, 187–188, 282–285
 for large groups, 181–185
 leadership techniques in, 189–191
 parent-volunteer, 228, 231–232
 planning of, 75–76, 181–182, 185–187
 selection of, 282–285
 for small groups, 185–191
Adaptation, to exceptional child, 24–40
Ad hoc committee, 233
Administrators, as resources, 103
Adoption, 257–259
Advocacy
 collaboration and, 55–56
 criteria for, 55
Affective learning, 15
African-American families, 249–250
Applied behavior analysis, 148, 149
Asian-American families, 251
Assertiveness strategies, 148, 149
Assessment
 of family needs, 92–101
 interview as, 83–92
 needs, 181–182
 psychosituational, 150–154, 169–177
Assessment conference, 71–74, 90–92, 276, 280–281

Association for Children and Adults with Learning Disabilities, 180
Attitudes, toward parent-teacher collaboration, 49–50
Autism, 28
Autism case study, 304–305
Awards, behavior and achievement, 123, 124, 125

Behavior
 definition of, 23
 observation of, 215–216, 217–218
 problems in, 150–154
 target, 150
Behavioral disorders case study, 302–303
Behavioral rehearsal, 221–222
Behavior and achievement awards, 123, 124, 125
Behavior change, strategies for, 148, 149, 202
Behavior log, in psychosituational assessment interview, 152–154
Behavior Log Form, 153, 324
Behavior Log Form (Spanish), 339
Behavior management
 leading to self-discipline, 11–12
 from training conference, 148–154
Behavior modification
 interviewing techniques for, 150–154
 lesson plan for, 207–209
 training program for, 205–207
Brainstorming, 147
Bronfenbrenner's social context theory, 24–40

347

Buckley Amendment of Public Law 93–380, 57
Bureaucratic transition, 267–268

Camp programs, 198
Carbondale Special Education Cooperative, 131
Case studies, 301–309
  autism, 304–305
  behavioral disorders, 302–303
  Down's syndrome, 302
  educable mental retardation, 301–302
  learning disabilities, 305–306
  moderate mental retardation, 302, 306–307, 307–308
  multiple handicaps, 308–309
  nonexceptional, 304
  profound hearing impairment, 303–304
Child abuse, 253–257
Child care, 198
Children
  abused, 253–257
  with exceptionalities, 21–41, 265–266
  home visits and, 159–161
  needs of, 9–17
  parent-teacher collaboration benefits for, 50–51
  participation of, in parent-teacher conference, 161–163
  transitions of, 265–266
Chronic sorrow, theory of, 22
Classroom activities, parent sharing in, 222–225
Closed questions, 85, 190
Coincidental Teaching, 236, 237
Collaboration. *See also* Parent-teacher collaboration
  continuum of, 75–76
  effective, 51–56
  with extended family members, 252–253
  family, 247–260
  with minority families, 62, 88, 247–260
  parent-teacher, 47–63
  with siblings, 252–253
  transition and, 266–268
Committee
  ad hoc, 233
  parent advisory, 181–182, 233

parents on, 233–234
Communication
  barriers to, 80–81, 84
  collaboration and, 52
  daily reports, 111–113, 118–119
  interpersonal, 79–83, 148, 149
  interview and, 83–92
  with minority parents, 121, 129
  newsletters, 130–131, 132–137, 138
  notebook for, 118–119, 120, 125–126
  in parent-teacher collaboration, 79–92
  periodic reports, 113–118
  telephone, 110–111, 127–130
  written, 110–111, 111–127
Communication groups, 198–201
  Parent Effectiveness Training, 199
  Systematic Training for Effective Parenting, 199–201
Community programs, parent involvement in, 213, 232
Conference(s). *See also* Meetings
  assessment, 71–74, 90–92, 276, 280–281
  effective, 188
  evaluation of, 183, 184, 195
  group activities and, 178–191
  guidelines for conducting, 182–184
  individualized education program, 154–159, 276
  intake, 71–74, 86–90, 276, 280–281
  leadership techniques in, 189–191
  models for, 194–211
  parents' negative reactions to, 163–165
  parent-teacher, 141–165, 178–191
  for planning activities, 75–76
  preparation for, 143–144, 145, 146, 147, 181–182, 185–187
  problem-solving, 145–148, 201–202
  progress report, 142–145, 146, 147
  for selecting goals and objectives, 74–75, 281–282
  by telephone, 129

348

three-way, 161–163
training, 148–154, 198–201, 205–210
Congruence, 23, 24
Consultation, Heron and Harris model for, 147–148
Content evaluation, 76, 77
Contexts, interrelationships among, 24–25, 36–38
Continuum of collaboration, 75–76
"Co-op Connection," 131, 132–137
Counseling, of families, 259–260
Counselors
  in IEP conferences, 156
  as resources, 102
Court cases, 56–57
Cultural abuse, 256–257
Cultural sensitivity, 81–82, 88
Culture(s)
  diverse, 248–252
  family and, 5

Daily reports, 111–113
  communication notebook, 118–119, 120
  general, 112
  issues addressed by, 112
  specific, 113
Denied abuse, 257
Descriptive language, 79, 80
Development, 23
Diagnosticians, as resources, 102
Directive techniques, 189
Discipline, 11–12
Discussion groups, 202–204
Distance-regulating abuse, 245
Down's syndrome, 27, 28
Down's syndrome case study, 302
Down Syndrome Congress, 180
Due process, 59

Ecological perspective, 23, 24–40
Ecological survey, 89, 90
Ecology, 23
Ecomap, 94–100
Educable mental retardation case study, 301–302
Education
  legislation and, 56–61
  parent-teacher collaboration in, 47–63
  social change and, 7–8

Education Amendments Law of 1974, 57
Education of All Handicapped Children Act of 1975, 58
Emotion, control of, 54
Environmental variables, 150–154
Evaluation
  of activities, 76–77, 183, 184, 195, 285–288
  in assessment interview, 91, 92
  content, 76, 77, 285, 286
  form for, 287–288
  in problem-solving conferences, 147, 202
  process, 76–77, 285–286
  of pupil progress, 114–117
Evaluative language, 80
Exceptionality
  adapting to child with, 24–40
  nature of, 27–29
Exosystem, of adaptation, 24, 34–36
Expertise, 53–54
Explore, freedom to, 13–14
Extended family members, collaboration with, 252–253
External social supports, 34–36

Family
  African-American, 249–250
  Asian-American, 251
  assessing needs of, 92–101
  child abuse and, 253–257
  collaboration and, 247–260
  composition of, 4, 5
  counseling of, 259–260
  definition of, 4
  from diverse cultures, 248–252
  with exceptional children, 21–41
  functioning of, 32–33
  Hispanic-American, 250
  low-income, 251–252
  Native American, 251
  relationships within, 30–34
  resources of, 35
  responsibilities of, 269
  school and, 36, 265–266
  social agencies and, 36–37
  social change and, 5–7
  social interactions of, 35
  as social system, 4–5
  substitute care and, 257–259
  transitions in, 264–271

Family collaboration, 247–260
Family transitions, 264–271
 collaboration and, 266–268
 exceptional children and, 265–266
 strategies for, 268–271
Fathers' adaptation to exceptional child, 26
Father's day open house, 197–198
Feedback, in child development, 14–15
Foster care, 257–259
Freedom to explore, 13–14

Gender, in coping with stress, 26
Goals, selection of, 74–75, 281–282
Grades, 111
Group activities (meetings), 178–191
 for communication, 198–201
 for discussion, 202–204
 effectiveness of, 188
 group size for, 179–181
 guidelines for, 182–184
 for large group, 179–180, 181–185, 195
 leadership techniques for, 189–191
 planning in, 181–182, 185–187
 problem-solving, 201–202
 revitalization of, 184–185
 for small group, 180, 181, 185–191, 225
 structure in, 187–188
 for training, 205–210

Handicap, characteristics of, 28–29
Helplessness, and child abuse, 255
Heron and Harris consultation model, 147–148
Hispanic-American families, 250
Home-based teachers, parents as, 234–238
Home programs, 213, 232, 237–238
Home visits, 159–161, 276
Homework, parent-supervised, 235
Honesty, in collaboration, 35
Hostility, in assessment interview, 91, 93

IEP (individualized education program), 58

Implementation of activities, 75–76, 182–184, 187–188, 282–285
Individualized education program (IEP), 86
 conferences for, 154–159, 276
 Public Law 94–142 and, 58–60, 154, 209
 training for, 207–210
Inferential language, 79–80
Informational meetings, 195–198
Information gathering
 in problem-solving conferences, 147
 techniques for, 79–92
Instructional coaching, parent training in, 216–219
Instructors, parents as, 226
Intake conference, 71–74, 86–90, 276, 280–281
Integrative social perspective, 22–24
Intellectual development, of child, 12–13
Interpersonal communication, 79–83, 148, 149
Interrelationships, 36–38
Interview
 in assessment conference, 91–93
 in parent-teacher collaboration, 79, 83–92
 psychosituational, 150–154, 169–177
Interview questions, 91–93
Intrafamilial relationships, 30–34

Joy of living, 15–16

"Kiddie Kapers," 131, 138

Language
 as barrier, in Hispanic-Americans, 250
 collaboration and, 250
 descriptive, 79, 80
 evaluative, 80
 inferential, 79–80
 use of, in collaboration, 79–83
Language skills, 13
Large-group activities, 179–180, 181–185, 195
Leadership techniques, in meetings, 189–191

Learning, affective, 15
Learning disabilities case study, 305–306
Legislation, and education, 56–61
Lending library, as home study program, 237–238
Lesson Plan, 207–209
Letters, 119–127
 of introduction, 121
 thank you, 123
 welcome, 121–122, 275, 277, 278
Listening, skill of, 82–83, 85
Love
 as children's need, 10–11
 parental, 10–11
Low-income families, 251–252

Macrosystem, of adaptation, 24, 38–40
Medical professionals, as resources, 103
Meeting Evaluation Form, 183, 184, 325
Meeting Evaluation Form (Spanish), 340
Meetings. *See also* Conference(s); Group activities
 communication, 198–201
 discussion, 202–204
 IEP, 154–159
 informational, 195–198
 models for, 194–211
 open house, 197–198
 orientation, 195–196, 225, 275, 276–280
 parent-student parallel, 198
Mesosystem, of adaptation, 24, 36–38
Microsystem, of adaptation, 24, 30–34
Mills v. Washington, D.C., Board of Education (1972), 56
Minority families
 African-American, 249–250
 Asian-American, 251
 collaboration and, 62, 88, 247–260
 Hispanic-American, 250
 low-income, 251–252
 Native American, 251
 telephone communication with, 129
 written communication with, 121

Model
 Heron and Harris, for consultation, 147–148
 for parent-teacher collaboration, 68–104, 274–289
 for problem-solving conferences, 148, 149
Modeling, 219–221
Moderate mental retardation case study, 302, 306–307, 307–308
Monthly calendar, 124, 127, 285, 298, 299
Mother-father relationships, 30
Mothers' adaptation to exceptional child, 26, 27–29, 30–31
Multiple handicaps case study, 308–309
Mutual affection, in assessment interview, 91, 93

National Association for Retarded Citizens, 180
National School Volunteer Program, 227
National Society for Children and Adults with Autism, 180
Native American families, 251
Needs
 of abused children, 254–255
 of children, 9–17
 of families, 92–101
 of parents, 38
Needs assessment, 181–182
Negative reactions to conferencing, 163–165
Newsletter, 130–131, 132–137, 138
Nondirective techniques, 189
Nonexceptional case study, 304
Notebook
 communication, 118–119, 120
 student handbook, 125–126
Notes, 119–127
 for behavior and achievement, 123, 124, 125
 for praise, 123, 126
Notices, 119–127
Nourishment, 16–17

Objectives
 selection of, 74–75, 281–282
 statement of, 147
Observation, parent training in, 215–216, 217–218

Observation Check Sheet, 216, 217–218
Ontogenic system, of adaptation, 24, 25–30
Open-ended questions, 85–86, 92, 94, 190
Open house, 197–198
Orientation meeting(s), 195–196, 225, 275, 276–280
Orientation Meeting Agenda, 196, 276–280
Orientation Meeting Handout, 196

Paraprofessionals
 parents as, 222–226
 as resources, 101, 102
Parent advisory committee, 181–182, 233
Parent Advocacy Coalition of Educational Rights, 180
Parental love, 10–11
Parent associations, as support groups, 239–240
Parent Career Day, 226
Parent-child relationships, 30–31
Parent collaboration. *See also* Parent-teacher collaboration
 lack of, 61–63
 rights and responsibilities in, 56–61
 social change and, 5–8
 with teachers, 47–63
Parent Collaboration Log, 276, 279–280, 328–329
Parent Collaboration Log (Spanish), 344–345
Parent Collaboration Program Evaluation Form, 286, 287–288, 330–331
Parent Collaboration Program Evaluation Form (Spanish), 346–347
Parent Conference Preparation Questionnaire, 145, 147
Parent Effectiveness Training (PET), 198, 199
Parent handout for conference preparation, 145, 146
Parenting, 3–18
 art of, 8–9
 children's needs in, 9–17
 of children with exceptionalities, 21–41
 family and, 4–5
 intellectual development of children, 12–13
 love and, 10–11
 providing feedback, 14–15
 providing physical care, 16–17
 self discipline of children, 11–12
 social change and, 5–8
 stigma and, 39–40
Parent involvement, 37–38. *See also* Parent collaboration; Parent training
 in IEP meetings, 154–159, 207–210
 in problem-solving conferences, 145–148, 201–202
 in progress reports, 142–145, 146, 147
Parent partner programs, 228–230, 240
Parent resource(s), 238–240
Parent resource center, 238–239
Parent roles, 8–9, 222–238
 on committees, 233–234
 as home-based teachers, 234–238
 as instructors, 226
 as paraprofessionals, 222–226
 as partners, 240
 as resources, 239–240
 as support teachers, 222
 as trainers, 239
 as tutors, 235–236
 as volunteers, 227–233
Parents. *See also* Family; Parenting
 attitudes of, 150–154, 160, 162
 needs of, 38
 neggative reactions of, to conferencing, 163–165
 personality factors of, 26–27
 as resources, 239–240
 responsibilities of, 9–17, 56–61, 269
 rights of, 56–61
 roles of, 8–9, 222–238
Parents' Activities From, 94, 97–99, 281, 282, 293–294, 296–297, 322–323
Parents' Activities Form (Spanish), 337–338
Parents' Needs Form, 94–97, 281, 291–293, 294–296, 319–321
Parents' Needs Form (Spanish), 334–336

Parent-student parallel programs, 198
Parent-teacher collaboration, 47–63
　assessing family needs in, 92–101
　attitudes toward, 49–50
　benefits of, 50–51
　for communication notebook, 118–119, 120
　communication skills in, 79–92
　continuum of, 75–76
　in daily reports, 111, 112
　in diverse cultures, 248–252
　effective, 49–50, 51–56
　group activities for, 178–191
　information-gathering techniques in, 79–92
　interview in, 83–92
　lack of, 61–63
　model for, 68–104, 274–289
　need for, 48–49
　premises for, 214
　for report cards, 113–114
　resources for, 101–103
　through telephone contacts, 127–130
　types of, 48
Parent-teacher conferences, 141–165
　as home visits, 159–161
　for individualized education program, 154–159, 276
　parents' negative reactions to, 163–165
　for problem solving, 145–148, 149
　for progress report, 142–145, 146, 147
　student participation and, 161–163
　for training, 148–154, 198–201
Parent training, 37
　in behavioral rehearsal, 221–222
　conferences for, 148–154, 198–201
　for IEP process, 207–210
　in instructional coaching, 216–219
　in modeling, 219–221
　in observation, 215–216, 217–218
　as paraprofessionals, 225
　Parent Effectiveness Training, 199
　programs for, 205–210
　in role playing, 221
　in simulation, 222
　Systematic Training for Effective Parenting, 199–201
　techniques for, 215–222
Parent-volunteer activities, 228, 231–232
Parent-Volunteer Questionnaire, 228–230, 326–327
Parent-Volunteer Questionnaire (Spanish), 341–343
Passport, 118–119, 120
Patience, in collaboration, 55
Pennsylvania Association for Retarded Children v. the Commonwealth of Pennsylvania (1971), 56
Periodic reports, 113–118. *See also* Report cards
Permissiveness of autonomy, 91, 92
Personal factors for coping with stress, 25–30
Personality factors
　in collaboration, 52–56
　copying with stress and, 26–27
PET (Parent Effectiveness Training), 198
Phases, of parent-teacher collaboration model, 71–77, 280–288
Physical care of child, 16–17
Planning activities, 75–76, 181–182, 185–187
Praise note, 123, 126
Preconference Report, outline for, 143
Prereading skills, 13
Preschool
　services for, 37
　transition from 265–266
Prescriptive-teaching methodology, 69
Pressuring, 91, 93
Prior experience, in adaptation, 27
Problem-solving conferences, 145–148, 149, 201–202
Problem-solving groups, 201–202
Problem-Solving Model, 149
Process evaluation, 76–77
Professional(s)
　at IEP conferences, 156–158
　at intake conference, 89
　as resources, 101, 102–103
　as social support, 34–35

353

Professional abuse, 255–256
Profound hearing impairment case study, 303–304
Program Development Form, 77, 78, 282, 283, 284, 318
Program Development Form (Spanish), 333
Progress report conferences, 142–145, 146, 147
Protocol Psychosituational Interview One, 169–174
Protocol Psychosituational Interview Two, 174–177
Psychologists, as resources, 102
Psychosituational assessment interview
 examples of, 169–177
 training conferences and, 150–154
Public Law 93–112, 57
Public Law 93–247, 253–254
Public Law 93–380, 57
Public Law 94–142
 collaboration and, 48, 68
 conferences and, 141, 154
 in IEP training, 209
 provisions of, 58–60
Public Law 99–457
 family involvement and, 60, 68
 transitions and, 266
Pupil Progress Report
 overall evaluation, 114–116
 sample subject area evaluation, 117

Questions
 for assessment interview, 91–93
 closed, 85, 190
 open-ended, 85–86, 92, 94, 190

Rehabilitation Act of 1973, 57
Reinforcement, by parents, 15
Religion, and adaptation, 27
Report(s)
 daily, 111–113
 periodic, 113–118
Report cards, 111, 113–114, 276
 overall evaluation, Pupil Progress Report, 114–116
 sample subject area evaluation, Pupil Progress Report, 117
 verbal, 142–145

Resource(s)
 for parents, 238–239
 for parent-teacher collaboration, 101–103
Resource center, for parents, 238–239
Responsibilities of parents
 in collaboration, 56–61
 in transitions, 269
"Responsive Parenting" program, 232–233
Review conference, 77
Revitalization of meetings, 184–185
Rewards, communication notebook and, 118
Rights, of parents, 56–61
Role playing, parent training in, 221

Safety, of children, 16–17
School
 family and, 36, 265–266
 transition from, 266
 transition to, 265–266
 social change and, 7–8
School programs, parent involvement in, 213, 222–238
School visit, what to look for in (form), 219–220
Self-acceptance, and adaptation, 27
Self-assessment, 12
Self-awareness, and collaboration, 53
Self-control, 11, 12
Self-discipline, 11–12
Shopping parent, 34
Sibling(s)
 collaboration and, 252–253
 relationships with child, 31–32
Significant others, 33
Simulation training for parents, 222
Small-group activities, 180, 181, 185–191, 225
Social agencies, and family, 36–37
Social change, 6
 family and, 5–7
 parent collaboration and, 5–8
 schooling and, 7–8
Social class, and adaptation, 27
Social contexts, 24–25, 25–40
Social interactions, of family, 35

Social support
  coping with stress and, 33
  external, 34–36
  parent associations as, 239–240
Social system, family as, 4–5
Social system perspective, 22–24, 40–41
Social workers, as resources, 102–103
Societal beliefs, in adaptation, 38–40
Societal values, in adaptation, 38–40
Special education teachers
  in IEP meetings, 154–155
  as resources, 101, 102
  as support, 255
Spina Bifida Association of America, 180
Stage theory, 22–23
Stand-in abuse, 256
STEP (Systematic Training for Effective Parenting), 198
Stigma, 31–32, 39–40
Stress
  coping with, 25–30
  management of, for parents, 210
Structure, in group activities, 187–188
Student handbook, 125–216
Student participation
  in parent-student parallel programs, 198
  in parent-teacher conference, 161–163
Subject area evaluation, 117
Substitute care, 257–259
Supper meetings, 204
Support groups
  as discussion groups, 204
  parent associations as, 239–240
Support teachers, parents as, 222
Systematic Training for Effective Parenting (STEP), 198, 199–201
Systems approach, in adaptation, 21–41, 255

Target behavior, 150–154
Teacher collaboration. *See also* Parent-Teacher collaboration
  benefits of, 51
  with parents, 47–63

Teachers
  effective, 49–50, 53–56
  as resources, 101, 102
Telephone communication, 110–111, 127–130, 275
  documentation for, 128
  miniconferences by, 129
  with minority parents, 129
Telephone Documentation Sheets, 128
Tenth Annual Report to Congress on the Implementation of the Education of the Handicapped Act, 7
Territoriality, 248
Thank you letter, 123
Three-way conference, 161–163
Time line, for transitions, 270
Training conferences, 148–154, 198–201, 205–210
Training groups, 205–210
  for IEP process, 207–210
  parent, 205–207
Training programs, 198–201
  behavioral rehearsal, 221–222
  behavior modification, 205–207
  instructional coaching, 216–219
  modeling, 219–221
  observation, 215–216
  Parent Effectiveness Training, 199
  role playing, 221
  Systematic Training for Effective Parenting, 199–201
  techniques for, 215–222
Transactional Family Systems Model, 236–237
Transferred abuse, 256
Transgenerational abuse, 256
Transition(s), 264
  bureaucratic, 267–268
  collaboration and, 266–268
  in families, 264–271
  issues of, 210
  from preschool to public school, 265–266
  from school to work, 266
  strategies for, 268–271
Transition Plan Time Line, 270
Tutors, parents as, 235–236

Universalizing, 189–190

355

Verbal contract, for group activities, 187–188
Volunteers, parents as, 227–233

Welcome letters, 121–122, 275, 277, 278
Work, transition to, 266
Written communication, 110–111, 111–127
   daily reports, 111–113
   daily, positive communication notebook, 118–119, 120
   letters, 119–127
   for minority parents, 121
   newsletter, 130–131, 132–137, 138
   notes, 119–127
   periodic reports, 113–118
   report cards, 111, 113–114, 114–116, 117, 276
   student handbook, 125–126
Writer's Suitcase, 236, 237